I0813223

"Jim Nestingen had a gift for sharing complex theological concepts in ways that apply to everyone and can be understood by anyone. He always communicated these truths with an eye on forgiveness, and the Gospel of Jesus Christ, which delivers the forgiveness of sins, is at the heart of everything Nestingen wrote. *The Essential Nestingen* is an expression of this legacy that will resonate for generations to come."

—Rev. Thomas Eggold, Emmanual Lutheran Church (Fort Wayne, IN)

"If you are like me, dear reader, your bookshelf includes a number of volumes that you purchased with the best of intentions but have not gotten around to reading. I urge you not only to buy this book, but also to read it and take it to heart. Start with the first essay, where Jim asks, "Is it possible to preach repentance without getting crucified for it?" This is no abstract philosophical question. It is born of Jim's own experience. I am confident that once you read the first essay, you will be hooked and you will not be able to put this book down."

—Pastor Michael Albrecht, Saint James Lutheran Church

"Nestingen was ever excited to share God's generous forgiveness to any sinner within earshot. One word summarizes his ministry: freedom! Freeing sinners from the law's accusations was the core of his work. Due to this freedom, God's people can treasure life; indeed, have fun. Few theologians have done theology as guided by a pastor's heart or have connected so ably with working pastors. This book will allow Nestingen to continue to teach and inspire future generations to be ambassadors of freedom."

—Mark Mattes, Lutheran Bible Institute Chair in Theology,
Grand View University, Des Moines, Iowa

"In life, Jim was a storyteller, and his favorite story to tell was Christ 'for you' from the pages of Luther's little Catechism. His vast theological breadth was always met with a profound pastoral depth. Jim's whole career testified that theology was for proclamation. The present volume provides a blessed opportunity to sit down with Jim, and learn from one of the greatest catechists, pastors, professors, and storytellers of our age."

—Philip Bartelt, Pastor, Lutheran Church of the Good Shepherd

"Everything James Arne Nestingen did and said was for the life and wellbeing of the Church. Accordingly, in this volume we find a down-to-earth, practical theology that exhibits a deep appreciation for the breadth of forgiveness and a delight in the cross and resurrection of our Lord. Decades of careful research and devotion to Scripture and the Lutheran Confessions are laid before us. Here is proclaimed nothing but the Christ who belongs to, and was sent for, sinners."

—Berett J. Steffen, Pastor, St. John Lutheran Church—Bingen, Decatur, IN

"*The Essential Nestingen* is a fitting tribute, honoring a legacy of profound pastoral wisdom and insight. Throughout this collection of writings is the comfort of Christ's crucified in order to deliver actual forgiveness to real sinners. Far from academic abstraction, this book captures Nestingen's visceral pastoral depth, making this collection a vital resource for preaching, catechesis, and pastoral care. It's a volume I'll keep within easy reach."

—Marsh Shamburger, Pastor/Holy Cross Evangelical Lutheran Church (Rocklin, CA)

"According to Christ, a faithful steward (ὁ πιστὸς οἰκονόμος; latin: "fidelis dispensator") gives the members of the household their portion of food in due season (Luke 12:42). Jim Nestingen, in this collection of essays, continues to act as "fidelis dispensator". By making explicit, what is so often ignored by present-day theologians and church leaders, he encourages and enables the reader to join in that very life-giving rhythm of receiving and distributing the gospel goods."

—Armin Wenz, Professor for New Testament, Oberursel, Germany

"Dr. Nestingen had an uncanny ability to know all the subtle ways that Christians are attacked and tempted to unbelief. He was an exceptionally pastoral church historian! These penetrating essays will help us face those attacks, repent, and lead us to cast every sin, accusation, and even our own good works all on Christ by faith, so that He alone remains our Lord and our righteousness."

—Jason D. Lane, Associate Professor of Historical Theology at Concordia Seminary, St. Louis

"Dr. Pless and 1517 deserve our thanks and praise for giving Dr. Jim Nestingen the opportunity to influence the next generation of pastors and theologians for the Church. What is "Essential Nestingen" must also be essential to all theologians of the Church!"

—Rev. John F. Bradosky, Bishop Emeritus, North American Lutheran Church

THE ESSENTIAL

Westingen

The Essential Nestingen

Essays on Preaching, Catechism, & the Reformation

Edited by
John T. Pless
&
Foreword by
Robert Kolb

The Essential Nestingen: Essays on Preaching, Catechism, and the Reformation

Published by:
1517 Academic, an imprint of 1517.
PO Box 54032
Irvine, CA 92619-4032

Publisher's Cataloging-In-Publication Data
(Prepared by Cassidy Cataloguing, Inc.)

Names: Pless, John T., 1953- editor. | Kolb, Robert, 1941- writer of foreword.
Title: The essential Nestingen : essays on preaching, catechism, and the Reformation / edited by John T. Pless ; foreword by Robert Kolb.
Description: Irvine, CA : 1517 Academic, an imprint of 1517, [2025] | Includes bibliographical references and index.
Identifiers: ISBN: 978-1-964419-12-1 (hardcover) | 978-1-964419-13-8 (paperback) | 978-1-964419-14-5 (ebook)
Subjects: LCSH: Nestingen, James Arne. | Lutheran teachers—United States. | Lutheran Church—United States—Clergy. | Preaching. | Lutheran Church—Catechisms. | Reformation. | LCGFT: Essays. | BISAC: RELIGION / Sermons / Christian. | RELIGION / Christianity / Lutheran. | RELIGION / Christian Ministry / Preaching.
Classification: LCC: BX8080.N44 E77 2025 | DDC: 284.1092—dc23

Printed in the United States of America.
Cover art by Zachariah James Stuef.

We are grateful to *Lutheran Quarterly*, *Concordia Journal*, *Logia*, *Word & World*, *Lutheran Theological Journal*, *Concordia Theological Quarterly*, and *Dialog* for their cooperation and permission to include previously published materials from their periodicals in this volume.

FOREWORD

James Arne Nestingen (1945-2022)

James Nestingen, a man who delighted in delivering the goods, the Good of the gospel of Jesus Christ, published far less than he should have in print (although recordings of his oral presentations do make it possible to enjoy his delivery of the new life Christ has won for his people). Thus, his friend John Pless has done us a great favor by collecting some gems that he composed for publication. They convey something of his desire to proclaim nothing but Christ Jesus and him crucified.

I do not remember our first meeting, but Jim Nestingen and I knew each other for forty-some years.* He reminded me of one of my Norwegian uncles, jolly but deeply serious, sympathetic as he heard the bruised and battered but sharp enough on occasion to bruise and batter others—something of the Viking in him indeed. An elder of a Laestadian congregation audited some of Jim's classes and often came to his office for a post-lecture chat. In one, Jim mentioned the bad blood between him and a colleague, eliciting the reaction from the Finnish brother, "that cannot be!" He insisted that Jim call the colleague, and the elder accompanied Jim to the colleague's office. He charged them to repent and then to absolve each other. The dispute did not end, but it took place in the shadow of that moment of forgiveness and reconciliation.

Our Norwegian immigrant cultural background took second place to the heritage of faith that bound us together. Our parents had grounded our thinking and shaped our way of life in Luther's Small Catechism. He was a product of a little parsonage on the prairie; Jim's formation took place in the culture shaped in the Dakotas and Minnesota by those of

* The following text is adapted from a tribute to Professor Nestingen that appeared on the website "concordiatheology.org" of Concordia Seminary, Saint Louis in January 2023 and is used with the permission of the editors.

whom the novelist Ole Rolvaag wrote in *Giants in the Earth* and *Peder Victorious*. He knew the harshness of life on the North Dakota plains and how richly the Lord blesses when the wheat prospers.

Jim was Old Synod, that is, his roots lay in the Norwegian Evangelical Lutheran Church of America, which had sent professors and students to Concordia Seminary in Saint Louis before the Civil War and had represented the same position on the doctrine of predestination in the Predestinarian controversy of the 1870s and 1880s as the Missouri Synod in which I grew up. He presumed that the people who came to him trusting in Jesus Christ had been chosen before the foundation of the world to be his own, and he viewed his calling as God's commission to make the election of his chosen people come true in the lives of those to whom he, Jim, was privileged to bring the means of grace, the Word of promise of forgiveness and new life in our Lord.

Jim could talk to anyone. He was able to bring the love of Jesus to a fearful, distressed student, and he could parlay with the best of theologians. His friendship formed in Toronto with Gustaf Wingren illustrates his ability to listen and learn even when he disagreed. The deeper Jim plunged into telling the gospel and bestowing the promise, the deeper his Norwegian brogue became. One morning, I went to his Luther Seminary office from mine at Concordia College in Saint Paul. He had left me a note to come to a classroom where he was speaking to a group of pastors from North Dakota. They lived in an area where their congregations and their culture were perishing as agriculture became ever more commercialized, and most of the farm children were leaving for towns and cities. He talked of the joy of ministry in bringing comfort and encouragement through the presence of Christ to those who recognized that their communities were withering and their congregations were diminishing numerically. He brought these pastors the comfort and power of the gospel in the midst of such a crisis through the theology of the cross. He cultivated these pastors' appreciation for the gift of serving through sharing Christ's presence in the face of the pervading sense of loss that filled their people. His consolation sounded all the more convincing as the Norwegian rhythms and tones grew more pronounced.

Jim knew and felt the law of God: "Uuuuh, Bob, it cuts ya to the quick." Both the deeply earnest lines in his face and the broad smile of delight when he spoke of the cross and empty tomb suggested that, although he would never have said it in these words, his heart was strangely warmed by thinking of Christ's sacrificial and triumphant love. The story is told that hc was substituting for a pastor in a congregation in which members came to the altar rail to receive absolution before the distribution of the Lord's body and blood. When Jim came to the last person who was kneeling before him, the young man backed up. Jim reached out toward him, and he stepped back. He turned away from the altar, and Jim hitched up his robes, climbed over the altar rail that had been closed for the distribution. He ran the poor guy down and forgave him his sins whether he liked it or not. Jim probably figured that if the Lord had to be chasing down James Arne Nestingen continually to straighten him out, he himself could do that for another who felt the burden of his sin. Whether my account is totally accurate or not, it is a faithful portrayal of this preacher of forgiveness and life.

As the fresh translation of the Book of Concord was developing, Jim proposed to Tim Wengert and me a pair of companion volumes. The task fell to Jim and me. Jim went to editors at Augsburg/Fortress and convinced them to invite us to produce what became *Sources and Contexts of the Book of Concord* (2001) and *The Lutheran Confessions, History and Theology of the Book of Concord* (2012). For the latter volume, we recruited Chuck Arand since neither one of us knew the ancient creeds as well as he did. Jim was perfectionist. He always thought one more draft was necessary when I found his work superb. I finally laid down the law to both of them: "I am sending to our editor the last draft you have written." Jim later told me that he had been very angry with me at that point but that he had come to recognize that the readers he wanted to serve would never have seen our work had I not done that. His regard for the precious word of life and salvation in Jesus Christ led him to want to polish it always just one more time.

Jim deeply desired to share with others the heritage that we shared in the riches of the Lutheran confessional documents. He had begun to do just that in print in 1975 with his outstanding guide to Luther's Small Catechism, co-authored with Gerhard Forde, *Free to Be*. Several works followed in print, all aiming to bring the gospel of Christ and the insights of the Wittenberg heritage to a broad audience: *Martin Luther: A Life (2009), Martin Luther: His Life and His Teachings (2004), Manger in the Mountains (2000), The Faith We Hold: the Living Witness of Luther and the Augsburg Confession (1983), and Roots of Our Faith (1978)*. But Jim's medium was the public proclamation in sermon or lecture. The blessings of the electronic age permit us to find him on our screens nowadays, at countless websites, including that of "Doxology" and "1517.org."

You might say that Forde and Nestingen deserved each other, teacher and pupil, both ardent confessors of the gospel of Christ and the theology of Martin Luther, both concerned deeply about the urgency of calling to repentance and the growing need for clear application of the consolation of Christ's gift of new life at the turn of the twenty-first century. Because of their growing up in the combat zone between Pietist followers of Hans Nielsen Hauge and the defenders of the Formula of Concord's understanding of grace, they saw how easily the gospel becomes just slightly conditional if we look for the assurance of our salvation anywhere but to cross and empty tomb, to God's absolving power in oral, written, and sacramental forms. They knew how to tell secure sinners how wrathful God is with them and how to tell broken sinners how deeply God loves them. Jim once commented, in reference to differences with colleagues, that he and Forde "outpastored them." As Gerhard's Parkinson's disease was making it ever more uncomfortable for him to venture alone into public settings, Jim accompanied his mentor and friend to the tenth International Congress for Luther Research in Copenhagen in 2002. Gerhard had served as president of the eighth Congress nine years earlier at Luther Seminary in Saint Paul. Jim assured Gerhard that he would not depart from his side, and Gerhard was enjoying the lectures and time with colleagues when Jim got an invitation to do something in Copenhagen for a few hours. It was among my highest honors that the two of them agreed that I could substitute for him as Gerhard's support for the afternoon. We had a great time together, as we had had nearly twenty years earlier when we partnered in teaching Lutheran Confessions for an academic quarter at Luther.

There were mornings when I would drive the few miles to Jim's and Carolyn's home after she had left for work. He was just taking his freshly baked bread out of the oven as I arrived, and we feasted the morning away on great bread and great theology. His commitment to practicing theology under the discipline of the proper distinction of law and gospel guided his thoughts as we searched the Scriptures to answer pressing questions of the day. His goal of helping sinners repent so that they could prosper as Christ's people under his promise came through in his lectures in classroom and conferences and in our discussions at his kitchen table on how to bring this joy and peace in our Lord that we shared to others.

We last saw each other and got to chat a bit when he and I were asked by the music folks at 1517 Legacy to confer over a new presentation of the Small Catechism by my former student, the insightful Marcus Grey—you may know him as "Flame." Flame's music style is closer to Jim's tastes than mine, I suppose, but he provoked Jim and me into the kind of exchanges we had always had as we probed the truth delivered by Dr. Luther for children of all ages. That book remained Jim's *vade-mecum* for the journey.

The next time we see each other, he may still be baking bread, but I know that he will be rejoicing in his Savior the way he always has.

Robert Kolb
Saint Louis USA, the Ascension of our Lord 2024

INTRODUCTION

James Arne Nestingen (1945-2022) was the son of a North Dakota Lutheran parsonage. Although he was a world-class theologian who was in demand as a lecturer not only in North America but also in South America, Australia, Asia, and Europe, Jim was never far from his roots on the Midwestern prairies or from the simple truth of Luther's Small Catechism. Jim's love for Luther's Catechism is demonstrated in what would be his most popular book, *Free to Be,* a catechetical text that he authored with his mentor, Gerhard Forde (1927-2005), published by Augsburg Publishing House (where Jim worked for a time as an editor) in 1975 and again in a revised edition in 1983. This book has sold over two million copies.

After earning his BA from Concordia College in Moorhead, MN, in 1967, Jim enrolled in Luther Seminary, earning his MDiv there in 1971. Ordained in the former American Lutheran Church, Jim served as pastor of Faith Lutheran Church in Coquille, Oregon, from 1971-1974 and at St. Ansgar's Lutheran Church in Toronto from 1978-1980. Accepted in the doctoral program at St. Michael's College in the University of Toronto, Jim would study with the renowned Thomist scholar Harry J. Mc Sorely (1931-2017), who had authored an important historical study of Luther's debate with Erasmus published in 1969 under the title, *Luther Right or Wrong?* Jim was awarded the ThD at the university in 1984.

Jim's academic career would demonstrate an ongoing engagement with Luther's *The Bondage of the Will.* This was more than a scholarly pursuit. Jim realized that Luther's controversial book was an exercise in pastoral theology and preaching. Like his beloved teacher, Gerhard Forde, Nestingen recognized that Luther wrote his book not as a philosopher out to win a debate but as a pastor whose aim was to bring the certainty of Gospel consolation to broken sinners. Forde had intended to write a full-length commentary on *The Bondage of the Will.* When Parkinson's disease robbed him of the capacity to complete the project, Steven Paulson edited Forde's partially done manuscript, and it was published in the *Lutheran Quarterly Book Series* in 2005 as *The Captivation of the Will: Luther vs. Erasmus on Freedom and Bondage.* Jim wrote an extensive introduction (23 pages) to this short book. This introduction is more than a helpful roadmap to Luther's arguments; it serves as a summary of Nestingen's rejection of every attempt to substitute psychological categories for theological assertions. In the end, "There is just one thing left: preaching."[1]

Jim's theological thinking was shaped in the midst of a debate going on in American Lutheranism over the power of the human will and the doctrine of election.[2] This debate was embodied in the controversy between Herman A. Preus (1896-1995) and George Aus (1903-1977) on the faculty at Luther Seminary while Jim was a student there. Preus held to the teaching of the Formula of Concord while Aus was prepared to grant the human will some freedom in conversion. Preus insisted on the centrality of the doctrine of justification by faith alone while Aus worried that his colleague was weak on sanctification. Preus held firmly to the infallible authority of the Holy Scriptures; Aus was more open to methods of historical criticism mediated by Ole Hallesby (1879-1961) of the free theological faculty in Oslo. Jim, like Forde, was influenced by Preus.

Other notable theological influences on Jim would include Bo Giertz (1905-1998), especially his novel, *The Hammer of God* and the Luther scholar, Hans Joachim Iwand (1899-1960), his New Testament professor and later colleague at Luther Seminary, Roy Harrisville, Jr (1922-2023), Kjell Ove Nilssen (1934-2019), a Swedish Luther scholar who was a visiting professor at Luther Seminary from 1967-1970 while Nestingen was a student, and the Finnish Luther scholar, Lennart Pinomaa (1901-1996) who was the author of *Faith Victorious: A Study of Luther's Theology.* Apart from Forde, perhaps the theologian with the most impact on Jim was Gustaf Wingren (1910-2000). Nestingen's treatment of the law in creation and his reception of Luther's doctrine of vocation bear the marks of this Swedish theologian. In the festschrift for Forde, *By Faith Alone: Essays on Justification in Honor of Gerhard O. Forde,* Jim contributed the chapter, "Examining Sources: Influences on Gerhard Forde's Theology." This essay not only gives insights into the theological influences at work in Forde, but it also provides a good picture of how these sources mediated through Forde would leave their imprint on Jim as well.

I first met Jim Nestingen through Dr. Robert Kolb in the summer of 1984. I was ordained the previous year and was serving University

Lutheran Chapel in Minneapolis; Jim was teaching church history at Luther Seminary. Bob had called me to see if I could give Jim a ride to a meeting of the Concordia Academy on the campus of Wartburg Seminary in Dubuque. The hours to Dubuque and then back to the Twin Cities slipped by as I quickly discovered a kindred spirit in my travel companion.

That trip would mark the beginning of a long and cherished friendship. In those early days, Jim, Bob, Dr. Kenneth Korby (1924-2006), and I would often meet for conversation. We worked with Lowell Green (1926-2014) to bring the Concordia Academy to Luther Seminary and again to University Lutheran Chapel. Jim was always an encouraging and thoughtful supporter of my work in campus ministry.

As a young pastor, I wanted to introduce the practice of individual confession and absolution at the chapel. I announced times when I would be available in the chancel to hear confession and speak absolution, but I didn't have any takers. I confided my frustration in Jim. He reminded me that a pastor should always have "ears for the confession of sin." He suggested that I not wait for students to come to me. Instead, to listen for those who were confessing their sins over a beer or cup of coffee, in a conversation at the student center, or in a chance meeting in some setting away from the chapel. Jim said that they may not immediately identify their problem as sin, but "you are a Lutheran, so you'll know sin when you hear it." Jim said that I should respond by saying, do you know what you just said? You confessed your sin, now I'm going to absolve you." Then Jim said, "haul off and say the words. . ..As called and ordained servant of Christ, I forgive you all your sins in the name of the Father and of the Son and of the Holy Spirit." With this advice, Jim rescued the practice of confession and absolution for me. I've used his advice ever since.

In 2000, I was called to the faculty of Concordia Theological Seminary in Fort Wayne. Jim encouraged me to accept the call and was full of encouragement as headed out on this new venture. Moving from the Twin Cities to Indiana meant that I would not have occasions to stop by his office on the Luther campus or get together for lunch in Dinkytown by the University of Minnesota campus, but the friendship remained and deepened as other doors would be open.

I was pleased that Jim was able to visit the Fort Wayne campus on several occasions. He was a speaker at our annual Confessions Symposium twice and he taught an intensive term STM course. His "fireside chat" on Luther's treatise on the enslaved will was one of his most energetic and memorable presentations making an impact on students that continues to the present. In typical, Nestingen fashion, Jim mocked much of contemporary theology as "Erasmus in drag." That year the fourth year class invited Jim to return to Fort Wayne as guest speaker for their spring banquet.

A recording of the fireside chat on the bound will would somehow make its way to Norway prompting Jarle Blindheim to invite Jim and me to speak for their Lutheran Study Days in Bergen. We did this together two summers in a row, focusing on the Small Catechism and Luther's teaching on vocation. Given his own Norwegian heritage, Jim fit right in and won the hearts and minds of participants with his down to earth humor and his practical applications of Lutheran theology to daily life.

A major intersection with Jim over the last dozen years was the official dialogue between the North American Lutheran Church (NALC), Lutheran Church-Canada (LCC), and The Lutheran Church-Missouri Synod (LCMS). Initially meeting twice a year, this group shared in honest and open theological discussion and sought ways the church bodies to work together in areas of common concern. Over a series of meetings, the dialogue engaged discussion of the understanding of law and gospel. Some of the fruits of that discussion, including a statement, "God's Word Forever Shall Abide: A Guiding Statement on the Character and Proper Use of the Sacred Scriptures" were harvested in the *Necessary Distinction: A Continuing Conversation on Law & Gospel* (CPH 2017) coedited by Jim, Albert Collver, and myself. In this volume, Jim contributed the essay on Romans 10:4, which in many ways, serves as a crystallization of thinking on law and gospel proclamation.

It was a delight to be together with Jim and Carolyn for the 500th anniversary of the Reformation in Wittenberg on October 31, 2017, as the NALC, LCC, and LCMS dialogue met at the Old Latin School to mark the occasion. Jim and Carolyn almost missed that event due to the fact Jim discovered that his passport had expired when he arrived at the Minneapolis airport. Determined not to miss being in Germany for the party, Jim rushed to the passport office in the Twin Cities to see if something could be done. Fortunately, the director of the office recognized Jim's North Dakota accent and discovered that he grew up in her hometown. She managed to expedite a passport renewal and Jim and Carolyn were on a flight to Germany by the end of the day! Jim didn't miss the party and with his sparkling knowledge of Luther and Wittenberg, he was a perfect guide to the city and the treasures to found there.

Jim was an active member of the dialogue right up to his death. He attended the most recent meeting by zoom in November and he was looking forward to the face to face meeting scheduled for Fort Wayne in April 2023. I was looking forward to once again hosting a fireside chat with our students. The Lord had other plans for Jim. His deep insights into the Scriptures and the Confessions, his humor and warmth will be deeply missed in the dialogue. From a human point of view, Jim is irreplaceable.

During the final years of his life, Jim was an active participant in 1517, an organization devoted to proclaiming and defending the Gospel of Jesus Christ as it was articulated by Luther. Jim found ready and eager hearers at 1517's *Here We Still Stand Conferences* held each October in San Diego. At the conference in 2018, Jim was presented with a festschrift under the title, *Handing over the Goods: Determined to Proclaim Nothing but Christ Jesus and Him Crucified: Essays in Honor of James Arne Nestingen* edited by Steven D. Paulson and Scott L. Keith. The volume echoed the themes of Jim's life and calling all clustered around "handing over the goods" packed in the word of the cross. It was a memorable evening of joy and thanksgiving for those of us privileged to be there with our friend, mentor, and colleague.

When Mark Mattes called me on the afternoon of December 31, 2022, with the news of Jim's death, I like many others was shocked and numbed. Later that evening, I went to what was one of Jim's last written works, a short essay, "The Theology of the Cross in the Lord's Prayer" now published in *Luther's Large Catechism with Annotations and Notes.* I was especially struck and comforted by the concluding words of that essay, so strong with the promise of the resurrection. I'll let Jim have the last word:

> ". . .Jesus teaches us to conclude the Lord's Prayer with two magnificent petitions: 'Lead us not into temptation' and 'Deliver us from evil.' In the Sixth Petition, we turn our temptations to 'false belief, despair, and other great shame and vice' over to Christ Jesus. He can handle—in fact, has handled—decisively what we can't. When he takes the field, 'even when we are so tempted,' the devil has to tuck his tail between his legs and flee. The 'strong man' is bound and we are free. And then faith can hear the rumbling promise progressing through the battlefield as our mighty fortress opens its doors and the Prince of Peace takes the field to win His ultimate victory against the forces remaining since Good Friday and Easter. Then we will be able to say the last Amen."[3]

Jim has uttered his final Amen and we who remain on the battlefield give thanks to Christ Jesus for the victory he now enjoys.

Jim's works do follow him. Most important are those "living letters" (see 2 Corinthians 3:2-3) encoded in those closest to him: his wife, Carolyn, his sons and their wives, his grandchildren in whom he had such great delight. Then there are the countless number of students whose lives and ministries were molded and shaped by his teaching all across the globe. The volume that you now hold in your hands brings together several significant essays that exemplify the potency of Jim's scholarship always pressed in the service of the Gospel of the crucified and risen Christ Jesus. For those who had Jim as a teacher or heard him speak at one of the many conferences that featured him as a lecture, these essays will bring to mind the clarity of Jim's thought, his knowledge of Luther and the Lutheran Confessions, but most of all his commitment to the saving Gospel. It is is my hope that this depository of Jim's wisdom might also stimulate faithfulness in a new generation of confessors. The words of the Psalmist may well serve as summary of Jim's work and the aim of this volume: "I will open my mouth in a parable; I will utter dark sayings from of old, things that our fathers have told us. We will not hide them from their children, but tell them to the coming generation the glorious deeds of the Lord, and his might, and the wonders that he has done" (Psalm 78:2-4 ESV).

John T. Pless, M.Div.; D. Litt
Assistant Professor of Pastoral Ministry & Mission
Concordia Theological Seminary
Fort Wayne, IN
Commemoration of the Augsburg Confession
25 June 2024

Notes

1. James A. Nestingen "Introduction: Luther and Erasmus on the Bondage of the Will" in *The Captivation of the Will: Luther vs. Erasmus on Freedom and Bondage* by Gerhard O. Forde, edited by Steven Paulson (Grand Rapids: Eerdmans, 2005), 23.
2. For a lively reflection of this controversy, see Roy Harrisville Jr. "Contested Election Memoir" *Lutheran Quarterly* (Fall 2020), 346-349. Also see Mark Grandquist, *A History of Luther Seminary 1869-2019* (Minneapolis: Fortress Press, 2019), 109-110.
3. James Nestingen, "The Theology of the Cross in the Lord's Prayer" in *Luther's Large Catechism with Annotations and Contemporary Applications* ed. John T. Pless and Larry M. Vogel (Saint Louis: Concordia Publishing House, 2023), 520.

TABLE OF CONTENTS

I

PREACHING AND PASTORAL THEOLOGY

PREACHING REPENTANCE

*In this essay, Nestingen takes up the question of the relationship between repentance and the Gospel—Is repentance a condition for or a consequence of the Gospel?—examining the missteps of the Antinomians who legalized the Gospel by making it a preaching of repentance in place of the promise of the forgiveness of sins. The Law works the knowledge of sin, but recognition of sin is not yet repentance. Nestingen says, "Without the gospel, the law is indiscriminate; it merely drives creating an appetite which, in the realm of the legal, is insatiable." The law is to be preached, uncovering sin in the ordinary places of human life. The law is not the preacher's ultimate word; that word is the Gospel. This article originally appeared in **Lutheran Quarterly**, 3:1989 JTP+*

Preaching Repentance Is a Problem

Theologically, there is no question about its priority. When the New Testament sums up the message of Jesus and the apostles, it identifies repentance with faith as the gospel's consequence: "The kingdom of God is at hand: repent and believe in the gospel" (Mark 1:15). "And Peter said to them, 'Repent, and be baptized every one of you in the name of Jesus Christ for the forgiveness of your sins . . .'" (Acts 2:38).

The Lutheran Confessions are equally adamant. Article twelve of the Augsburg Confession, in fact, speaks as though repentance were a condition for the forgiveness of sins. And when Luther in *The Small Catechism* addresses the significance of baptism, he describes a daily death by drowning in repentance that continues throughout the life of the faithful.

Yet even to name the theological priority of repentance is to come perilously close to undergoing it. For the preacher who is engaged by a text which calls for repentance immediately confronts a whole range of difficulties.

One difficulty is theological. The Lutheran witness to the gospel insists that it is an unconditional word of pardon and release in Christ. With much of the talk of repentance, there is the suggestion of a condition to be achieved. How can repentance be preached without giving the lie to the gospel?

Another difficulty is pastoral. The traditional language of repentance—sorrow over sin, contrition, desire to make amends—describes various dispositions of the heart. Such states are difficult to discern unambiguously. The problem is compounded when, in situations of pastoral authority, a person is called to assess repentance and make recommendations for action. Are there any signs of repentance which manifest its presence strongly enough to give those in authority sound footing?

Still another difficulty is perhaps even more basic: survival. There may have been good reason for the fact that the prophets generally lived out of town, not in parsonages, and not on housing allowances, either. Preaching repentance requires a willingness to stand against the hearer, to speak directly of matters that may call up conflict. How do you stand over and against people you are called to live in relation to? Is it possible to preach repentance without getting crucified for it?

Faced with such questions, one reasonable alternative would be to inquire of the Lutheran heritage to see what it might have to suggest. According to the church constitutions, model or otherwise, we are obligated to do just this. And there is the possibility, too, of finding something helpful.

It has to be acknowledged, however, that the generation of Lutheran theologians currently in its ascendancy has, by and large, worked by a different procedure. This has been to identify a problem such as repentance; to attribute the problem to some personal, psychological difficulty of Luther or to a failure of the larger tradition; and then to run a shopping trip through various metaphors, models, or ecumenical alternatives for attractive solutions.

The generation that came to its theological calling in the late 1950s and early 1960s, amidst Bobby Sox and the excitement of Kennedy's new frontier, has been around long enough now that it should be possible to evaluate this procedure, to ask what it has produced. There has been some fine scholarship, especially concerning Barth and some other neo-orthodox theologians. There have been some outstanding exegetes. And in the corners, among those by and large excluded by their contemporaries, there has even been some fine Luther research.

But it is equally clear that pushing off from the heritage, this generation of theologians—with few but significant exceptions—has defined its calling by pushing off against the preaching of the church. Theology has been professionalized; it has become a guild unto itself. Turned in upon themselves, the theologians have kept the church at a safe distance, treating preaching as incidental instead of as the goal of theological reflection. And so the church, with rare exceptions, has passed over this generation of theologians when it has sought leadership, leaving the guild to its own standards and devices, and telling the schools, with increasingly slim financing, to fend for themselves.

Given such results, more importantly, given the church's calling to serve the witness of the gospel, there is good reason for trying something different. And there is precedent. Karl Barth, Karl Rahner, Hans Joachim Iwand, so too, Abraham Joshua Heschel, or Emil Fackenheim, instead of rejecting their various traditions, went deep into them and built intelligently from what they had received to become the great theologians of the century. The best theologians in contemporary American Lutheranism have done the same.

In relation to repentance, there is especially good reason for proceeding to the heritage to see what it provides. The first of the Ninety-five Theses reads, "When our Lord Jesus Christ said, 'Repent,' he willed the entire life of the believer to be one of repentance," indicating how fundamental repentance is to Luther's thought.[1] In addition, a major source in his discussion of repentance is only recently being translated, so that it is now possible to get a deeper insight into Luther's understanding of the role of the gospel in repentance. And there is the deep sense, in Luther as well as in the confessional discussion, that repentance is not the end but the beginning of freedom, so that as the law breaks false alternatives, the gospel takes hold to break open the liberty of faith.

Repentance and the Law

Some years ago, Gerhard Ebeling raised a question all the more critical for the infrequency of its being asked: If the law is known by its uses, who is the user?[2] If this question is addressed to Luther and the Lutheran confessions, the answer is surprising. The law is defined in a particularly concrete way that leaves the identity of the law's user an open question. Accordingly, repentance begins in the generic stuff of everyday life.

The word "law" is one of the most complex in the Lutheran vocabulary, capable of any number of inflections. But for the purpose of analysis, it can be said that Luther uses the term in basically two ways: he speaks of law at the level of what it signifies or requires, and he speaks of it in terms of what it does to its hearer.

The Catechisms, Small and Large, are some of the best examples of Luther's treatment of the requirements of the law. He explains the commandments in simple and direct language, identifying both what is enjoined and what is demanded. All the requirements of the law come down to two, the faith called for in the first table and the love of the neighbor set forth in the second.

Yet the very clarity of Luther's discussion masks the concrete way in which he moves at this level. On the First Commandment, for example, he does not begin with the Scripture, the Creed, or the classical language of Western theism—God's omnipotence, omniscience, or omnipresence. Instead, Luther opens the discussion with a naked, seemingly naive inquiry: What is it to have a God? What do you have if you have one? How does it work?

> Answer: A god is that to which we look for all good and in which we find refuge in every time of need. To have a god is nothing else than to trust and believe him with our whole heart.[3]

The warrant of Luther's argument is that having a god is a fundamental requirement of life. To be human is to be a creature, to receive life from outside one's self rather than from within. Thus, it is to be vulnerable, to be found in need, to have to look outside of the self for help, to suffer misfortune and distress that requires some reliable form of assistance. The experience of life demands a god, insisting on it with such determination that everyone has one and, in fact, serves one.

That's the way a god works. God is whatever you depend upon for help. If your god doesn't provide for you in a time of trouble, you must provide for it and, in the end, be consumed by the relationship. Thus, there can only be one god per person—a god demands such a level of fear, love, and trust as to exclude any other possibility.

Luther's explanations of the rest of the first table and all of the second follow the same logic. Having a god, it is necessary to use the god's name for its proper purposes and to hear what the god has in mind. By the same token, since having neighbors is a necessary feature of human life, there are some requirements involved in getting along with them: what happens with your original neighbors, your parents, has a way of playing itself out in the whole neighborhood. If there is going to be life in the neighborhood, killing must be kept under control; sexual disorder makes the neighbors nervous; a minimal level of property rights, the expectation of truth-telling and an elastic public trust are constitutive of communal peace.

Set up this way, Luther's interpretation of what the law requires is analytical—a descriptive examination of the minimal conditions necessary for the determining relationships of life. The commandments hold not because God gave them to Moses, because they are found in Scripture, or because Torah is actually gift. They hold because they make explicit what is implicit in the ebb and flow of human interrelatedness, summarizing the non-negotiables of creaturely life.[4]

Because the law is so embedded in daily relationships, it is ineradicable. Johann Agricola, Luther's old friend, who, after a stint of teaching Latin in Eisleben, came back to haunt him as the antinomian, argued that the law could be set aside in favor of the gospel. Luther answered in the Antinomian Disputations by sending Agricola back to school, this time in the declensions of the law. What the law signifies is eternal, Luther argues (2:46).[5] While the law is "emptied" or "quieted" in Christ for the believer,[6] it makes its requirements known wherever sin and death are at work (5:12). Thus, "they are completely ignorant and deceivers of souls who endeavor to abolish the law from the church. For that is not only foolish and impious but completely impossible" (5:15-16). It is a theoretical and conceptual resolution of the law, "a play put on in an empty theater" (5:32), as Luther himself put it, a conceptual trick that equates absence with ignored presence.

The second level in Luther's discussion of law describes it in terms of its impact or function in the hearer. At this level, the law makes itself known by what it does.

> Whatever shows sins, wrath or death, exercises the office of the law. For to reveal sin is nothing else nor can be nothing else than law, or the most proper effect and power of the law. (2:18-19)

Significantly, the Formula of Concord—after a generation and a half of feuding over definitions of the law—returns to this level of the definition in its fifth article, citing the same passage from Luther's argument against Agricola.[7]

This second level is predicated on the first. Because the law is in the fabric of human relationships, it bears itself out in experience, particularly in relation to the First Commandment. The law is the accusing voice which sounds in the conscience. But the voice's speech may be inchoate—it may sound in a vague sense of dread, in being ill at ease, or in an apprehension of jeopardy. And the accusation itself may be difficult to formulate: in relation to the First Commandment, it concerns faith and thus involves a sense of place, purpose, or belonging. But like the wolf in John 10, the law at this level doesn't announce its presence—the only sign of its work may be evidence that something is missing, a sense of loss that refuses reduction to specificity.

The law may attack in this manner during some monumental point of passage: the death of a parent, irretrievable failure in something that has been life-orienting or purpose-giving, the death of a child, the end of a marriage, middle age's realization of mortality. Such an experience is a death in its own right, the real effect of the law, just because it cancels out what has been life-shaping.

But this attack of the law doesn't necessarily always appear in such large proportions. It may arise from the bumps of a house settling at night in winter cold; from a spouse or child's unanticipated delay in returning home; from a minor slip at work, or from reading about the most recent civic disturbances in the newspaper. However it happens, whether in something major or seemingly minor, in relation to the First Commandment, the law's accusation is aimed at faith. Its result is despair.

Compared to the first table, the law's attack on matters of the second is exactly that: secondary. But just because the law's demands are inherent to life itself, moral disobedience also has its requital. The proportion is not necessarily one-to-one—Luther is as aware as the psalmists of the wicked, seeking financial consultants while the righteous suffer. But if the proportions vary, the rule generally holds. "Victimless crimes" are just another illusion, a moral sleight-of-hand in which insensitivity empties the theater. The law doesn't turn away its eye.

So, there is hardly a family that does not taste some deep levels of conflict, gaining first-hand experience of the way troubles play themselves out. The sense of hostility in communal life—whether in traffic or with competing neighbors—constricts it. The sexuality considered private and merely recreational has a way of implicating the public, and so on.

Again, this is a descriptive, indicative analysis. It is not that the law always should or must accuse. Rather, the law always approaches those in need, those who are troubled, those driven to the edge, as an accuser. In this age, under these conditions, law works this way. Its requirements, as good and just and right and true as they may be, are never neutral.

They bear themselves out in attack that may vary in degree but proceed, nevertheless, relentlessly.

Because the law works this way, the question of its user is open-ended. As Luther understood it, the law can become its own user—an aimless, purposeless power which simply makes demands or states conditions, continuing to expect fulfillment no matter what. This happens when, as Luther put it in the great Galatians commentary, "the law ascends into the conscience and attempts to rule there." The law makes ultimate claims for itself, conditioning the most important relationships of life on obedience to its demands. When the law makes its ultimate claims, it becomes a torturer, ceaselessly grinding away at its demands and accusations.

If the law can be its own user, other powers may take hold of it as well. The devil can use the law, offering release on the basis of obedience to its conditions, only to disappoint and so confound the faith of anyone foolish enough to have accepted the original premise—that the law frees. There is a close relationship here. Allied with the devil, the law is also allied with sin and death. They are existential forces, powers of the age, that contend against the gospel and the Creator for the heart of the creature.

Placed in such a league, the preacher can only become a user of the law in a secondary sense. Since the law plays itself out anonymously without stating its identity, it remains implicit in situations until it is stated. Much of its power is in its all-pervasive hiddenness, its anonymity. Stating it, making it explicit, identifying the law as law is already an attack on its claim to ultimacy. Naming it brings the law out of its hiddenness, sets out the requirement in recognizable terms, and consequently gives the hearer standing in relation to it.

This is the preacher's use of the law; this is why when Luther speaks of the commandment, *Gottes Gebot*, he does so in such positive terms. That which is unconditionally conditional in its relentless demand becomes in the speaking, in the naming, merely conditional. It is no longer high above you, but near to hand, as Moses and Paul have it (Deut. 30; Rom. 10).

So the preacher uses the law neither to become the accuser nor to make the accusation—that's the law's work. Rather, the preacher speaks the unspoken word, bringing to expression what is unexpressed, identifying the point where the law stands against the hearer. One of the best examples is the story of Nathan and David. Nathan's quiet parable brought the law into focus for David so that he could hear through all the illusions and denials the conclusion the law required. Nathan merely stated in what must have been a very quiet and thoughtful way what was already clear but unexpressed, "You are the one" (2 Sam 12:7).

This is the beginning of repentance. The law comes first. Before any other word is spoken, it is at work in the conditions of human interrelatedness, making its requirements and bearing out its accusations. Such is generic human experience, the seemingly ceaseless round of encountering limits and living with the consequences—the crises, minor or major, of having to have a god and neighbors, of living in the callings of everyday. Here, the law is being itself, doing what law does, grinding out despair and pride as though it feared a shortage.

Repentance starts in just such hiddenness, in the garden variety nuisances and pangs of the day. But if it is going to be anything but garden variety, if it is going to continue on as repentance, there must be a voice—a witness, a preacher who has the kindness to name the limit, to identify the accuser, to speak against the law by naming the law, showing the law its limits and its true master.

The Gospel and Repentance

The relationship of the gospel and repentance is disputed in Lutheranism. Philip Melanchthon floated some theological trial balloons on the matter in the later 1540s and 50s, raising a controversy as a result. The issue was settled in the fifth article of the Formula of Concord. Nowadays, mentioning the gospel in relation to repentance doesn't recall Melanchthon so much as it suggests, at least to some more careful Lutheran observers, *prima facie* evidence of Barthianism.

This is one of the unfortunate results of the Antinomian Disputations being left untranslated for so long. Apparently, the original translators—in German as well as English—took Luther's verdict on an early stage of the antinomian controversy as applicable to the whole of it. He dismissed that battle as a "war of words." His own Disputations, a set of six issued for public academic debate between 1536 and 1539, are far superior to such a verdict. For, in the theses which he prepared for the debates, he gave extended and careful attention to the contribution of the gospel to repentance.

Once again, the starting point is Ebeling's question—the true agency of the law, its ultimate user. So far, three possible users have been identified: the law itself, the devil, and, in a smaller way, the preacher. The preacher's use of the law, however, already anticipates and is only possible in light of the fourth and only legitimate user: the Holy Spirit, working through the gospel.

There is a strange collection of passages in some of Luther's writings where, caught up in the argument and in what almost appears to be a kind of transport, he directly addresses the law as though it were another person. One of the best of these is contained in the transcript of one of his exchanges with Agricola:

> Although, moreover, we say that despair is useful, it is not so by virtue of the law, but of the Holy Spirit, who does not make a robber or devil of the law but a teacher. Thus, whenever the law is dealt with, the nature and power and effect of the law is dealt with—that which it is able to do by itself. But when the law pretends that it follows or penetrates the gospel, 'Hear, quiet down, O law, see lest you jump your fences. You ought to be a teacher, not a robber, you can terrify, but beware, you may not entirely crush, as you once did to Cain, Saul, Judas; remember that you are a teacher. Here is your office, not of a devil or robber but of a teacher.' But these things are not by virtue of the law, but of the gospel and the Holy Spirit as interpreter of the law.[8]

Without the gospel, the law is indiscriminate. It merely drives, creating an appetite which, in the realm of the legal itself, is insatiable. So any port in the storm; when the trouble starts, any god will do. There is not one gospel; there are gospels by the thousands, all of them promising either to accommodate or possibly even to silence the voice of the law. "When in doubt, buy an appliance"; smoke a Lucky or drink a Miller, or try a new hairspray, or find an ample bosom, or shop 'til you drop; or whatever it takes to give the lightness of being some weight of significance.

In fact, the law offers itself as gospel. It makes one promise after another—offering to restore order, to give a new ethical tone, to elicit genuine striving that will put apathy to flight—all on a condition of minimal obedience. But in the end, the masquerade is broken and, along with it, the last, desperate illusion—that somehow, the sinner can also become a user of the law. The law turns on its deluded manager with quiet ruthlessness, dealing out disappointments that turn to cynicism, which culminates in despair. It is the foreplay of death. They are all the same in the dark.

The one and only gospel takes hold of the law in order to bring it to its true end, placing it under the power of Christ. The random hunting of the law, its aimless self-use, is brought to a point, its true point, its telos (Rom. 10:4). Only when it has been brought to its end does the law become a teacher, driving to the gospel. This happens at both levels of the law, in relation to what it signifies or requires and in relation to its accusation.

At the level of requirement, Christ brings the law to its end by fulfilling it in the believer. As he kept the First Commandment himself, Christ fulfills it in the believer by bringing into being the faith required. This fulfillment or restoration, as Luther calls it, is the subject of an argument that extends through several theses in the Antinomian Disputations.

> 4:35. But in truth, faith in Christ justifies, alone fulfills the law, alone does good works, without the law. 36. It alone accepts the remission of sin and spontaneously does good works through love. 37. Truly, it is after justification [that] good works follow spontaneously without the law, that is, without the help or coercion [of the law]. 38. In summary: The law is neither useful nor necessary to good works, much less for salvation. 39. But on the contrary, justification, good works, and wholeness are necessary to the fulfillment of the law. 40. For Christ comes to save that which was lost and to restore all things, as Peter says. 41. Therefore, the law is not destroyed by Christ, but restored, so that Adam might be just as he was, and even better.

Faith is the turning point. Rather than taking God on at the level of requirement, as though the law were some list out of a job jar, in Christ, faith meets God in the relationship signified by the First Commandment: as God. Related now, grounded in Christ, faith is free to go about its business in relation to both God and the neighbor. As Luther says at another point, "whoever believes this is brought back to the point from which Adam and Eve fell"—set free to live as a creature in relation to the Creator and the creation.

As Christ brings the requirement of the law to its end by fulfilling it, he brings its accusative function to its end by silencing it. This happens in the absolution, through the forgiveness of sins. Luther spells this out in another series of theses.

> 2:45. For the law as it was before Christ, certainly accusing us, under Christ is placated through the remission of sins and therefore is to be fulfilled in the Spirit. 46. Thus after Christ, in the future life will then be fulfilled even that new creature which [the law] in the meantime demanded. 47. Therefore the law in all eternity will never be abolished but will remain either to be fulfilled in the damned or already fulfilled in the blessed.

Through the forgiveness of sin, the law loses its basis for accusation and consequently falls silent—it is "quieted," "placated," or "emptied." The silence of the law in Christ contributes directly to its fulfillment. When the law stops its nagging and denouncing, a person can finally begin to live with what it really signifies: faith, hope, and love.

At the level of the law's requirement as well as at the level of its function, the end is an eschatological promise. The restoration begun is not yet complete. The "new creature" will only be himself or herself "what the law in the meantime demanded" when all things have been completely restored in the future life.

The meantime occurs under the sign of the *simul.* Brought under the power of Christ in faith, the believer begins to fulfill the law and, in eschatological earnest, experiences the silencing of the law's accusation—its mouth is stuffed. But until the final restoration, the law is always getting the gag off to shatter the silence once more.

> 5:40. Insofar as Christ is now raised in us, so far are we without the law, sin and death. 41. Insofar as he truly is not yet raised in us, so far are we under the law, sin and death. 42. Therefore the law (and likewise the gospel) is to be taught without distinction to the pious just as to the wicked.

The *simul* itself will only finally be resolved at the last day. Then the law, sin and death will all have lost their power, and Christ will rule in the undisputed sovereignty of the gospel.

Preaching repentance in the meantime involves, as Luther points out, both law and gospel. By stating explicitly what is implicitly demanded in creaturely relationships, by identifying the point where God stands against us, the preacher is already placing the law under the gospel's control. But if the law is actually going to end in the gospel, if repentance is truly to find its end in faith, then the gospel itself must become even more explicit than the law.

This is a critical point in the dialectic, one often overlooked. If nature abhors a vacuum, the heart will not tolerate even the hint of one. To preach against the law and all the false gospels used to appease it without naming the name of the one who is the law's true end is merely to entrench false alternatives. If it takes good money to drive out bad, only the gospel can expose all of its counterfeits. So Jesus' own preaching of repentance begins not with the abstract demand or an attempt to convince people of their need for the kingdom of God, but with announcement of the dawn of the kingdom. Repentance and faith are the gift and consequence of the kingdom's presence, not prior conditions for its arrival.

This is risky business in traditional Lutheran discussions because here, the gospel is entering into the law's realm, in effect, overlapping it. But Luther spoke of just this overlap, and as early as in the Commentary on Hebrews where he discussed God's alien and strange work.[9] By working this way, Luther argued, God takes the devil's weapons, that is, what Satan would use to drive to despair and unbelief, and uses them to drive to faith. So the Spirit, through the gospel, takes hold of the law and, without intermixing them, joins them to make them both function in the very same words. For Luther, the best example of this overlap is the First Commandment itself. It is both law and gospel, law in that it is aimed at unbelief, stating both requirement and accusation, and gospel in that it actually bestows what it demands: "I am the Lord, your God." The great "I am" sayings of John's gospel have the same character. When Jesus says, "I am the resurrection and the life," he simultaneously grants the gifts of which he speaks and excludes all other possibilities. Law and gospel function in the very same words.

When the unconditional character of the gospel is turned into an ideology, conceptualized as though it were just another theory about how God deals with us, this overlap is lost. Having lost its edge, the gospel turns to mush, to an unqualified endorsement or a universalism of unlimited tolerance. It doesn't have what in this age, under the simul, always remains its characteristic bite.

As well grounded in Luther's own theological reflection as they may be, such considerations may seem to put an impossible burden on the preacher. The law is in the web of things; the gospel is an alien word, sounded from without. If the law doesn't get through the ear, it will get its pound of flesh in another way. But if the gospel is to challenge all of its pretenders—the illusions and evasions, the false alternatives—it must be spoken. Finding a way to speak it so that it retains its bite can be extraordinarily difficult.

There is a formal way of speaking the gospel in which the church has historically expressed its confidence: absolution. In the direct and personal declaration of the forgiveness of sin in Christ, the gospel overlaps the law, both confirming its accusation and bringing the law to its end. Only sinners are forgiven; if you are forgiven, you must be the one. Yet it is the very act of the absolution, with the freedom it brings, that allows the conclusion of repentance, "I am a sinner," to be drawn. Precisely here, freedom dawns.

Though the rituals of absolution—private confession or the public confession which opens worship—have by and large passed from use in Lutheran congregations, there are still strategic points at which it must be spoken. One is in the pulpit. As in the Smalcald Articles, Luther equated preaching with the declaration of forgiveness.[10] Good preaching always moves toward such a directly personal word of assurance and hope. Another such point is in person-to-person conversations, such as counseling or calling. It is reported that Karl Menninger said that some seventy or eighty percent of the people who want to talk to a counselor are looking for absolution. It is a matter of uttering it, of taking courage in hand and actually speaking the word of pardon in Christ's name. *The Lutheran Book of Worship* provides rites for the recovery of both private and public absolution.

But it is the genius of the Word that it is so preeminently capable of moving beyond what is formal or ritualized into more personal address. The gospel is never generic—it is always "for you." In direct contact, the gospel can be spoken in personal terms directly related to the situation of the hearer.

Far and away, the example of such preaching is the story of Zacchaeus. When Jesus saw that little man dangling so far out on a limb, he didn't confront him with the abstractions of justice. Zacchaeus had undoubtedly heard all of that before and simply redoubled his security. Instead, Jesus spoke a word that is both law and gospel at the same time, marking the overlap: "Zacchaeus, I am coming to your house today" (Luke 19:5). His presence at table was law. He broke through all the illusions and evasions that had allowed Zacchaeus to keep a safe distance from those he was exploiting. It was also gospel. Jesus, at the same time, broke through the opprobrium, the rejection, the condemnation that came with the distance. "And Zacchaeus stood and said to the Lord, 'Behold, Lord, the half of my goods I give to the poor; and if I have defrauded anyone of anything, I restore it fourfold'" (Luke 19:8).

Under the power of the gospel, repentance can come to its true end: faith. Beginning in the generic stuff of daily life—in family struggles, the frustrations of work, the problems of the larger community, or in some deeper crisis—repentance is set in motion as we are dislodged. This is the law's work, to demand that we find lodging and continually to dislodge us. When the gospel enters, it overlaps the law, confirming its requirement and accusation by bringing the law to its true end in Christ. The believer, then, experiences the peace which comes when the law's voice is silenced. The conscience comes to rest in Christ and so under the power of the gospel. The believer begins actually to fulfill the law.

Repentance and freedom are correlative. For, in the light of the utter self-giving of Christ, a person begins to see the web of self-preservation in himself or herself; to see through and so to loathe the self for its illusions, evasions, and entanglements. And in the light of Christ, a person actually begins to know God for who he is—not a theistic projection attempting to catch up with his pretensions, but the one Mary mistook for the gardener, the one who, after Simon Peter had been sifted like wheat, made a bishop of him. This is the freedom of the gospel—freedom from all that entangles, freedom for life as a creature in relation to God, the neighbor, and the earth.

Repentance and the Preacher

On the basis of this analysis, it is possible to address the three problems mentioned at the beginning: the condition implied in repentance, the question of the marks of repentance, and the situation of the preacher.

First, repentance is not a prerequisite for but a consequence of the gospel. In this sense, the gospel could conceivably be called conditional—there is no faith without repentance. But anyone who wants to construe such a condition as though it were something to be achieved should not be allowed simply to talk about what good it would do the neighbors! Without the gospel, what is passed off as repentance will always go false in one way or another. It will degenerate into the cheap absolution of self-hatred, the perverse self-justification that thrives on its own put-downs. Or it will become a personal achievement that justifies the self's unyielding judgment of the others. If repentance is mere demand, the self will always lose itself one way or another, whether by drowning in its own mire or by claiming the ability to walk on it and then, after a brief delay, drowning just the same.

True repentance happens along the lines of the prayer of St. Augustine that drove Pelagius crazy, "Give what you command, and command what you will." By providing the good money that drives out the bad, the gospel saves the self from becoming its own project. Then the law can rest, and happily, because its work is completed. And the joy of repentance is fulfilled in the easy laughter of faith.

Secondly, the problem of identifying repentance in progress is more difficult, for it is not so much a theological as a political question. Theologically, the marks of repentance have traditionally been identified as sorrow over sin and a resolve to make amends, that is, to be restored to the relationship. According to Luther's analysis, these would be the appropriate marks to look for in a pastoral relationship, as persons are cared for in repentance.

But the question becomes considerably more complicated when it involves the *polis*, the larger community of the congregation, the church and possibly even state authorities. Then, it becomes a political problem in the true sense of the term—that is, a problem of community order. The community may demand an evaluation of repentance to see if it is real or simply claimed. It may also be necessary to determine whether or not the person or people involved have come to terms with the situation sufficiently to be trusted once more.

Recognizing the problem as political is helpful in such situations because it allows a more limited burden of proof. Pastors undoubtedly have both the authority and the responsibility to speak God's word of judgment, addressing the person's relationship to God. But in such political situations, the question that complicates also helps to simplify the matter: it is the person's relationship with the community that is at stake. This changes the evidence requirement—while the deeper question of the person's relationship to God is not to be neglected, in such circumstances, what the community seeks is evidence of reliability in relation to itself.

In this context, there may still not be a hard and fast set of criteria. But there are some outward signs which do manifest a person's willingness to deal penitently with the people who have been offended. One sign is truth-telling, the willingness to take responsibility for what has happened. The normal escapes—it was the other's fault, the circumstances were bad, I couldn't help it, and so forth—all indicate evasion. While it may take some time to develop, straightforward acknowledgment of the offense and, with it, acceptance of responsibility indicate that the person is coming to terms with what has happened.

Another mark is to deal directly with those who have been offended. Denial requires a safe distance, just enough so that the offense may remain theoretical and the people offended mere abstractions. Facing the offense and the offended directly breaks the distance and gives external evidence of an internal willingness to deal responsibly with the matters. David did not give Nathan a lesson in the nature of sexual addiction or the risks of military engagement. Neither did Zacchaeus offer Jesus a Chamber-of-Commerce course in the free market economy.

Both marks require patience, however. Early denials may merely set the stage for later confessions; unwillingness to face those offended may recede as a person gains confidence of a future shaped by forgiveness. One of the arts of hearing confessions is timing—as urgent as the situation may be, the Word also has its due season. Sometimes, the absolution can only be spoken after a thorough confession; at other times, there will be no confession without a prior absolution. Discerning the time, however, is more difficult in the abstract than it is in actual conversation. There is often a palpable sense of when further confession or immediate absolution is demanded.

Finally, the answer to Ebeling's question indicates the helpfulness of Luther's analysis for preachers. If it is assumed that the preacher is the user of the law in an unqualified way, then the preacher is put into an impossible situation. The preacher must literally be the Holy Spirit, calling, gathering, enlightening, sanctifying, keeping and thus bringing to repentance and faith every believer in every congregation that calls! Under such circumstances, it would make sense to break off the story of Jonah while he is in full flight, summing it up with an appeal to go and do likewise.

The fact that the Holy Spirit is the ultimate user of both law and gospel frees the preacher to preach and to do so in the close pastoral relation to the congregation that characterizes effective ministry. If it is the work of the law to accuse and denounce, the preacher is called to a more limited responsibility: to destroy the law's anonymity by naming it, to identify what is beginning in the law so that the gospel, by overlapping it, can bring repentance to its true end: faith in Christ. The preacher destroys the law's cover through the full-square declaration of the gospel, by declaring its end in Christ through the forgiveness of sin, and then by going about the quiet business of nurturing the new life that comes forth with the Word.

There is still plenty of risk here. To make explicit what is implicit is to be identified with what has become explicit in the law. To hit the overlap, to preach the gospel in such a way that it retains its bite is to be held responsible for the tooth marks that follow.

Preaching Repentance

The gospel is far more difficult to handle than the law. There is no resurrection without crucifixion. But in this connection, at least the crucifixion is for the right reason. And there's company in it, true companionship, the fellowship of his sufferings.

Notes

1. *Luther's Works*, American Edition, 56 vols., eds., Pelikan and Lehmann (St. Louis and Philadelphia: Concordia and Fortress, 1955ff.), 31:25. Hereafter cited as LW.

2. "The Doctrine of the *Triplex Usus Legis*," in *Word and Faith*, Gerhard Ebeling, tr., James Leitch (London: SCM Press, 1963), 71.

3. *Book of Concord*, ed., Theodore Tappert (Philadelphia: Fortress, 1959), 365. Hereafter cited as BC.

4. The best analysis of Luther's interpretation of the place of the commandments is Heinrich Bornkamm's *Luther and the Old Testament*, translators., Eric and Ruth Gritsch (Philadelphia: Fortress, 1969).

5. The Antinomian Disputations are found in *Luthers Werke*, Weimar Edition, 57 vols., eds. J. F. K. Knaake et al (Weimar, 1883ff.), 39:1.334-358. They are cited here by disputation number (1-6), followed by the number of the particular thesis. (Hereafter *Luthers Werke* is cited as WA.)

6. WA 39:2.433. There are summary transcripts of the first three debates involving the Antinomian Disputations on pages 359-584.

7. BC, 561.

8. WA 39:1.445.

9. LW 29:135.

10. BC, 310.

DISTINGUISHING LAW AND GOSPEL: A FUNCTIONAL VIEW

This essay was originally a lecture at Concordia Seminary in St. Louis. It was subsequently published in the **Concordia Journal** *(January 1996). In this paper, Nestingen traces the route of the controversy over definitions of Law and Gospel leading up to Article V of the Formula of Concord. The essay, though, is more than a history lesson as Nestingen demonstrates how the content and function of both God's Law and His Gospel are held together in preaching. Some critics of Nestingen (and Forde and Paulson) assert, but do not demonstrate, that they are mere existentialists who dismiss the need for the historical events of the cross and resurrection. Nestingen answers the unfounded worries of the critics when he states: "If the Law is merely arbitrary, detached from life or the necessities of relationship, it loses its authority. By the same token, when the function of the Gospel is separated from the content, the Gospel turns Christless—it becomes a generic word of acceptance which, having been detached from its source, gets applied willy-nilly to serve the purposes of its purported preacher. No one will ever be saved by the notion of inclusiveness or universal goodwill." JTP+*

As both Luther and Walther insisted, the proper distinction of Law and Gospel is fundamental to sound preaching. The contemporary experience of the church bears out the truth of their arguments.

When Law and Gospel are improperly distinguished, both are undermined. Separated from the Law, the Gospel gets absorbed into an ideology of tolerance in which indiscriminateness is equated with grace. Separated from the Gospel, the Law becomes an insatiable demand hammering away at the conscience until it destroys a person.

When Law and Gospel are properly distinguished, however, both are established. The Law can be set forth in its full-scale demand so that it lights the way to order and, through the work of the Spirit, drives us to Christ. The Gospel can be declared in all of its purity so that forgiveness of sins and deliverance from the powers of death and the devil are bestowed in the presence of our crucified and risen Lord.

Yet even within the Reformation itself, the church experienced difficulty with the distinction. This occurred most publicly in the 1540s when Melanchthon proposed to include the preaching of repentance within the realm of the Gospel. Flacius, ever vigilant, challenged quickly, arguing that this, in fact, transforms the Gospel from a gift of grace into another command. During the ensuing controversy, the issue shifted back and forth between the question of the relationship of Gospel with repentance and the manner of definition.

Pastors also experience difficulty with the distinction. It happens both ways, with Law and Gospel. A preacher goes into the pulpit intent on declaring a word of Law and discovers that rather than constraining and accusing, the proclamation appears to be comforting and encouraging the hearers. On the other side, there is the dreadful dilemma of attempting to speak a word of hope and joy, only to realize that the hearer is unmoved or descending even deeper into despair.

Taken historically and pastorally, then, there is ample reason to look into the proprieties of distinguishing Law and Gospel, specifically the manner of definition. In what follows, this will be attempted at two levels: first of all, historically, through analysis of Article V of the Formula of Concord, and then secondly, pastorally, with some consideration of the situation of the preacher.

I The Story of a Controversy

The controversy settled in Article V differs from others that preceded the Formula of Concord in that it is more compact and consequently has the appearance of being somewhat less complicated.

At least the history of the controversy can be summed up quickly. In a disputation held in one of the most difficult years in Lutheran history, 1548, Melanchthon offered the opinion that the Gospel must be involved in repentance. Always alert to Philip's theological experimentation, Matthias Flacius Illyricus promptly challenged. Flacius argued in classical Lutheran terms that to tie repentance to the Gospel was effectively to qualify it, thereby depriving the Gospel of its true comfort.[1]

Familiar as he had been with this type of argument, Melanchthon shifted ground. He backed away from the substance of what he had argued in the disputation, taking cover in theological method. He had used the term Gospel in a wider sense, he said, one that would include the whole doctrine of Christ and His work. Thus, repentance would be included.

Melanchthon's explanation appears to have satisfied Flacius, who backed off and let the matter rest until a similar argument was made, this time in the even more acrid theological atmosphere of 1556. Once again, the spark was struck off in a disputation, Melanchthon returning to the substance of what he had argued in 1548. But this time, Philip did not back down. Instead, his students took up the conflict, arguing, among other things, that since there is no commandment in the Decalog that explicitly sets out a requirement for repentance, the Gospel must be added to set forth the demand.

Flacius led the attack again, equating Melanchthon's arguments with Johann Agricola's earlier antinomian attempts to derive repentance from the preaching of the Gospel. Flacius was joined by Nicholas von Amsdorf and Johannes Wigand, the controversy carrying right into the early part of the 1570s.

If the conflict itself was fairly simple, however, the Formula of Concord's sophistication in handling it appears when the settlement is examined closely.

The Formula settled the controversy by entrenching Melanchthon's first reply to Flacius. It acknowledges a legitimate, Biblical use of the term Gospel in a wider sense, to include "the entire doctrine of Christ,"[2] while at the same time holding out for a more specific sense of the term when the Law and the Gospel are opposed to one another. The Gospel, "strictly speaking," is "precisely a comforting and joyful message that does not reprove or terrify but comforts consciences that are frightened by the Law, directs them solely to the merit of Christ, and raises them up again by the delightful proclamation of God's grace and favor acquired through the merits of Christ."[3]

Two features of this settlement, both of them commonly passed over, should be noted. To begin with, the Formula allows the substance of Melanchthon's earlier argument to stand unrepudiated. Luther and Melanchthon had both made statements that the Gospel, "strictly speaking," is necessary if there is to be genuine repentance. Luther argues the point in the Antinomian Disputations, Melanchthon, in Article IV of the Apology.[4] But neither of them went beyond their assertions to spell out a specific doctrinal relationship.

Aware of earlier discussions, the authors of the Formula are careful to carry them forward.[5] They clearly repudiate the excesses of the later Philippist polemics, insisting that the Gospel cannot be considered a "proclamation of conviction or reproof," that it must be "exclusively a proclamation of grace."[6] But they also specifically acknowledge a contribution of the Gospel to repentance, holding that "both doctrines are always together, and both of them have to be urged side by side, but in proper order and with the correct distinction."[7] The Gospel, properly defined, is an unconditional word of pardon and release in Christ. No demand, even for repentance, can be allowed to compromise it. But at the same time, the Gospel clearly contributes to the realization of repentance in its hearers.

The specific nature of the relationship between the Gospel and repentance should be more fully explored by contemporary Lutheran theologians and preachers. For at this point, as commonly elsewhere, the Biblically grounded theological reflection of the Lutheran confessors also has experiential warrant. Left bereft of any hope of God's grace, a sinner will flee judgment rather than come to terms with it in repentance. Similarly, the Gospel has a way of intensifying a believer's sense of inadequacy even as it declares the sufficiency of Christ's work—the closer you get to the light, the more you see! Further theological and pastoral analysis of the contributions of the Gospel to repentance would break down some of the common stereotypes and contribute to the vitality of Law-Gospel preaching.[8]

There is another matter that should be noticed in Article V of the Formula. Attempting to escape Flacius' critique, Melanchthon took refuge in theological method. The authors of the Formula accepted his wider definition, but taking up the method, go Melanchthon one better.

In the cases of both Law and Gospel, the authors of the Formula begin with definitions that specify the content. The Law "is a divine doctrine which teaches what is right and God-pleasing and which condemns everything that is sinful and contrary to God's will"; the Gospel is "the kind of doctrine that teaches what a man who has not kept the law and is condemned by it should believe, namely, that Christ has satisfied and paid for all guilt and without man's merit has obtained and won for him forgiveness of sin, the 'righteousness that avails before God,' and eternal life."[9]

But having defined Law and Gospel by their different content, in both cases the Formula moves to an additional level of definition in which verbs and adverbs are used to describe the way Law and Gospel actually work or function.

The definitive activity of the Law is that it condemns sin, a mark so characteristic that having described it, the Formula will say, "Everything which condemns sin is and belongs to the proclamation of law."[10]

Similarly, the Gospel is a "*comforting* and joyful message which *does not reprove* or *terrify* but *comforts* consciences that are frightened by the Law, *directs* them solely to the merit of Christ and *raises* them up again by the delightful proclamation of God's grace and favor acquired through the merits of Christ."[11]

To put it in a phrase, the Formula of Concord supplements its definitions of Law and Gospel by moving from content to function. The description of what Law and Gospel are is not considered complete until they have also been defined in terms of what they do.

In the case of the Law, in fact, the function is so idiosyncratic that it pushes out the limits of definition by content. As "a divine doctrine," the Law certainly contains specific requirements—its content cannot be obviated. But in a fallen world, among endlessly inventive sinners, the Law must continually be shutting down the exceptions. Thus, anything and therefore also everything that participates in the definitive function—condemnation, accusation; crushing or exposure—is part of the Law's proclamation.

'Under this definition, the term law is being given a wider sense than Melanchthon accords it in the Apology. "By 'law' in this discussion," he wrote, "we mean the commandments of the Decalogue wherever they appear in Scripture."[12] A pedantic use of this equation may have been part of the difficulty for the Philippists. Either way, the Formula clearly broadens the sense. It takes up what had been a test case, a dispute over whether the passion story is Law or Gospel, to point out that other Biblical words besides the commandments can also condemn.[13] And it invokes Luther's authority to show that the Law is more all-encompassing, "Everything that preaches about our sin and the wrath of God, no matter how or when it happens, is the proclamation of the law."[14] Taken in the broad sense given to it by Luther and the Formula, the Law cannot be confined to the Ten Commandments. Just as "anything that does not proceed from faith is sin" (Rom 14:23), so anything outside of Christ is under the Law. Moral requirements, the law of the state, familial pressures, personal expectations—even a blown leaf, to take one of Luther's favorite examples—can all preach the Law. For each one of them can condemn—the rustling leaf probably most effectively because it makes its threats implicitly—letting the imagination fill them out.

The Gospel also functions. It is comforting and joyful; it comforts consciences and raises them up again. But where the Law's functions press the limits of definition by content, the Gospel's function points back to its source, the one who is the essential content of the Gospel, Christ Jesus. He is both Alpha and Omega, the beginning and the end. There can be no gift without the giver; theologically, there can be no function without the content.

This is true of both Law and Gospel. A functional definition of Law, even one as broad as Luther's and the Formula's, will work only as long as there is some prior content. If the Law is merely arbitrary, detached from life or the necessities of relationship, it loses its authority. By the same token, when the function of the Gospel is separated from the content, the Gospel turns Christless—it becomes a generic word of acceptance which, having been detached from its source, gets applied willy-nilly to serve the purposes of its purported preacher. No one will ever be saved by the notion of inclusiveness or universal goodwill.

The problem that develops when a functional definition is detached from a definition by content appears in existential theologies. The Law is no longer a divine requirement but a category of existential analysis. Likewise, faith is detached from Christ and becomes a form of authentic existence.

This difficulty is also evident in current preaching. Christ gets treated as a concept, grace as a disposition or policy, and the Gospel as idea. The *extra nos* is lost, the crucifixion and resurrection of Jesus of Nazareth, born of the Virgin Mary, being rendered theoretical.

The Formula of Concord holds content and function together, moving to the level of function to fill out the definition more concretely. As the authors of the Formula knew, they had precedent for their method. They cite Luther directly, using his language to describe the functions of both Law and Gospel.[15] The troubles the older Melanchthon and his students ran into illustrate what happens when content alone is used to define Law and Gospel; the Formula uses Luther's more balanced functional view to bring an essential corrective.

II A Distinction that Matters

When Article V of the Formula of Concord is examined for its implications for preaching, it introduces an additional level of consideration in distinguishing Law and Gospel.

At its basic level, the distinction is grammatical-doctrinal. The Law speaks with the voice of Moses, saying, "Thou shalt," "Thou shalt not," "You haven't," "You did," "If you wouldn't." The Gospel rings with the voice of Christ, saying, "I am the good shepherd. The good shepherd lays down his life for the sheep." "No one shall snatch you out of my hand." "Nothing shall separate you from the love of God in Christ Jesus our Lord."

Now much would be gained if preachers would simply mind this fundamental level of definition. Then, texts that set forth the Law would be proclaimed as such. And texts that declare the promise of Christ would bring Him home to the hearer in all of His grace and goodness.

Standing in a heritage that includes Luther, the younger Melanchthon, Flacius, Chemnitz, Bach, Walther, Koren, and the rest, this should be a bare minimum expectation. If grammatically-doctrinally, a text has the sound of Moses about it, there can be no turning a deaf ear. The Law claims the pulpit. On the other hand, when Christ is at work in the Word to bring comfort and peace, there should be no lectures on the possibility. The preacher's job, then, is to bestow Christ's gift in the words and images of the text.

But now when it re-introduces a functional definition, the Formula takes the preacher to the other level of consideration. If the first level examines the original grammar and doctrine of the text, the second level examines the way the word functions for the hearer, that is, its effect.

For example, the Sacraments and the absolution would be at the grammatical-doctrinal level unquestionably Gospel. Yet their very intensity has a way of stirring the conscience of the believer so that people become profoundly self-aware in their participation. As such, just because they are such powerful expressions of the Gospel, the Sacraments, and the absolution can gain the effect of Law.

It is for this reason that writing in the Small Catechism, Luther takes up the question of worthy participation in the Lord's Supper. He had dealt with a deep sense of his own unworthiness during his earlier days as a monk. In his ministry, he had to serve people who experienced anxiety about their faith in the reception of the Sacrament. With such firsthand knowledge of the difficulty, Luther used the fourth question in the explanation to encourage those caught in themselves to simply turn to the words "given and shed for you for the remission of sins." Experience had taught him to tend the Gospel in the Sacraments rather than simply assuming its presence.

A faithful pastor, sensitive to the function of the Word in the congregation, learns to guard the consciences of the faithful, just as Luther did. "There is many a slip 'twixt cup and lip"; just so, there may be worlds of difference between the preacher's mouth and the hearers' ears. What is grammatically, doctrinally without question the pure word of the Gospel may become the harshest word of condemnation if the function is not also discerned.

Not so long before he died, I had opportunity to talk about this topic with Alvin Nathaniel Rogness, formerly president of Luther Seminary in St. Paul. He began to reminisce, as older people sometimes do, about sermons he had heard on joy, calling them the most annihilating voice of the Law in his experience. It is easy to see how this happens. Given a text like Philippians 4, "rejoice in the Lord always, again I say, rejoice," the preacher sets out to meditate on the joy of the Gospel. But in fact, something different happens in the heart of the hearer.

Accepting the preacher's premise, the hearer says, "Yes, it is only right; I should have this joy. But I don't have it. It must be because I am not devout enough, sincere enough, or haven't given myself completely." The voice which in the pulpit is perceived to be full of grace enters a disquieted conscience and turns vicious.

Thus, the proper distinction of Law and Gospel must move beyond stereotypes, those within the Lutheran community, as well as beyond it. The distinction begins grammatically, doctrinally, in recognition of the textual differences between command and promise. But taking up the grammar or doctrine, as important as such a step is, is just the beginning. Knowing the traditions, circumstances, and struggles of the hearers, a faithful pastor also seeks to discern—with the help of Article V of the Formula, among others—how the text will work for the hearer. If it is grammatically a word of Law, it should be the same functionally so that the hearer has no doubt about the one to whom the Word is being addressed. More difficultly, if the Gospel is going to be the Gospel, it must really do the Gospel's work, imparting Christ's gifts to the hearer.

Such consideration is only possible in the knowledge and conviction that, ultimately, it is the Spirit who wields Law and Gospel in the hearts of our hearers. Yet at the same time that this relieves us of the final responsibility, it shows us our penultimate duties. We cannot bring about repentance or create faith. But we can use words in a neighborly way, seeking with them to be of service to both the Word and the hearer.

This is the awesomeness of our calling. We are called to be craftsmen, to handle rightly the word of truth so that God's Word of truth takes form on human lips and enters the hearing of our congregations fit for their ears. May God grant us the wisdom and discernment necessary to such a calling.

Notes

1. There is a fine summary of the controversy in F. Bente, *Historical Introductions to the Book of Concord* (St. Louis: Concordia, 1921, 1965), pp. 171ff.
2. BC 478, 6.
3. BC 478, 7.
4. In the first of the six disputations against the antinomians, Luther argues that the Gospel is necessary before a person can make the good resolve, the second part of repentance, WA 39.11,345. In the Apology, Melanchthon argues that the preaching of the Law is not enough to produce repentance, that the Gospel must be added, BC 144, 257; 145, 260.
5. The Solid Declaration quotes one of Melanchthon's statements from the Apology, and a couple of paragraphs later cites the Antinomian Disputations, BC 561, 15, 17; WA 39. 1, 348. The citation to the disputations is not footnoted as such in the Tappert edition of the Book of Concord.
6. BC 479, 11.
7. BC 561, 15.
8. For some further consideration of the connection, see an article by the author, "Preaching for Repentance," Lutheran Quarterly 3.3 (Fall 1989): 249-266.
9. BC 478, 3 and 5.
10. BC 478, 4.
11. BC 478, 7; emphasis mine.
12. BC 108, 6.
13. BC 560, 12.
14. Ibid.
15. BC 560, 12; 561, 17.

FORGIVENESS OF SINS AND RESTORATION TO OFFICE

*Originally published in **Logia** (Epiphany 1993), this essay was presented at a meeting of the bishops of the former American Lutheran Church. The bishops requested Nestingen to provide theological guidance on how to address the issues of pastors who have been removed from office for unethical behavior. Nestingen begins with the question of what God's forgiveness does do and then speaks of the New Testament qualifications for those who bear the office. Nestingen argues that the absolution is eschatological but not necessarily therapeutic. That is to say, God's forgiveness provides Christ's righteousness to the broken sinner, delivering from sin, death, and the devil, but it does not repair the breach of trust with the community that has occurred. The office is not a matter of status or entitlement but a place of service for the sake of the Gospel and well-being of the church. He notes that a former pastor who demands restoration to office as a right misunderstands both the nature of the office and the New Testament expectations for fidelity. One may be forgiven, but for the good of the community, not restored to the office. This essay is a fine example of Nestingen's clear thinking—evangelical, scriptural, and churchly. Those who accuse Nestingen of Antinomianism have not grasped the argument he makes in this essay. JTP+*

There are two theological issues involved in the question of restoring to the pastoral office those who have lost it through some public offense. The first is the nature of forgiveness; the second, qualifications for the office of the ministry. To provide perspective for further discussion of the problem, these issues are considered here in light of the New Testament and the Lutheran tradition.

The Forgiveness of Sin

Understandings of forgiveness and sin in both the New Testament and the Lutheran Confessions are controlled by what might be called eschatological afterthought. Instead of moving from an analysis of the problem to a proffered solution, they move backward from the solution to the problem. This reversal, in which the work of Christ takes priority, radicalizes the concepts of forgiveness and sin.

The driving force of New Testament theology is its eschatology. The cross and the resurrection of Jesus are understood as disclosure of both his identity and the creation's future. He is identified as Lord (Rom 1:3; 14:9), as the ultimate authority placed in control of all things so that at his name every knee shall bow, on the earth, above the earth, and under it (Phil 2:9-11). The early Christian confession, "Jesus is Lord," is an assertion of his power. Raised from the dead, he has been given authority over all things.

Identifying Jesus as Lord, the resurrection discloses the future of the earth as well. The classic expression of this hope is in 1 Corinthians 15, where Paul speaks of Christ subjecting all of the other powers (finally death) to his control and then, in effect, handing things over to the Creator (vv. 20-28). If the language remains strange, the hope that it expresses is certain: the ultimate purpose of Christ's work is the restoration of the creation to its rightful owner. Taking on all the other powers that have claimed sovereignty, Christ is establishing his claim so that he will be manifest as "the one in whom all things hold together" (Col 1:17) and so that the creation will finally be what it was meant to be.

There were early Christian communities, such as Corinth, where anticipation of the resurrection in this life undermined the cross. Counteracting this, Paul's letters and the Gospels tie the resurrection and the cross together as closely as possible. Paul's power-in-weakness discussion toward the end of 2 Corinthians, for example, is to show that the power of the resurrection is to be had only under the sign of the cross. Similarly, in the Gospels, the risen Christ always appears with his wounds so that the continuity of the risen and the crucified are beyond any doubt. The resurrection is the vindication of Jesus' crucifixion. In the light of his rising, the one who was "crucified outside the camp" (Heb 13:11-13) under the curse of the law (Gal 3:13) among the godless (the two thieves, Golgotha) is known for who he is and what he does; he is the Lord of all, giving himself under the sign of the opposite in the midst of rejection and shame.

It is in the light of this hope, held in varying degrees of anticipation by all of the New Testament writers, that matters of forgiveness and sin are considered. The hope functions as the first premise in the line of reasoning, with everything else falling into place behind it.

Forgiveness is the entrance to new life in Christ. By forgiving sin, Christ takes the sinner under his lordship, gathering a new community of those who are being freed from the other powers that have held them. Forgiveness is thus equivalent to justification, both being rooted in the presence of the Spirit of the resurrected Lord. Forgiven, the believer is incorporated into Christ to be conformed to his image (Rom 8:29), dying with him to be raised with him.

The classic text here is John 20:19-23. The risen Christ makes his first appearance to his disciples as they are attempting to protect themselves by hiding in an upper room. He appears among them without knock or warning and then, without statement of intention or explanation, breathes on them, granting the Holy Spirit in the power to forgive and retain sin. The forgiveness of sins is the present equivalent of the resurrection of the dead.

This connection is maintained throughout the New Testament. Even before his limbs are unlocked, the paralytic has already received new life in Christ's words of forgiveness (Mark 2:3-12). Zacchaeus and other tax collectors, prostitutes, and sinners of all kinds (Luke 19:1-10; Matt 9:10-12; 21:31)—"the off scouring of all things" as Paul speaks of the early community (1 Cor 4:13)—are all treated accordingly. Forgiveness breaks them out of a situation in which their future is shaped by their sin and puts them into a relationship in which the future is given to them in Christ.

Once the eschatological purpose of Christ's work and the power of forgiveness are clear, the basis of the New Testament's discussion of sin becomes apparent. It is no longer simply a moral problem, a chronic appetite for the titillating. Rather, as Paul declares in Romans, "anything that does not proceed from faith is sin" (Rom 14:23). Since faith defines the relationship between the risen Lord and those who have been called into his community, anything—anything in its broadest and most inclusive sense—that undermines this relationship in any way not only is sin but also reveals the power of sin. It is a turning away once again from the Creator to the creature. The creature becomes ensnared all over again by the powers that identify the passing age, death, the devil, the law.

For all of the emphasis on the power of forgiveness, some question remains about the possibility of restoring to the community one who has fallen away from it. The problematic text is Hebrews 6:4-8, where any return from apostasy without repentance is flatly denied. Paul, in dealing with a similar problem in Corinth, where members of the community apparently had come to the conclusion that the power of the resurrection so protected them that it was no longer possible for them to sin, instructs the community to drive these evildoers out of the fellowship (1 Cor 5).

Matthew and Luke, on the other side, give close attention to the restoration of the lost. Matthew 18:12-14 speaks of the restoration of "the little ones"; the well-known parables of the lost sheep, the lost coin, and the prodigal in Luke 15 broaden it to a concern for the lost of any kind. Matthew 18:15-17 provides specific instructions for restoring sinners to the community or finally excluding them; Luke 17:3 calls for unlimited forgiveness on condition of repentance.

It may be that this range of data represents continuing discussion of the problem of discipline in the New Testament community. As hope for an imminent *eschaton* cooled, problems of community discipline had to be dealt with, policies being developed accordingly. Whatever the case, the eschatological power of forgiveness, at least in the Pauline writings and the Gospels, is such that it blurs any clear line between sinners and saints. The exegesis of Romans 7 that Luther appealed to for the *simul* may be disputed by some, but the presence of Peter—whose apostasy was known in such detail that it is one of the most fully documented stories in the Gospels—in a position of leadership in the early community makes it clear that forgiveness was not considered a one-time clearance. Rather, it is the hallmark of the early Christian witness in the power of the crucified and risen Christ.

The logic of this New Testament eschatological afterthought carries over into the Lutheran tradition. Luther himself was driven by apocalyptic expectations that, in turn, animated his whole witness. While the tradition after him cooled the drive of Luther's hope, Lutheran teaching still reflects the basic features of that eschatology, at least in its classic documents. Unlike the Augustinian tradition from which he came, Luther does not begin his theology with an assumption about the law. Instead, he begins christologically and reasons backward from the work of Christ to forgiveness, the law, and sin. If Christ alone saves, then there can be no other force in human experience capable of saving. Forgiveness must, therefore, be understood in relation to justification as the saving declaration of God in Christ. Unable to save, the law has to serve some other necessary but ancillary purpose. Sin can then be spoken of on two levels: in relation to faith and in relation to the law.

"Where there is forgiveness of sins, there is also life and salvation" (SC VI, 6). For Luther, as for the New Testament, forgiveness is never simply a negative transaction dependent on perceived guilt. Rather, it is a future-opening, freedom-bestowing gift in which the believer lives. Baptized into the forgiveness of sin, living under promise, renewed in faith, the believer receives life in Christ under the sign of absolution. Forgiveness and justification are two aspects of the same event: being incorporated into Christ, being defined by him in a life-determining relationship.

This said, the law is put in its place. It is "demythologized," confined to its proper realm. Unable to save, it is doing the work of law when it states the Creator's demands upon his creatures. And it is doing its best when it brings home, in an inchoate, indiscriminate way, the need for some kind of help. It is only when the gospel takes control of the law that this "second use" actually serves its proper end: driving a person to Christ. Otherwise, left to its own resources, the law simply drives and keeps driving insatiably. Under the power of the gospel, however, it is used by the Holy Spirit. Then and only then can it convict of sin. The confession of sin is the confession of faith.

For Luther and the early Lutherans, the sin of which the Holy Spirit convicts through the law is "person sin," "root or hereditary sin," the sin of the first table of the Commandments. It is unbelief, the idolatrous quest of the heart that seeks in the creature what the Creator alone can give. This is the realm of "unbelief, despair, and other great and shameful sins" (SC III, 16), an arena of life in which human inability to fear, love, or trust God above all things is revealed. Here, the believer is driven to confess, "I believe that I cannot by my own reason or strength believe in Jesus Christ my Lord or come to him, but the Holy Spirit has called me through the Gospel . . ." (SC II, 6).

The sins of the second table follow out of the sin of the first. Fearing, loving, and trusting something other than God, the sinner is at odds with the neighbor as well. But here, maybe surprisingly, the law can be of some help. In the second table, there is some possibility of self-discipline, of community restraint, and encouragement. The law cannot produce faith, but it can, by its coercive power, place some check on the sinful self. It can even go further, encouraging a civil righteousness, which is a positive good.

There is no question about the possibility of restoring the sinner to community in the Lutheran tradition. The confession of faith that the Holy Spirit has "enlightened" and "sanctified" stands side by side with the conviction that "in the church, day after day, he fully forgives my sins and the sins of all believers" (SC II, 6). The sanctified are sinners who continue to live in forgiveness until the last day. Impenitent sinners, those who have not been moved to penance by the gospel, may be excluded from the church, however. This "lesser excommunication" is carried out for the sake of witness to the one being sent away, in hopes that restoration will result.

Qualifications for Office

There are two primary traditions of ministry in the New Testament, one defining it in terms of charismatic power, the other in terms of apostolic authority. Each sets its own standards for ministry. But in both cases ministry belongs to the community; it is neither a personal endowment nor a right of the individual. The tradition of ministry rooted in charismatic power is the oldest in the New Testament and characteristic of the Pauline congregations. Romans 12 and 1 Corinthians 11-13 define its basic features. As the Spirit of the risen Lord takes believers under the power of grace (χάρις), they are endowed with gifts of grace (χαρίσματα) that range from prophetic speech to financial stewardship and administration. The gift is the believer's calling, the particular piece of the action assigned in the endowment: "Having gifts that differ according to the grace given to us, let us use them" (Rom 12:6). The gift is also for what has been given: "each according to the measure God has assigned" (Rom 12:3, "but let each one test his own work . . . for each man will have to bear his own load" (Gal 6:4-5).

The Spirit's specific endowment or gift of power is the one qualification for ministry, which is understood to be the continuing work of the risen Christ through the community. Paul vehemently resisted any attempt to establish other requirements, as for instance, in Galatia, where outsiders came insisting on obedience to a particular understanding of the law. At the same time, however, he set a test for ministry, namely, edification, building up the body (1 Cor 14). This test was to be a basis for challenging self-serving and disruptive ministries.

The second tradition, in which ministry is defined in terms of apostolic authority, grew up a little later in the New Testament church, possibly in reaction to the disorder of the Pauline congregations. Whereas for Paul and his communities, ministry was the continuing work of the Holy Spirit carried out through a body of incorporated individuals, in the later tradition, ministry was seen as the work of the Holy Spirit mediated through offices. The apostles themselves were not replaced when they died; there was no continuation of an office of "apostle" in the Christian community. There arose, however, a tradition of derived authority in which the ministry is handed on through the succession of offices.

Luke-Acts holds a variation of this understanding of ministry, but the primary source for this tradition is the Pastoral Epistles. The threefold ministry of bishop, presbyter, and deacon became the working structure of the early church. The clergy appear to have taken over the ministry that, in the earlier tradition, had belonged to the whole congregation. Now, it became ordered, delegated, and passed along from office to office. Qualifications for office were set out in terms of desired personal characteristics. In 1 Timothy 3:2, for instance, a bishop should be "above reproach, the husband of one wife, temperate, sensible, dignified," while a deacon must be "serious, not double-tongued, not addicted to much wine, not greedy for gain" (v. 8). Using these qualifications, congregations could seek persons to lead them in ministry.

Whether ministry is by charismatic power bestowed from above or by apostolic authority delegated through office, it is clearly neither a possession nor a right of the individual. In Paul's understanding, the charismatic gift is a commission to service; unused or exploited, it turns on its bearer in indictment. In the Pastorals, those who do not live up to the qualifications of the office are unfit for it.

The Lutheran tradition of ministry combines characteristics of both of these traditions, a factor in the continuing disputes about it. Ministry is defined eschatologically in terms of the Spirit's work. The means of the Spirit's working, however, is not a person, an office, or the community itself, but rather the word and sacraments. It is a confessional understanding in the sense that the ministry is defined by confessing, by the declaration of the word, and the administration of the sacraments.

The Augustana provides the classic definition. Article V lays down the working premise: the Spirit works faith through the means of grace. The fact that the Spirit works through the word requires speakers establishing an office. The speaking, in turn, brings about a gathering of hearers (Articles VII and VIII). But as it establishes both the office of the ministry and the gathering of the church, the word also limits both. Articles XIV and XXVII limit the office of the ministry: it is not a personal prerogative but a calling (XIV). As such, its authority is limited to what is given in the word itself (XXVIII). While the gathering is not limited as explicitly, the word clearly defines its boundaries as well: the gathering requires speakers of the word (V and XIV), and it is subject to the word proclaimed to it (XXVIII).

The essential qualification for ministry in the Lutheran Confessions, then, is the word itself. A pastor called to speak it must know it and be able to tell it in such a way that the community receives its service. The community may also set other appropriate standards for its pastors. The Augustana doesn't ask for anything more than a "regular call." But the "Treatise on the Power and Primacy of the Pope" speaks of ministry as a "right of the congregation" (Tr 24). Dependent on the word, the community has to have access to it and may then set standards for its speakers.

These standards certainly include the second table of the Commandments. As reluctant as he was to support coercive measures in matters of the first table, Luther left no question about expectations for personal discipline. Article VI of the Formula of Concord is an echo, though the language has changed somewhat. "The law is for the body," Luther argued. Personal discipline in matters of the second table is on the order of table manners—an elementary requirement to be handled without either fuss or concession.

So, for example, sexual trustworthiness, as defined in the Sixth Commandment, is a minimal standard that cannot be compromised without disrupting the community. In the case of pastors, it is demanded by the workings of the ministry itself. If a pastor is going to be relied upon to speak the word in the intimate contexts of daily life where people are the most vulnerable, that pastor must be sexually reliable. A pastor who is not predictable, who cannot be counted on to honor appropriate pastoral relations within the community, will not be able to function as a speaker of the word in it.

Some Suggestions

On the basis of these considerations, it is possible to draw out two implications that may be helpful in considering the problem of restoring to the pastoral office those who have lost it through some public offense.

First, the promise of forgiveness in Christ cannot be reduced to therapy, treated as entitlement, or abstracted into a general policy of tolerance. Forgiveness is therapeutic. Silencing the accusing voice of the law undermines the very basis of the attack on the conscience. Released, a person is no longer divided within at that point—there is healing in the self. In the absolution, guilt may end, the future may open; there may be a great sense of relief.

But eschatologically considered, the gift is inseparable from the giver. While restoring a person to a proper sense of self may be an appropriate therapeutic goal, in faith, the objective is different. In faith, the sought-for result is that one be brought into such a relationship with Christ as to be defined by him. If the goal of therapy is self-recovery, life in faith is self-loss, literally dying with Christ.

In neither case can forgiveness be considered entitlement. As powerfully as Christ's forgiveness functions, both therapeutically and eschatologically, it does not automatically resolve the question of restoration to office. Though the sin is forgiven, the sinner may have forfeited by public offense the trust necessary to function effectively in office. Likewise, considerations of the integrity of the witness may demand qualifications—for example, in relation to marital conduct—that automatically eliminate people who do not conform to them. As an institution of the earthly kingdom, the church is duty-bound to set standards of office that are appropriate to its function. Further, a person who invokes forgiveness in an attempt to override the legitimate concerns of the community for its proclamation can hardly be considered a penitent!

For the same reasons, the word of forgiveness in Christ cannot be abstracted or reduced to a general policy of tolerance. This reduction happens when forgiveness is treated as a concept and its implications pressed, either in relation to God as a universalism or in relation to other people as a principle of openness or general acceptance. Tolerance is negative; at best, it is a generalized willingness to overlook offense. In Christ, forgiveness is not an idea but an event that happens. As such, it is positive; a person is taken on in the specifics, the offense is dealt with, and a new relationship is established.

Second, the call to the ministry and the language of personal rights are antithetical. Biblically and confessionally, whether empowered by the Spirit or authorized by a succession of offices, ministry is always a trust that is given. The very concept of call involves the presence of others who take the initiative in seeking out a person for service. The language of rights, however, is by its nature individualistic. It defines powers or prerogatives that the individual already holds and which may not be taken by the community.

Only the gathering of believers, at whatever level they may be organized, can speak of a right to the ministry. Holding this right, they may set whatever theological, educational, moral, or other standards they consider appropriate to the call. The limit on their right, whether it is delegated to a bishop or exercised in a congregational procedure, is the word. No individual can claim as a right what the community of the saints bestows as a trust under the power of the Holy Spirit.

PREACHING THE CATECHISM

In this article, Nestingen demonstrates that he stands in the lineage of the great American Lutheran catechist J. Michel Reu (1869-1943) in his love for Luther's Small Catechism. With Christ Jesus at the center, the Small Catechism is the pattern for Christian faith and life. Nestingen gives Moses his due in the Ten Commandments and the Table of Duties but then notes that Moses has to keep his nose out of Christ's work. It is only when Moses won't stay home where he belongs that he creates trouble. The Small Catechism was born in the pulpit, and it served to shape the proclamation of preachers and the hearing of the baptized. Nestingen is confident that after all these years, the Small Catechism is a vital source in the life of individual Christians and the congregation corporately. This is a very practical article, as Nestingen has thoughtful suggestions for parish use. The article was first published in ***Word & World*** *(Winter 1990). JTP+*

Speaking of the Small Catechism's place in recent American Lutheran congregational life, Gerhard Frost, longtime professor of catechetics at Luther Seminary, once remarked, "For years, the catechism glowered at us menacingly. Then it went behind trees and hid, peeking out occasionally. Now we're hoping that it will come out and smile again."

Poetic as always, Frost sketches both a transformation and a prospectus. The transformation is in the catechism's standing. There were and are those of Frost's own generation who remember it with the intimacy of old love. For much of the generation that followed, however, the catechism was apparently something different: a stern taskmaster which turned up in confirmation class to set out the theological values of an enforcement-minded majority.

But if the generation now providing a good share of the leadership in American Lutheranism remembers the catechism in primarily negative terms, there is another generation after them that remembers it not at all. For these people, the catechism was, at best, an occasional visitor at Christian education.

Either way, recalled as a glower or sensed vaguely in concealment, the catechism has clearly lost the place that it has held in Lutheranism for centuries. It is no longer the working paradigm, encompassing the witness of Scripture in the language of daily experience to serve preaching and reflection on the church's faith and mission.

Given such a transformation, it may be mere poetry to speak of a prospectus. This much is certain: the catechism cannot become a vehicle for the recovery of a lost golden age of Lutheranism. The past wasn't so golden; now it's gone. Neither can the catechism be called back on terms of enforcement. That was a failure. If the catechism is to be for this and future generations of Lutherans what it was for those who went before us, it will only be because, as Frost put it, it has smiled again.

All of this may require an impertinent question, however: Does the catechism have a smile? In order for us to see it, the catechism has to get more than the piecemeal analysis it usually receives when the parts are taken individually, apart from their connection. It is when it comes together that the catechism does what it does best—setting out, in its simple yet profound way, the depths of law and gospel in life shaped by the cross. The catechism's smile occurs in its witness when it gets a chance to preach.

The purpose of this essay is to see the catechism smile—to listen to it preach—and then to consider preaching its own paradigm for the hearer both within and beyond the Christian community. This will involve, first of all, considering the preaching of the catechism itself and, secondly, reflection on ways in which the catechism can serve current preaching.

I. The Lutheran Paradigm

Historically examined, two factors shape the preaching in Luther's Small Catechism: first, its catholicism; second, its analysis of daily life shaped by the forces of law and gospel.

A. The Catechisms as Catholic Documents

Both of Luther's catechisms, the Small and the Large (or German), are inherently catholic documents. In part, this reflects the situation in which they were written—the Small in late 1528 and early 1529, the Large over a slightly more extended period in the same years.[1] But the catholicism of the catechisms also reflects the considered commitment of Luther and his fellow Wittenberg reformers. After having been blocked by circumstances and interdicted through the early years of the reformation, the Saxons in 1526 finally got what they took to be legal authority to proceed to the reform of the congregations. Planning methodically, they first wanted to survey the prevailing conditions. They established what later came to be institutionalized throughout the Lutheran reform: the visitations. Committees consisting of a couple of theologians and some canon lawyers were sent out to evaluate the circumstances and make recommendations. *Ad hoc* as they were, these visitation committees are the institutional seeds of what became the Lutheran church.

There was no such vision at the time, however. The visitations were for strictly provisional purposes. The local congregations had suffered serious neglect in the late Middle Ages; the reformation had contributed its own disruptions. There were problems aplenty, with immediate pressure for remedy. Something had to be done to tide the congregations over until church life was regularized according to the priority of the gospel.

But there was also something provisional in the agenda of the reformers themselves. Though time has dimmed its impact in Lutheranism, the original Lutherans were fully apocalyptic. Luther thought of himself in prophetic terms.[2] He was widely interpreted as a new Elijah, another John the Baptist, raised up as a harbinger of the end times to prepare for the apocalypse. This hope drove original Lutheran theological reflection; it also undermined any long-term structural or organizational reflection. Something had to be provided for the meantime; there would be no long-term.

With this apocalypticism, there was also what might be termed an ecumenical commitment. As currently conceived, ecumenism is a strategy for dealing with the multiplicity of denominations; in Luther's day, the oneness of the church was a matter of faith that had some sight to support it. Religious unity was commonly understood to be a non-negotiable requirement for public peace. The papacy was considered its visible expression. For all of their objections to the papacy, with all of their commitment to a conciliar settlement of the reform, Luther and the Wittenberg reformers viewed the prospects of separation from Rome with abiding horror. Even in lectures finally published in 1535, some fourteen years following his excommunication, Luther could say, "To be sure, we censure, we denounce, we plead, we warn; but we do not on this account disrupt the unity of the Spirit. . .A love that is able to bear nothing but the benefits done by another is fictitious."[3]

Situation and long-term commitment came together, then, to produce a catholic catechism. Excommunicant, apocalyptic prophet Luther remained profoundly catholic. So when he set to work to provide documents that would serve congregations in their disrupted life, he took classic documents of the catholic faith—the Ten Commandments, the Apostles' Creed, the Lord's Prayer—and added explanations of the indisputable sacraments, Baptism, and the Lord's Supper, and their nearest relation, Confession, and Absolution.

With all its problems, C. P. Krauth's old title, *The Conservative Reformation*, sums up Luther's orientation. Unlike the radical reformers and even the Calvinists, he did not set out to establish something separate but equal. Nor in his catechism did he publish some Lutheran gnosis or private, personal insight. Instead, he took over a catholic framework, confessing the faith in public formulas using the defining expressions of the Christian faith in command, promise, and prayer. As Old Testament professors habitually observe, the commandments are not Lutheran; they are originally Hebrew and have been taken over in the church. The Apostles' Creed was at Luther's time and remains the working creed of Western Christendom. The Lord's Prayer belongs to all believers, as do the sacraments. The catechism is not a sectarian document; it is the faith held by the church, set out for parents to teach their children. Catholic to the bone, the catechisms transcend later developments like parochialism or denominationalism. The goal is to grasp and define the center—what holds for all—so that those who use it can be sustained in transitional times.

B. Life under Law and Gospel

There is a novelty in Luther's catechism, however: the order. Unlike earlier catechisms, Luther places the commandments before the creed and the Lord's Prayer. According to Luther:

> There are three things which everyone must know in order to be saved. First, he must know what he ought to do and what he must leave undone. Then, as he has discovered that it is impossible for him to accomplish either with his own strength, he must know where to obtain, where to seek, and find the power that will enable him to do his duty. And, in the third place, he must know how to seek and obtain that aid.[4]

This innovation has been the subject of intense debate in recent theological discussion, virtually all of it resting on false assumptions about

Luther's presuppositions. Luther was not setting a theological priority in this sequence. Rather, as his own statement makes clear, his purpose was to follow the order of experience: life begins, is lived, and ends under the force of law; the gospel enters the realm of the law as an alien word, giving the faith, hope, and love necessary to live in such a context; prayer arises as both necessity and gift in life lived between law and gospel.

Luther's approach is radical in the truest sense of the term. Attempting to go beyond theological or psychological superstructures in which ideological commitments predominate, he wants to address the original questions of human life, not theoretically or conceptually, but actually, truthfully, in terms of what can be known: What does God expect of me? What does God do for me? How can I get hold of God to get some help? As usual for Luther, it is a thinking of the faith hammered out in temptation, where the irreducible issues of life and death, faith and unbelief emerge.

The Commandments. Approaching the catechism in this way, Luther exposits the commandments as the sum of the demands God makes in the down-to-earth conditions of daily life.[5] If you are a creature, possessing neither life nor the future in and of yourself, you are going to have to get help from somewhere; where you tum for such assistance divulges the identity of your god. Since you have to have a god, you have to be able to get hold of him or her or it; this requires a properly used name—not just a generic title, but a name to which your god will answer. And you have to hear from this god so that you know what your god demands and promises; time has to be taken from the everyday round for this hearing.

By the same token, creatures who receive life from outside of themselves have to get along with their neighbors. So we have to have parents, need protection to live, and require sexual order, basic property, a community in which words hold their value, and a context of trustfulness so that life can be lived in the open.

In interpreting the commandments, Luther attempts to read life from the bottom up to get to the non-negotiable requirements of the human condition. That the Ten Commandments were given to Moses, that they are in the Bible, that they are understood in the Old Testament as torah—all of this is incidental to their explication of the ineradicable minimums of creatureliness. Luther is not interested in ideal social orders or moral systems or whether the law is found in nature or conscience. He wants to get down to the barest bones, to life-constitutive requirements.

Luther does make assumptions, however. One is rooted in inexperience: Luther believed that a creature attempting to live under the commandments inevitably lives with disappointment. It may be full-fledged guilt (though that is usually a believer's problem); it may be the simple frustration of trying to make creaturely inventions work; it may be despair; it may be passing difficulty with a flaccid upper lip. Whatever, to live as a creature with non-negotiable conditions is to be continually confronted with limits and the consequences they impose: *lex semper accusat*.

There is also a Christological assumption. In the commandments, however, this premise is far more important for what it disallows than for what it proposes.

Like Paul, Luther was convinced that since Christ saves, the commandments can't.[6] They can order life for the time being; the law is doing its best when it accuses. But the commandments were not, are not, and never will be meant to save. That is Christ's job; where he is at work, the commandments and the law they explicate have no saving force. The requirements of life may be non-negotiable, but they are not the last word—that belongs to Christ alone. Consequently, the law can never be more than penultimate—that is the limit of its allowance.

This christological assumption is not necessary to the interpretation of the law's requirements, however. Christ can interpret it, no questions asked, but so can a rabbi, a moral philosopher, or even an ayatollah, for that matter—the minimums hold for all people, be they Christians, Jews, Moslems, or California gurus of inner peace. So, there is no attempt to find a Christian law—we already have enough to handle as creatures. Moses does a good job as far as he goes; in the penultimate realm, Christ doesn't go into competition with him. But then Moses has to keep his nose out of Christ's work, too. It's when he won't stay at home that Moses gets into trouble.

The Creed. Luther's explanations of the creed are similarly rooted in the language of daily experience. Technical terms and theological concepts critical to the reformation—even slogans like the Word alone, grace alone, faith alone—fall into the deep background as Luther sets forth a direct declaration of God's work for us. The goal is the simple one: to get to the bottom of what God has done, is doing, and can be expected to do for us.

The explanation of the first article amplifies what has already been stated in the commandments. Creaturely life is shaped by the gifts provided—"food and clothing, home and family, daily work and everything else I need"—and by the ongoing experience of the obligation. The obligation has already been focused in the commandments. But here, there is an additional force mentioned: "Therefore surely I ought. . ." The gifts of daily life, in Luther's explanation, as well as in daily circumstance, become the basis of obligation. Gifted, we face the demands that come with the gifts themselves. The demands are in the workings of interrelatedness, arising out of the conditions of life itself. They are consequently as unyielding as the stubborn particularity of each individual.

But in the explanation of the second article, just as in Bach's *Clavierübung* (also an exposition of the catechism), there is a new flow to the music—open, expansive, and free. For here Christ makes his entry, taking on all of the powers of sin and death with their claims, demands, and bondage; Christ takes us under a lordship which has as its trademark his own gracious self-giving. "He has redeemed me, a lost and condemned person, bought and freed me," all so that "I may be his own, live under him and serve him."

For Luther, the transfer described here is no abstraction, no theologoumenon. Christ's work is literally to "at-one" us, to restore us to the creatureliness lost in all of our attempts at self-transcendence.[7] His gift is that he takes us on precisely at the point of our bondage, where we are gripped by obligations that are not only moral demands but impingements, obsessions, resentments, addictions—all of them turning us in upon ourselves, inciting the desperate desire to become our own creators, to have life and the future within ourselves, at our beck and call. Taking hold of us here, Christ bestows himself in the forgiveness of sin and the promise of the resurrection to free us from the web of our self-seeking and to bestow the open-endedness that only he can give. He bestows peace by bringing the conscience to rest in himself. It is Christ's business—his calling and his accomplishment—to restore creation and creature to their creator, or in Luther's words, "to make us what Adam and Eve were meant to be, only better."

Luther's very contention for the immediate reality of Christ's work sets up the dialectic in the explanation of the third article. Being told that Christ has actually freed her, a Christian can only confess to seeing evidence of the opposite: "I believe that I cannot by my own reason or strength believe in Jesus Christ my Lord or come to him. . ." That is one pole of the dialectic. Yet, given the identity of the one who both creates and redeems, there is another pole: "He has called, gathered, enlightened, sanctified, and kept." Redeemed, the believer receives the gifts yet lives in hope of the future realization of them, observing the daily reality of unbelief yet living in the confidence that the Spirit is setting him apart, restoring her to her creaturely purpose. So, for the time being, until the last day, the true identity of the believer exists in the absolution alone. There, in the oral declaration of forgiveness, the future is disclosed, life is given, and the power of the resurrection is unleashed.

The Lord's Prayer. The doubleness that emerges in the third article of the creed characterizes Luther's entire explanation of the Lord's Prayer—the least known part of the catechism, yet the masterwork of it. Living in the context of law, but under the power of the gospel, the believer is simultaneously an unbeliever. Gripped in Christ, he gets caught up in immortality games all over again; caught in desires for control, she is freed once more in forgiveness. Thus, a believer must learn "where to seek and obtain the aid" needed to live in the tension, for this tension is the crucible of daily life.

The explanations of the Lord's Prayer acknowledge the tension while declaring the help that can be expected from God.[8] The old Adam or Eve, who prays, "hallowed be my name, my kingdom come, my will be done," is prayed against; the new self, who lives in the Word and in faith, is prayed for because only the one who is relentlessly committed to both creature and creation will sustain the self-created in the absolution. By the same token, the old self's relentless seeking of daily bread in all its forms meets its Waterloo in the realization of God's gifts, a realization for which we must pray because our hearts become as hard as adamant. Rather than being a patch on the old self's inner tube, forgiveness emerges as the force of the new creation, the very basis of freedom with God and the neighbor. The old self's heroism is just the reverse side of "unbelief, despair, and other great and shameful sins"; yet "even though we are so tempted," we continue to pray for God's preserving grace, knowing that finally only he can deliver us from every evil.

As beautiful as they are, the other parts of the catechism—the explanations of the sacraments, the keys, confession, and absolution—concern what could be considered technical matters. For Luther, the catechism *per se* was the first three parts. The explanations of the sacraments were added because of the circumstance of the reformation, in particular, some of the seemingly perpetual confusion around the means of grace. Yet Luther isn't satisfied with mere clarification. He goes to the root to emphasize that it is God who is at work in Word and sacraments to reclaim creature and creation. So, in each case, he spells out the relationship of Word and element and examines the implication for life in faith.

It is no wonder that Luther considered the catechism (along with the *Bondage of the Will*) his finest work. It is also no wonder that the catechism held such a deep grip on Lutheranism until recent times. Setting out the heart of the catholic faith, Luther also reads daily experience and depicts the rhythms of life in terms of law and gospel, unbelief and faith, death and resurrection. Born under the law, living in the midst of obligation and the bondage that comes when we resist our limits, we are graced by the gospel of Jesus Christ, who recreates, making us creatures again—people of the earth, fit for God, the neighbor, and the earth itself.

Taken together, the themes of the catechism's preaching form a paradigm—a way of understanding the Word of God and human experience for the sake of continuing witness. It is a paradigm with both feet on the ground, an assessment of daily life and the gospel emphasizing the reality of the obligations that confront and the gifts of grace that sustain us. As stoically responsible as it is about the demands of creatureliness—one of its focal points—it breaks into a smile when it sets out the other: the even deeper and more abiding reality of God's grace in Christ.

II. The Paradigm and Preaching

A paradigm such as that proposed by the catechism does two things: it offers organizing principles which simplify the complex—clarifying and focusing the conversations of those who share it—and it provides a basis for speaking with those who don't hold it, keying particular themes that open up possibilities for extending the conversation. The catechism's paradigm serves preaching in both ways, providing a shared language within the community and a basis for speaking to those outside of it.

The generation that produced the Formula of Concord referred to the Small Catechism in a phrase that until a generation or two ago was commonplace: "the layman's Bible."[9] While the title has some overtones which aren't so helpful, it suggests the catechism's paradigmatic function. Amidst the welter of biblical assertions, ideas, forms, and arguments, the catechism highlights themes it takes to be crucial in the deepest sense. It does this not to exclude, but to underscore—asserting that whatever else the Bible can and does say, it is a book of law and gospel in which the last word is the declaration of Christ. So doing, it weights such themes as sin and grace or death and resurrection—themes which by any generally accepted criterion are central in Scripture.

This weighting has performed a helpful service within the Lutheran community. Since the reformation, there have been dramatic changes in the way law is understood. Yet, among Lutherans, the commandments and their explanations give specificity to the consideration of law, so that even those who argue for a Lutheran misunderstanding have something concrete to deal with. Similarly, where you find Lutherans, you can generally expect to hear something of the grace of God. The explanation of the second article has a way of focusing on God's gracious act in Christ, so that grace itself doesn't float off into some conceptual ether or get reduced to mere tolerance. So, too, the *simul* set out in the explanation of the third article and of the Lord's Prayer still has a way of bringing a deep comfort to people battling with an abiding sense of their own unbelief.

In this way, the catechism serves as a multiplication table or, for the more advanced perhaps, a calculus of the faith. It establishes a shared vocabulary, defines essentials, and lays down a basis for reflection. Talking pastorally or reflecting theologically with a person nurtured in the catechism, there is always a common point of reference, an oral word echoing out of the years which can now once more be spoken to specify the demand or the promise.

This internal community function of the catechism is particularly important in a context where there are so many competing paradigms. The public schools have one—a pop-psych interpretation of the child as a self-contained individual replete with all the necessities for coping with life if only the artifices are removed so that feelings can be freely expressed. The marketplace has another—using advertising to present an image of selfhood, which is actively in charge of its destiny, shopping for its fate, but at the same time only truly in control when in possession of the particular product. Television religion has its own version of the marketplace paradigm, only in theirs, the essential product is different, and "shop 'til you drop" takes on a different meaning.

These public paradigms have been very effective in undermining the Lutheran witness. Each of them is premised on a free will, which classical Lutheranism regards as myth and *prima facie* evidence of rebellion; each of them tries to manage or manipulate the free will they've posited in some particular direction, insisting on the necessity of law to contain it, while Lutheranism's classic declaration is the freedom of the gospel. Conflict comes at every level. Not surprisingly, until they discover how the old Lutheran paradigm makes sense of experience in the light of grace, people often respond to it with some shock and offense. "You mean there's no free will—you've got to be kidding!"

But this turns the question over to the other side: Given the offense, can the Lutheran paradigm speak to those outside it, those who don't have an oral point of reference echoing out of the past but who live in the common paradigms of the culture? If the old Lutheran way of reckoning is to have any value, it must be catholic and oriented to life experience. Failing that, it will become what it was not and never should be: a gnosis, a secret knowledge preserved only by and for the insiders.

There have been many critiques of Lutheranism aimed at just this point, though they don't all have equal claims to quality. There is something funny about Krister Stendahl's argument before a group of psychologists and psychiatrists that people don't feel guilty anymore![10] But whatever the source or quality of the complaint, it is at least asking the right questions: How is Christ proclaimed? How is Christ brought home to those who don't know him?

The problem in the critiques themselves and in many attempts to reply, hinges on a false assumption about the relation of law and gospel, particularly concerning the firstness of the law. That the law comes first is to Luther and the original Lutherans not a prescription to be fulfilled by a pastor or witness who, armed with the law, seeks to inculcate guilt or need. Rather, it is a description of what is commonly known: that we have our lives in the context of law, living under limits, in the midst of demands and various forms of accusation or imposition, and that we don't generally begin to examine our illusions of control until the situation is uncomfortable enough to require it. In this sense, the law must come first; gospel preaching that doesn't recognize or deal with this firstness loses contact with the realities of daily life, becoming one more illusion of transcendence.

This does not mean that the law must always come first in witness, however, as though one could only hook after having sufficiently jabbed. To a person already afflicted, the gospel may be the first word: Christ is for you! On the other hand, to a person who imagines himself possessed of a robust conscience, free from any demand or accusation, another word may claim priority: You are the one!

In either case, what is required is some sense not only of the text but of the hearer and of how they meet. And it is just here that the old Lutheran paradigm starts to hit its stride. For its assumptions are keyed to daily experience: creatures who do not have life in themselves experience law as limit and accusation—not simply in a moral sense, but more broadly as entrapment, containment, the terrors of recognized mortality. It is Christ, "a man born of woman, born under the law," whose work it is to enter into such obligation, impingement, and terror and speak the word: "In the world you will have tribulation, but be of good cheer; I have overcome the world."

Some of the best research into the origins of Lutheranism indicates that what gave it a compelling quality for its sixteenth-century adherents was the doctrine of vocation.[11] The Lutheran witness desacralized or de-pietized the religious overlay, which encumbered and ultimately devalued everyday life in the sixteenth century. At the same time, it re-valued the common stuff of the family, work, and citizenship, declaring the freedom of the gospel bestowed in Christ to enter into these earthly relations.

The genius of the Lutheran paradigm for contemporary witness is at the same point. It attacks all the mythologies of fulfillment, self-transcendence through self-actualization, creating a new world through product relationships—the secular pieties and all their religious counterparts—by telling the truth about the limits and impingements of creaturely life. But it does so by speaking a word that is beyond goals, accomplishments, lifestyles, and alternatives: in Christ, God has come to reclaim creature and creation for himself, and so sets us free to live in the very good for which we were created.

Preaching the catechism to the outsider is not so much a matter of handing it out on the street or using it directly in evangelism calls. Rather, the catechism specifies some things to look for and some ways to address them. There is no point, as Dietrich Bonhoeffer declared long ago, in invading people's closets to drag out dirty linen. There is every good reason, however, to be sensitive to the points where the law is bearing down, enclosing, pinching, and driving so that the word of grace can be addressed to just such points. Jesus didn't affirm the frustrations of the blind, telling them how much he understood—he gave them sight. In the same way, he didn't tell the poor about his humble origins in Nazareth—he preached good news to them.

That's how the catechism can work in witness. It sets up a paradigm for sober-minded discernment of law and gospel, a witness which acknowledges the reality of the day but at the same time declares the hope and freedom given in the midst of it.

With this, there is a remaining question: How or when? In Luther's day, there were several Sunday services—it was customary to continue preaching on the catechism at one of them while following the lectionary in others. Given the competition for leisure time nowadays, that is an unimaginable luxury. But there are times when the rhythm of the church year offers a particular opportunity.

The most appropriate time for preaching on the catechism is Lent, the traditional season of instruction when the catechumens used to be prepared for baptism. To take one of the chief parts of the catechism each year, for example, would provide themes for five years of Lenten preaching. Or, by pushing hard, one might be able to cover the whole catechism in Lent, though there would hardly be any time for digestion and discussion. Just think: something besides Lenten dramas.

Another possibility is breaking into the lectionary for a series of sermons on each of the parts, once a year over a succession of years or for an entire year early in the pastor's ministry in a particular parish. There is every good reason to be loyal to the lectionary. But the value of preaching a sermon on each of the commandments, for example, or on each article or each petition, is such that even the lectionary might yield. The Sundays late in Pentecost, from the time school starts until American Thanksgiving, are good ones for a series on the commandments. The Sundays of Lent are good for preaching on the creed or the Lord's Prayer.

There are lectionary texts that lend themselves to preaching on the sacraments. The anti-sacramentalism of American Protestantism affects Lutherans also. They have to be taught and regularly. This should not be merely inculcating the latest fashions in sacramental piety but the deep-down gifts of Word and element.

With such use—clarifying and focusing the discussion inside; opening up the Word in terms recognizable to those outside—the catechism may regain something of its hold as the living confession of Lutheranism. But the catechism is more interested in witness than in gaining power, and so it may smile prematurely—just for the sheer joy of being able to say it again, to name the name that is above every other.

Notes

1. The best introduction to the catechism in English is still J. Michael Reu, *Dr. Martin Luther's Small Catechism: A History of its Origin, its Distribution, and its Use* (Chicago: Wartburg, 1929).
2. Karl Holl, "Martin Luther on Luther," in *Interpreters of Luther: Essays in Honor of Wilhelm Pauck*, ed. Jaroslav Pelikan (Philadelphia: Fortress, 1968) 9-35.
3. Luther's Works, 27.392f
4. Quoted by John C. Mattes and M. Reu, Luther's Small Catechism: A Jubilee Offering (Minneapolis: Augsburg, 1929) 15.
5. Heinrich Bornkamm, Luther and the Old Testament (Philadelphia: Fortress, 1969).

6. WA 39.1,354.

7. Gerhard Forde, "The Work of Christ," in *Christian Dogmatics*, ed. Carl E. Braaten and Robert W. Jenson (Philadelphia: Fortress, 1984) 79-98.

8. Herbert Girgensohn, *Teaching Luther's Catechism* (Philadelphia: Muhlenberg, 1959) 1.199-306

9. *The Book of Concord*, ed. Theodore Tappert (Philadelphia: Muhlenberg, 1959) 465

10. Krister Stendahl, "The Apostle Paul and the Introspective Conscience of the West," in *Paul Among Jews and Gentiles* (Philadelphia: Fortress, 1976) 78-96.

11. Steven Ozment, *The Reformation in the Cities: The Appeal of Protestantism to Sixteenth Century Germany and Switzerland* (New Haven: Yale University, 1975).

FLOOD LOGIC: TENDING THE MEANS OF GRACE

*The Gospel and the sacraments invite contention with objections to "how they work." In this short piece, Nestingen unfolds the "logic" of preaching and the sacraments. Christ Jesus pulls us outside of ourselves by a promise that comes from Him, not us. It was published in **Logia** (Easter 2009). JTP+*

In a death-driven world, word and sacrament evoke perennial contention. Proclaimed or administered, they bestow here and now the fruits of Christ's death and resurrection. No wonder preaching, baptism, and the Supper—along with absolution—get swamped with such vitriol. Sin, death, and the devil do not surrender without a fight. So, the complaints cascade, the impious and the pious alike protesting Christ Jesus' encroachment on sinners. What chance does a preacher have?

Augustana V, with accompanying articles, defines the pastor's calling in this context. Preaching, baptizing, serving at the table—with absolution—set the terms of the office. But as Robert W. Jenson once argued, the language describing this combination of responsibilities implies a second: tending word and sacrament, serving their course in the community and beyond. Thus, having handed over the goods delivered by the text, having passed along the gifts granted by Christ Jesus through word and element, the preacher wades into the contention that follows. Because they are so counter-intuitive, standing directly in the face of all the usual human assumptions, the means of grace have to be taught, their workings clarified, and the questions they raise addressed.

This said, however, a danger prowls within the second task. Word and sacrament are from faith to faith - the preached and sacramental word embodies the power of the Holy Spirit to create the faith required. The common explanations and defenses invite both preacher and hearer to move from the faith-producing word to a secondary position behind it, in which the explanation or defense displaces the promise and so becomes itself the object of faith. For just this reason, Luther described the old Adam as the original theologian. Asking, "Did God really say?" signals unbelief. The promise of the gospel stands on its own, exposing its theoretical and theological supports as wanting.

Yet, with the danger noted, it may be helpful to take a closer look at the difference between the usual assumptions and the logic of the means of grace. Luther used the term *alien* to describe both the gospel and the righteousness it creates. It is alien in that it comes from without, from outside of the usual structures and systems, and enters our ears extraneously to reorient, more radically to re-create, those who hear it. Because of this, the gospel has a logic of its own in which the resurrection makes all the difference.

Subject-object logic, the process of reasoning employed in common forms of thought, assumes the power of death even if it can only acknowledge death's presence implicitly. As Leo Tolstoy wrote in *The Death of Ivan Ilyich*, the proposition that Gaius is a man, men are mortal; therefore, Gaius will die always seems true as applied to Gaius but never as applied to myself. Death holds the self loosely, thereby fostering illusions of immortality. But when its grip closes—in imposition and limitation, fear or sorrow, pain, and loss—the illusion shatters even as the self hastens to put the remains together again. If everyday logic seeks to keep any contact with the larger human enterprise, it has to acknowledge the power of death as it surfaces in threat and limitation. Failure to register the forces loose in creaturely life turns the reasoning towards enthusiasm. Like a hot air balloon, it rises.

In contrast, the first premise of the logic of the gospel—the reasoning set in motion by the means of grace—is laid down by Good Friday and Easter. With the words "crucified, dead, and buried," the Apostles' Creed anchors the starting point in the hard realities of every day. Incarnate, Christ Jesus went under the power of death, becoming its victim. In any other human way of thinking, this would not be the first but the last word. As Cleopas said, speaking in the past perfect for himself and the other disciple on the road to Emmaus, "We had thought he was the one to redeem Israel" (Luke 24:21). In other words, they thought it was all over. But the risen Christ literally turned the tables, making himself known in the breaking of the bread. The crucified, dead, and buried one has become the risen one. Jesus lives.

The reality of the resurrection declared, however, the Gospels, particularly Mark and the Apostle Paul, insist that Good Friday cannot, therefore, be pushed out of the syllogism. The resurrection does not annul the cross but establishes it. The risen Christ always appears with his wounds. So Paul writes to his enthusiastic Corinthians, "We have this treasure"—the power of the resurrection is present—but we have it "in earthen vessels," that is, under controverted circumstances, "to show that the transcendent power belongs to God and not to us" (2 Cor 4:7). In the present situation, any circumstance prior to the *eschaton*, Easter manifests itself under the sign of Good Friday, in the cross.

Just so, Easter explodes into abundance (John 10:10), the lavish overflow of the wedding at Cana, or the feeding of the five thousand. Marked by the cross, the resurrection cannot be contained, but breaks open the cornucopia, bringing a new future in which Christ Jesus pours himself out to overthrow all of the powers—sin, death, and the devil—that have bound, diminished, demanded, and destroyed the creation. Accordingly, loss has lost, emptiness has been filled to overflowing, enough has become wanton excess with no sign of surfeit.

This turns the ordinary thinking about word and sacrament on its head. The logic of death rules out any external source of life or power. In this way of thinking, discussion of baptismal practice focuses relentlessly on the qualifications of the baptized, the pastor, the congregation, or the water itself. One way or another, someone or something present has to energize the sacrament to make it work. In fact, in a strange form of perversity, guarding this requirement gets taken as a hallmark of fidelity. In the logic of the resurrection—which Gerhard Forde liked to call "flood logic," or the logic of abundance—death cannot contain the risen Christ. He is loose, out there, seeking his own to bestow himself in a death and resurrection like his. The qualifications of the baptized only become an issue in thinking about how to shape ministry most effectively to that particular person or people.

The same thing happens to the absolution. The dead giveaway of the old logic shows up in the protest, "Yes, but there are sinners in the congregation who may not have repented sufficiently." Once the focus has shifted from God's word in Christ to the hearts of the hearers, the conclusion follows: therefore, the absolution has to be qualified in favor of those who truly repent.

This protest fails at several levels. Of course, there are sinners in the congregation—the risen Christ keeps dragging them into the pews. "Compel them to enter," he says. Pastorally, it doesn't work as the protest assumes. The truly penitent are just for that reason confused about themselves, never satisfied with their own repentance, while the truly impenitent are more than ready to offer themselves as models of moral rehabilitation. Further, the idea that the weeds and the wheat can be identified and separated betrays the origins of the objections—once again, hidden under piety, unbelief moves to stave off the crucified and risen Christ so that it can preserve its own prerogatives. Dressed in Sunday-go-to-meeting concerns, sin, and death masquerade with the devil as redeemers.

The logic of the resurrection proceeds in an entirely different way. "He who hears you hears me," Jesus said; "Whatsoever you loose on earth is loosed in heaven." The qualifications of the hearer may become a pastoral consideration—timing may demand further reflection by the penitent. But Holy Absolution does not depend on the piety of the pious—it bestows the gifts won by Jesus of Nazareth on Good Friday and Easter. Grace flows by the sheer, abounding goodness of the one who could not keep himself away from gluttons, drunkards, and tax collectors—a sordid mess. Of course, they cannot repent—that is not within human capacity. The Spirit of the risen Christ works repentance, tearing us loose from false attachments so that we can live in the freedom of the gospel.

In another strange turnabout, the logic that promotes the disqualification of sinners in baptism and absolution has recently turned into an indiscriminate inclusiveness around the Lord's Supper. Grace, which Paul describes in Romans as the power of the resurrection, has been reduced to an ideology that follows the logic of death. Since Christ forgives one, the reasoning holds he must, of necessity, forgive all. So everything specific, all of the sacrament's faith-creating relational quality, gets obviated in a generic grease that harks back to the slippery old evasion, "Love is never having to say you are sorry." By such thinking, even baptism itself is too much to ask. So it goes round and round. As Karl Barth once commented, we barely get bucked from one horse when we have got our foot in the stirrup of another. So, caught up in ourselves and our own pursuit, we run back and forth between exclusion and inclusion. The one consistency, at either end, is the desire to keep Christ Jesus at a distance.

The logic of the resurrection once again proceeds from a different starting point. The risen Christ's habits and predilections are apparent in the Gospels. Wherever he goes, he gathers sinners to himself, setting the table in the presence of his enemies to lay himself out for us. The promises, "This is my body given for you" and "This cup is the New Testament in my blood," grant what they declare: the presence of the Risen One. In this way, the sinner is exposed as the death-dealing, spiritual pretender intent on self-realization. At the same time, a new self arises, recognizable from the water of baptism and the words of absolution: a sinner now in Christ's grip.

"This is what makes our theology certain," Luther once wrote, "it takes us outside of ourselves." Just so, the logic of death turns us back on ourselves, in the end, leaving us empty-handed. The means of grace and so the logic of the gospel get set in motion by Christ's eager joy in taking hold of us to make us his own.

HANDING OVER THE GOODS

This short essay takes as its title, the signature Nestingen phrase of "handing over the goods." That is what good preaching does! It is not a persuasive appeal to make a decision but the proclamation of Christ as pure promise to the hearer. The Gospel is not an offer to be accepted (or rejected) but a gift to be received by faith alone. This little piece was published in ***Logia*** *(Easter 2009). JTP+*

In the face of it, the absurdity announces itself plainly: appealing to the old Adam to create the new, if it begets anything at all, can only propagate either hypocrisy or despair. Blood will tell. But for all of such transparency, secondhand evangelicalism makes its perennial appearances in Lutheran circles stridently denouncing the unconditional proclamation of the gospel, insisting that Christ's work depends on the acceptance of the hearer and that any other formulation undermines evangelism. It will never end.

The critical point at issue is the power of God's word. The living God—the Triune One who creates out of nothing, justifies sinners, and raises the dead—does all such work by speaking. Just so, Jeremiah describes the word of God as a hammer that breaks the rocks to pieces; Hebrews calls it a two-edged sword. Since it is God's own word, the gospel does what it says, performing in the hearer what it describes, accomplishing that which it declares. It is, as Paul says, the power of salvation.

Because it is God's speech, the gospel eliminates all qualifications. As Mark tells it, when a group of friends rolled back the roofing to lower a paralyzed friend to him during a sermon, Jesus acted unilaterally to break the paralysis and forgive. Likewise, when he stood at the door of the tomb weeping at the unbelief welling up all around him, Jesus did not say, "Lazarus, if you really want to, you can come forth." Nonsense. Faith and resurrection join as sovereign acts of the Triune God in sinners by which the old Adam gets put to death and the new being in Christ comes forth.

The dead giveaway in the derivative evangelicalism that appears among Lutherans flags itself in the language of appeal. That was Zwingli's move. He reduced language to its ability to signify or communicate information. So God's word, like the bread and wine of the sacrament, represents or symbolizes that which he wishes to pass along. Shorn of the power God invests in it, the word takes on the limitations of all other human speech: it must be interpreted, understood, and applied by the hearer to gain any force. Working from similar assumptions, cut-rate evangelicalism must of necessity speak of the gospel as an offer, qualified by the willingness of the hearer to accept or complete what God has begun. The biblical language of death and resurrection gets reduced to a personal decision, the new birth to an intense emotional experience which the sovereign self lets or allows, thereafter invoking it as though it were conversion.

When the gospel is reduced to an appeal or an offer, Christ Jesus gets replaced by the old Adam as the standard of proclamation. According to John, after a brief conversation with Mary at his own tomb, the first thing the risen Christ did was to seek out his fear-driven disciples in their hiding place to absolve them and commission them with the authority to forgive sinners. As Luther says in the Small Catechism, "Where there is forgiveness of sins, there is life and salvation." The absolution is the present form of the resurrection of the dead. Contrariwise, bargain-basement evangelicalism claims that the contemporary seeker finds absolution a downer—an observation offered as though it were *prima facie* grounds for eliminating services of confession. The sacrament, which according to the Apostle Paul proclaims the Lord's death until he comes, becomes a festival of inclusiveness in which even the requirement of baptism poses too much of an obstacle. The demands and accusations of biblical texts are passed over in silence, as though ignoring it makes the law go away. Grace becomes indistinguishable from tolerance. The old Adam, like a cat in a sunbeam, lies licking itself while the crucified and risen Lord Jesus joins the ranks of the unemployed.

Biblically and theologically untenable, such degenerate evangelicalism multiplies hypocrisy and despair. On the one side, those who are confident in their acceptance of the alleged offer (the very people whom Jesus relentlessly attacked in singularly exclusive language) repeatedly point to those they consider real sinners (those whom Jesus with equal persistence sought out) as evidence for the necessity of qualifying the gospel. On the other side, those whose self-awareness has been tenderized by the gospel can see enough of themselves in the light of Christ to be suspicious of their own willing and doing. Deprived of the comfort of Christ's unqualified goodness, they wander aimlessly in Bunyan's slough of despond, always seeking assurance, never certain. As Phil Hanson, the author of *Sick and Tired of Being Sick and Tired*, once said, "If you think you have a free will, try it the next time you've got the trots."

Rather than undermining evangelism, such traditionally Lutheran arguments actually radicalize it. The folk church habits that the immigrants brought to North America are certainly failing. The days when the church could set out the means of grace and then rely on public religiosity to keep people in range of a congregation are long gone. But blaming the lost sheep for being lost and then challenging them to find themselves in the detritus provides no alternative. Rather, the Triune God's empowering of the word by his Spirit frees its speakers from self-reliance and all of the apprehension that goes with it to hand over the goods—to speak freely, openly, confidently to anyone who will listen. Sinners are premium. By just such speaking, the Holy Spirit calls, gathers, enlightens, sanctifies, and keeps.

LUTHER ON MARRIAGE, VOCATION, AND THE CROSS

The Reformation would transform the understanding of marriage. No longer a sacrament that communicated saving grace to the couple and not a contractual agreement for legalized sexual relations, Luther spoke of marriage as a calling given to men and women in creation. Drawing on Luther's "The Estate of Marriage" (1522), Nestingen, in his typical lively conversation, accents how marriage as a life-long union of man and woman is lived under the cross by those who know the promise of the Gospel. This essay originally appeared in ***Word & World*** *(Winter 2003). JTP+*

In the middle 1530s, his health having become a trial, and with rumors circulating that he had abandoned the faith that had driven the reform movement, Luther wrote several documents summing up his confession. The best known is the *Smalcald Articles*, and there are several lesser-known sets of disputations. His statements at this point are important because in them Luther indicates what he himself regarded as central.

As Luther marked out the essentials, he stressed a combination that had first appeared in the 1520 treatise, *On Christian Liberty*. There he wrote that being justified by faith, "the Christian is a perfectly free lord of all, subject to none." Just so, the Christian is also "a perfectly dutiful servant of all, subject to all."[1] In the preface to the *Smalcald Articles*, he used somewhat different language to point to the same double focus, regarding it as the reform's achievement: "By God's grace our churches have now been. . .enlightened and supplied with the pure Word and the right use of the sacraments, with an understanding of the various callings and with true works. . ."[2] It is clear that in Luther's mind, the doctrines of justification and vocation went hand in hand as the twin centers of both his personal faith and theology of reform.

It was this combination that made marriage a perennial topic for Luther. In *The Babylonian Captivity of the Church*, he discussed marriage in the context of the Roman Catholic sacramental system. In 1522, he published a major treatise, *The Estate of Marriage*. His arguments there were a factor in convincing him that he should get married himself; he and Katherine von Bora were joined in wedlock in 1525. Thereafter, there are numerous references to marriage scattered through various writings, including a 1531 sermon on marriage and the Genesis commentary.

In recent years, there has been considerable interest in Luther's view of marriage. William H. Lazareth's *Luther on the Christian Home*, written in 1960, provides a definitive, systematic overview.[3] More recently, Scott Hendrix of Princeton University has written a more historical summary. His notes provide a virtually complete survey of the current state of the discussion.[4]

The purpose of this essay is to fill in further what Lazareth and Hendrix have done by locating Luther's treatment of marriage in a double context: one in relation to his doctrine of vocation, the other in relation to the theology of the cross. Justifying the godless, God restores sinners to the creatureliness for which we were intended, freeing the faithful to live in the down-to-earth relationships of the family. In this context, God brings about death and resurrection, repentance, and faith.

The Sources

In order to place Luther's treatment of marriage in context, it needs to be summarized. Luther's own writings on the topic are readily accessible, along with Lazareth's and Hendrix's works. But the arguments are straightforward enough to see the implications, even in condensed form.

A 1519 sermon on marriage reflects Luther's anchorage in the medieval Catholic tradition on marriage. Just a year later, in *The Babylonian Captivity of the Church*,[5] he developed two objections. The first was to the definition of marriage as a sacrament. Reviewing the sacramental system of the medieval church, Luther pointed out that unlike baptism and the Lord's Supper, there is neither a specific promise nor a special physical sign involved with marriage. Marriage is not a matter of the gospel but of the law. In this context, he also considered some of the church's treatment of marital issues, such as impediments to marriage and the legitimacy of divorce.

The second challenge was directed at celibacy requirements for priests, nuns, and monks. Earlier in 1520, in *To the German Nobility*, Luther argued that this was an illegitimate demand, expressing the hope that the church would "restore freedom to everybody and leave every man free to marry or not to marry."[6] In *The Babylonian Captivity*, he pushed the same point.

In 1523, Luther supported his objection to the celibacy requirement in a fuller way, offering an interpretation of 1 Cor 7 that Hendrix calls "revolutionary." The church had taken over Paul's apocalyptically driven considerations of marriage, interpreting them in terms of the old Roman understanding of spirit and flesh. The papacy insisted that genuine sanctification requires detachment from the flesh—so the celibacy requirement for priests and religious. Luther argued that marriage is also one of the gifts of God. In fact, as Hendrix points out, Luther held that "marriage is the most religious state of all," the "real religious order," because "nothing should be called religious except the inner life of faith in the heart, where the Spirit rules."[7]

Luther divides *The Estate of Marriage*, his most complete statement on the topic, into three parts: requirements for marriage, bases for divorce, and godly marriage. The first part is fairly traditional, though Luther objects to the church's enjoining of marriage to non-Christians on the ground "that marriage is an outward, bodily thing, like any other worldly undertaking."[8] In the second part, as Hendrix indicates, Luther's "new theology of marriage becomes clearer."[9] On the one hand, denying the sacramental character of marriage legitimizes the possibility of divorce. But on the other, living by faith puts the legal possibilities in another perspective. While he acknowledges legitimate grounds, such as adultery, Luther was reluctant to support divorce, arguing that faith takes priority, moving a person beyond the law's minimums.

In the third part of *The Estate*, Luther further developed his positive treatment of marriage. Having argued at the beginning of the treatise that God established marriage by creating male and female and commanding them to be fruitful and multiply, Luther argues that the basic requirement is respect for both sexes, which involves ignoring those who disparage women and marriage. Christians are to "firmly believe that God instituted [marriage], brought husband and wife together, and ordained that they should beget children and care for them."[10] In the course of this discussion, Luther makes one of his best-known statements on married life:

> Now observe that when that clever harlot, our natural reason. . .takes a look at married life, she turns up her nose and says, "Alas, must I rock the baby, wash its diapers, make its bed, smell its stench, stay up nights with it, take care of it when it cries, heal its rashes and sores, and on top of that care for my wife, provide for her, labor at my trade, take care of this and take care of that, do this and do that, endure this and endure that, and whatever else of bitterness and drudgery married life involves? What, should I make such a prisoner of myself? O you poor, wretched fellow, have you taken a wife? Fie, fie upon such wretchedness and bitterness! It is better to remain free and lead a peaceful, carefree life; I will become a priest or a nun and compel my children to do likewise."
>
> What then does Christian faith say to this? It opens its eyes, looks upon all these insignificant, distasteful and despised duties in the Spirit, and is aware that they are all adorned with divine approval as with the costliest gold and jewels. It says, "O God, because I am certain that thou has created me as a man and hast from my body begotten this child, I also know for a certainty that it meets with thy perfect pleasure. I confess to thee that I am not worthy to rock the little babe or wash its diapers, or to be entrusted with the care of the child and its mother. How is it that I, without any merit, have come to this distinction of being certain that I am serving thy creature and thy most precious will? O how gladly will I do so, though the duties should be even more insignificant and despised."[11]

While the statement clearly reflects some traditional, patriarchal assumptions, it also indicates that Luther was in process with them, moving with his understanding of marriage to a more positive view of the relationship between men and women and of women in general.

In 1525, theological considerations took on a more personal form. The fact that Katherine von Bora is remembered by her family name, not simply as Mrs. Martin Luther, solidly indicates the standing that she achieved, not only with her husband but in the Lutheran Reformation. She was an extraordinarily gifted person.[12] If she took over a traditional role, bearing six children while managing a splaying, multifarious household and looking after a husband prone to *Anfechtung* and increasingly to physical ills, she also established her individuality. Luther's subsequent comments on marriage reflect the love they shared. He said in a 1531 wedding sermon, "The ancient doctors have rightly preached that marriage is praiseworthy because of children, loyalty, and love. But the physical benefit is also a precious thing and justly extolled as the chief virtue of marriage, namely that spouses can rely upon each other and with confidence entrust everything they have on earth to each other so that it is as safe with one's spouse as with oneself."[13]

Vocation

Some years ago, Heiko Oberman demonstrated the force of apocalypticism in Luther's thought. The late fifteenth and early sixteenth centuries were alive with such expectation. As he worked with the biblical texts—particularly Paul's letters, but also the Psalms—Luther was caught up in this hope. "The waiting is for God to act," Oberman wrote, "to take the initiative."[14]

The impact clearly registers in the grammar of justification by faith but spills over throughout. In justification, the crucified and risen Christ is the subject of every verb, the triune God at work ceaselessly in him to restore both creature and creation. But as the explanations of the Apostles' Creed in the *Small Catechism* show, this grammar is not confined to the second article: God has created, given, and still preserves, provides, protects, and guards; in the face of unbelief, the Holy Spirit calls, gathers, enlightens, sanctifies, and keeps. In one of Luther's favorite images, the triune God is a red-hot oven full of love, pouring himself out.

This apocalyptic emphasis on God's continuing activity has a double effect on Luther's discussions of marriage and related matters of creation. For one thing, in the end, marriage and the household are interpreted *coram deo*, in terms of God's work as Creator in and through them. For another, Luther's way of thinking is set in motion. There are some givens characteristic of creation itself—the existence of females and males, for instance, or the fact that life springs from the relationship between them. These givens have to be registered. But as the fourth verse of "A Mighty Fortress, in its current translation, indicates, there is something beyond "goods, honor, child or spouse"—"God's kingdom is forever."[15] In this light, even the defining relationships of life become provisional: they are not fixed, eternal, unchanging but, as Luther interprets, have to be worked out in light of the specifics.

This noted, Luther numbers the household with church and government as God's three orders, ordinances, or, in an older translation, estates. The original German, *Stand*, like the English terms, easily loses the dynamism Luther has invested in it. The church is not simply an institution or a structure but an activity: it happens as a gathering in which the word is preached, and the sacraments administered. Similarly, but more provisionally in that it was instituted after the fall, government's defining characteristic is not a particular form but a function: it exists to restrain the effects of sin in public life, to work out the provisions necessary to approximate peace and justice in a fallen world.

The household, which, as Oswald Bayer has pointed out, includes marriage and the family as well as the work necessary to provide for them, is even more basic than government.[16] It is also defined by what God does through it: in this order, the Creator continues to give life to creature and creation, using wives and husbands as his "hands," "channels," or "masks" for this purpose.

As an order of creation, the household is regulated by law. The law gains its authority in this connection by formulating or codifying what is required in the workings of creaturely life in relationship. So, as Luther interprets the Fourth Commandment, honor is required by the workings of the family. Because life is fragile, because beginnings are so crucial to later life, mutual cherishing and deference are necessary to a family's well-being. Likewise, in the Sixth Commandment, married life, by the very givens of the relationship, requires sexual fidelity, so that infidelity signals its breakdown.

As codified requirement, however, the law is doubly vulnerable. For one thing, life inevitably gets more complicated than the code. Putting sinners together belly to belly for a lifetime is a risky proposition. The law runs along behind on short legs, trying to keep up with all the permutations and variations. Child protection policies, property laws, and divorce regulations further specify what is required in particular circumstances, but there is always something more, not yet part of the code. For this reason, as Luther once commented, "Every house needs its own Moses"—a law-speaker who can recognize the adjustments that need to be made. But this necessity also exposes the law to a second vulnerability: sinners always think they are the exceptions to the rule, as though the law's code were merely a paper summons to be accepted or dismissed at will. Adjustments are necessary, but beyond the code, the demands and requirements of life are still working themselves out. At that level, the law continues to work itself out in experience even if it can't get a hearing: the diapers need to be changed, no matter what the father or the mother thinks of the process.

Thus, in the Table of Duties at the end of the *Small Catechism*, Luther gathers up scriptural passages that describe the requirements that pertain to the three estates, including familial relationships and work.

The Ten Commandments stand in the background, stating the essential, creaturely minimums—what life demands of all, Christian or otherwise. The biblical word interprets these minimums in the perspective of faith, further specifying what is expected in the defining relationships. At the same time, with the word, God sanctifies the earthly connections, just as with the word, God sanctifies the sacramental elements.[17] Finally, quoting the command to love at the end of the Table of Duties, Luther emplaces the all-encompassing, all-embracing condition that not only sums up the law but makes the relationships workable.

"In the Spirit," the phrase Luther uses to note the turning point in the long citation above from *The Estate of Marriage*, all of this takes on a different appearance. What has been demanded by the law, whether codified or required in the actual workings of daily life, becomes a vocation—the Christian's calling. It becomes the specific opportunity for, and occasion of, service.

In point of fact, marriage and the family include many different callings: as son or daughter, as spouse, as mother or father, brother- or sister-in-law, uncle or aunt, cousin, and so forth. Each calling has its own particular characteristics as well as its timing. The relationship between parent and child changes, for example, as the child becomes an adult and the parent ages. Uncles and aunts have a particularly significant calling in helping nieces and nephews to leave home. But no matter what the calling, they are all life-conditioning, life-shaping-points at which, knowingly or without knowledge aforethought, a person actually functions as God's mask, hand, or channel.

The familial callings are so important, in fact, that in this connection, Luther can use language that he otherwise assiduously attacks and resists: called by God, the believer becomes God's partner and friend, working with God to look after the aging parent, to love a spouse, to give life to a child, and so to contribute to the future of the community. The partnership is not exclusive to the family-labor with head or hands, callings in church and state are all blessed by God as points of specific service. But the life-giving, life-shaping characteristics of the household give it a prior significance.

In this partnership, the believer is literally law-free—the relationship, whether as spouse or in some other familial connection, takes over. Caught up in it, the believer does without the law what the law requires. So older couples commended for the years of love and service to one another will generally reply that they didn't realize that there was an alternative—it just happened. This kind of lawlessness is a hallmark of grace, breaking loose in the down-to-earth connections of everyday life. In vocation, the sinner grasped by faith is becoming what Adam and Eve were intended to be, a free and joyous creature of the earth.

The Cross

In the fourth question on baptism in the *Small Catechism*, Luther asks what the sacrament signifies for daily living: "It signifies that the Old Adam in us with all sins and evil desires is to be drowned and die through daily contrition and repentance, and on the other hand that daily a new person is to come forth and rise up to live before God in righteousness and purity forever."[18]

Given the old Adam's eagerness for job jars, especially when the tasks appear manageable, the imperative in Luther's explanation is often misinterpreted. Then the drowning and the rising become obligations put upon the baptized, as though the old sinner in each of us should take charge of its demise and create the new being. If that were the case, baptism would signify either hypocrisy or despair.

Rather, as Luther points out again and again, the cross is not something to be sought. When the word is near, the cross is always close at hand; you don't find it, the cross finds you. So, the cross characterizes all vocations but becomes particularly evident in families. To be someone's son or daughter is to be on the receiving end of their gifts and limits, their strivings and fears, faith and unbelief. Even—perhaps it would be better to say, especially—in the healthiest families, self-loss is an inevitable aspect of these relationships. Putting sinners together multiplies the risk exponentially.

The call to bear the cross is a summons to enter these controverted family relationships by sharing them. There are, to be sure, situations where conditions can be changed. When that is the case, the possible improvements become an obligation to those in a position to be helpful. Bearing a cross needlessly is itself a form of self-justification. But as Sheldon Tostengard, professor emeritus at Luther Seminary, often says, "Angels and demons have the same backbone." What makes a family member gifted and delightful also makes them troublesome, so to slay the demon is also to kill the angel. At such points, attempting to lift one cross simply creates another.

Thus, with the cross, repentance is built right into marriage and the family. Exclamations like, "I can't take this anymore!" or "It can't go on like this!" are the old Adam's death cries. When the Holy Spirit takes over such desperation and turns it toward a new resolve in the troubled relationship, repentance has happened—even unawares. It is another indication, hidden in the contraries, that as the old Lutheran marriage service put it, "Nevertheless our gracious Father in heaven doth not forsake his children in an estate so holy and acceptable to him."[19] Marriage and the family being a point of crucifixion, they are also and at the same time a point of resurrection. Conditioning, limiting, bringing one another to the brink and sometimes seemingly beyond it, spouses still share in intimacies that approach the gospel of Christ Jesus and faith itself in their profound joys. Watching a child whose diapers are unforgettable emerge out of childhood, and the hormonal baths of adolescence into young adulthood becomes a foretaste of the resurrection. Even the ancillary delights of being an uncle or aunt, a relationship that features generous forms of authority without concomitant responsibilities, can be a foretaste of the new creation. At such points, the forgiveness of sins realizes itself, not as an occasional moral necessity, but as the reality of Christ's promise, opening up the deepest levels of freedom possible in creaturely life.

Martin Luther and Katherine von Bora both knew the cross of marriage. Katherine von Bora was dumped in a convent as a surplus daughter. She and Luther lost two children, one in infancy and another as a teenager, along with her beloved aunt, "Mume Lena," who had moved in with them to help out. Undoubtedly, when Luther talked about the cross in the family, Katherine von Bora thought of him lying there beside her, sometimes beset by dread, other times trying to give away their substance.

With this, however, as husband and wife Martin Luther and Katherine von Bora also shared in the daily resurrections characteristic of marriage. So, in his later years, as he talks about the household estate or order, Luther focused on the love that grows out of shared life. Thus, Scott Hendrix concludes his fine article with a translation of a passage from Luther's 1531 wedding sermon:

> God's word is actually inscribed on one's spouse. When a man looks at his wife as if she were the only woman on earth, and when a woman looks at her husband as if he were the only man on earth; yes, if no king or queen, not even the sun itself sparkles any more brightly and lights up your eyes more than your own husband or wife, then right there you are face to face with God speaking. God promises to you your wife or husband, actually gives your spouse to you, saying: "The man shall be yours; the

woman shall be yours. I am pleased beyond measure! Creatures earthly and heavenly are jumping for joy." For there is no jewelry more precious than God's Word; through it you come to regard your spouse as a gift of God and, as long you do that, you have no regrets.[20]

Notes

1. Martin Luther, "On Christian Liberty" (1520), *Luther's Works*, 55 vols., ed. Jaroslav Pelikan and Helmut Lehmann (Philadelphia: Fortress; St. Louis: Concordia, 1955-1986) 31:344 (hereafter LW).
2. Martin Luther, "Smalcald Articles," in *The Book of Concord: The Confessions of the Evangelical Lutheran Church*, ed. Robert Kolb and Timothy J. Wengert (Minneapolis: Fortress, 2000) 299 (hereafter BOC).
3. William H. Lazareth, *Luther on the Christian Home: An Application of the Social Ethics of the Reformation* (Philadelphia: Muhlenberg, 1960).
4. Scott Hendrix, "Luther on Marriage," Lutheran Quarterly 14 (2000) 335-350.
5. Martin Luther, "The Babylonian Captivity of the Church" (1520), LW 35:92-105.
6. Martin Luther, "To the German Nobility" (1520), LW 44:176.
7. Hendrix, "Luther on Marriage," 338, citing "Commentary on I Corinthians 7" (1523), LW 28:17.
8. Martin Luther, "The Estate of Marriage" (1523), LW 45:25.
9. Hendrix, "Luther on Marriage," 340.
10. Luther, "The Estate of Marriage," LW 45:38.
11. Ibid., 45:39-40.
12. Roland Bainton, *Women of the Reformation in Germany and Italy* (Minneapolis: Augsburg, 1971) 23-44.
13. *D. Martin Luthers Werke: Kritische Gesamtausgabe*, 60 vols. (Weimar: Herman Bohlaus Nachfolger, 1883- 1980) 34:52.5-9 (hereafter WA).
14. Heiko Augustinus Oberman, *Forerunners of the Reformation: The Shape of Late Medieval Thought*, trans. Paul L. Nyhus (New York: Holt, Rinehart and Winston, 1966) 14.
15. *Lutheran Book of Worship* (Minneapolis: Augsburg; Philadelphia: Fortress, 1978) hymn 229.
16. Oswald Bayer, "Nature and Institution: Luther's Doctrine of the Three Orders," trans. Luis Dreher, *Lutheran Quarterly* 12 (1998) 125-129.
17. Ibid., 141-143.
18. BOC, 360. Translating "*der alte Adam,*" "the old Adam," is a difficult problem. Rendering it "the old creature" may be more inclusive, but it is also more neutral and therefore doesn't appear to pick up the adversarial character of Luther's usage.
19. "Order for Marriage," in *Service Book and Hymnal of the Lutheran Church in America* (Minneapolis: Augsburg et al., 1958) 271.
20. WA 34:52.12-21, translated by Hendrix, "Luther on Marriage," 347.

II

THE CATECHISM

JUSTIFICATION BY FAITH IN LUTHER'S SMALL CATECHISM

Luther's Small Catechism is the gem of the Reformation. By means of the Small Catechism, in the form of wall charts and pamphlet, the evangelical proclamation of Christ took root in the homes and hearts of Christians around the world. As Nestingen so memorably puts it, the Small Catechism brought the parish altar into the family kitchen. Yet Luther does not use the term "justification" in the Small Catechism. In keeping with his intention to write a Catechism for "children and simple folk" Luther avoids complex terminology. He anchors his treatment of the Christian faith in the Second Article of the Apostles' Creed with its confession that Jesus Christ "has made me His own." The Ten Commandments begin where we live in creation under the demands that common to all humanity, but theologically the Catechism gets its focus from the person and work of Christ Jesus. Along the way, Nestingen imagines what the Small Catechism would have looked like if Melanchthon, not Luther had been the author. JTP+

Justification by faith and Luther's Small Catechism are both indisputably strategic to the Lutheran Reformation. Time and again, Luther insisted that justification was the central issue. Written just as the reformers were beginning to take a direct hand in parish life, the catechism—in the felicitous phrase of Elizabeth Eisenstein—moved the parish altar into the family kitchen, literally bringing the word home.[1] Ever since, it has remained the working confession of Lutheranism.

Put together, however, this double centrality provokes a perplexing question: What happened to justification in the catechism? Given Luther's statements and the common perception of Lutheranism, justification by faith should be prominently displayed. But in fact, a scholar of the caliber of Paul Althaus could say that both the language and concept of justification are altogether missing in the catechism.[2] Why? What would prompt Luther to pass over such a central theological concern at such a critical point?

Two possible answers suggest themselves, one traditional, the other more far reaching. Considering the first, it appears that the disappearance stems from Luther's understanding of the difference between doctrine and preaching. By this reckoning, the language of justification would be missing in the catechism because it does not belong in proclamation. But there is a second possibility—that, in fact, as in a game of hide-the-thimble, the concept of justification stands out so prominently that it gets overlooked. The following pages explore both possibilities.

Doctrine and Preaching

While neither sermonic nor a sermon, the Small Catechism is clearly oriented to preaching. Written for parents to use in the instruction of their children, it moves from the abstract to the particular, from implicit assumptions about the word it declares to the explicit declaration of that word in personal, confessional terms. So the explanations of each of the three articles of the Apostles' Creed move out from the Trinitarian doctrines, which clearly inform them, to get right to the level of faith: "I believe that God has created me and all that exists . . .," "I believe that Jesus Christ, true God, Son of the Father from eternity and true man, born of the Virgin Mary, is my Lord . . .," "I believe that I cannot . . . but the Holy Spirit has "As in the explanations of baptism and the Lord's Supper, everything comes down to the "for you."

This reflects Luther's concept of the relationship between doctrine and preaching. Doctrine, the church's officially defined theological affirmations, and theology, continued reflection on the word for the sake of its further declaration, both take place one step removed from preaching. Like the grammar of a language, doctrine is public, communal, and more fixed. Theology, like a scout or outrider, moves alongside at some distance to explore the edges, anticipating new developments and seeking ways to engage creatively. Either way, doctrine and theology are classically second-order discourse, talking about what happens at the first order, proclamation, the oral declaration of law, and gospel. To paraphrase an old formulation of Robert W. Jenson, they are what happen between the ear and the mouth, between the hearing of the word and its speaking.[3]

In this connection, Timothy Wengert and Robert Kolb have made a dramatically important but little-noticed improvement in the translation of the Small Catechism in their edition of the *Book of Concord*. Traditionally, Luther's catechetical questions have been translated, "What does this mean?" That is a secondorder question. So, not surprisingly, traditional explanations of the Small Catechism produced by the old immigrant Lutheran church bodies amplified Luther's explanations with doctrinal discussions. The First Article, for instance, became an occasion for introducing God's omnipotence, omniscience, and omnipresence. But as Wengert and Kolb more accurately translate Luther's original question, "*Was is das*?" "What is this?" it remains first order. The explanations are not so much explanations as they are means to advance the declaration. Luther certainly teaches, as do those who join him in use of the catechism for instruction in the defining statements of Christian faith, both word and sacrament, but he teaches by confessing.

A critical difference between law and gospel emerges here. In a basic way, the law functions by meaning or signifying what it demands. In the first or civil use, the law sets out requirements, prohibiting or requiring specific behaviors, that call for the understanding and subsequent conformity of the hearer. "The law says, 'Do this,' . . ." as Luther wrote in the Heidelberg Disputations (AE 31: 56).

But even the law cannot be confined to meaning or significance. It gets loose, in league with the other powers of this age, and so breaks in on its hearers, confronting, exposing, accusing. Thus, the Heidelberg quotation continues, "The law says, 'Do this,' and it is never done." The problem is far greater than mere knowledge or understanding. Until the Holy Spirit, in effect, halters it with the gospel, the law exercises its power far beyond schemes of meaning and significance at the deepest level of the conscience or sense of standing in the shaping relationships of life.

"What does this mean?" has a limited but appropriate place in relation to the law, but the gospel's true power comes home as the Spirit works in those who hear the gospel. So, in the Heidelberg Disputation, Luther juxtaposes the sentence quoted above with a second, "Grace says, 'Believe in this,' and everything is already done." The gospel creates what it demands, namely, faith.

So, for example, if the absolution were a matter of law, it would depend on the hearer to discern its meaning and apply it to himself. In that case, the human heart being the lonely hunter that it is, the absolution would be as powerless as any other human word—just another offer, an elusive but profoundly uncertain possibility. But in the absolution declared as God's word, the gospel overlaps the law. The absolution says "your sin," hereby confirming the law's indictments. Then the gospel takes over, claiming exclusive, unqualified sovereignty in the terms "is forgiven." Like the "is" of the words of institution in the Lord's Supper, this "is" accomplishes the reality that it declares. The Spirit of the risen Christ takes hold here, bringing the power of the resurrection to bear in the present on real sinners. So doing, the Holy Spirit gives the very faith that believes the absolving word, thus calling, gathering, enlightening, sanctifying, and keeping.

This examination of the way that Luther assumes the second order in the catechism to move to the first order, so to declare the word, explains what has happened to the language of the doctrine of justification by faith alone. In fact, the catechism is not a doctrinal document but a first-order confession. Thus, aside from the bare invocation of the two natures of Christ Jesus at the beginning of the explanation of the Second Article, there are no doctrinal references whatsoever—not even in the Lord's Prayer, where the theology of the cross shapes each of the explanations.

This indicates the role of doctrine in Luther's reflection.[4] Melanchthon, up to his ears from the beginning in curricular reform in Wittenberg and beyond, was above all a teacher—the *preceptor Germaniae*, as he has historically been called. For him, as well as for his students, doctrine was directed at teaching and so became an end in itself. But for Luther the importance of true or pure doctrine registered in the pulpit. To be sure, he commonly talked about justification by faith in his preaching, seeking to inform his parishioners' witness as well. But for Luther, the test or measure of doctrine is not a mathematical conformity to an established pattern, but the actual function, the preached and sacramental word. This is the point of the well-known question, *Was Christum treibt*, "How is Christ brought home?" Doctrine does not justify; Christ does, as the little catechism declares in its triune formulations.

The Concept of Justification

If the declaratory character of the catechism accounts for the absence of the language of justification, what about the concept? Here, Althaus's comment becomes more problematic. For Luther, justification by faith claimed supreme importance in the Reformation, specifically because of the way it informs preaching, providing the grammar of the unconditional word of the gospel. Dropping the theology altogether, especially in a document as critical as the catechism, would be completely out of character. There are good grounds, then, to suspect that justification functions in the catechism after all, but in a different form than expected, one easily passed over because it is implicit, and even controlling.

Wilhelm Maurer provides an important clue to the difference in his classic study of the *Augsburg Confession*. Maurer points to the difference of sequence between the catechism and the Augsburg Confession.[5] The explanations of the Apostles' Creed provide the point of comparison. Whereas it had traditionally been treated as twelve phrases, each ascribed to one of the apostles, Luther organized his explanations by the persons of the Trinity, so the First, Second, and Third Articles. His explanations are eschatological in the fullest sense of the term—the triune God claims every verb, the explanations setting out the impact of God's activity in personal terms in creation, redemption, and sanctification. At the same time, as will be demonstrated below, each explanation links to what follows or precedes, preserving the unity, one in three, three in one.

Melanchthon proposed a different sequence. It originally appeared in the Schwabach Articles, which Melanchthon took the major hand in editing in 1528 and then revised thoroughly at Augsburg to make the statement more ecumenically appealing to Emperor Charles V. Though Luther saw an earlier text, he did not examine the final copy until after it had been presented at Augsburg as the Augsburg Confession. Though he had some assistance from Chancellor Bruck and others at Augsburg, Melanchthon did all of the final revising without Luther's consultations.

Following the Schwabach Articles in the Augsburg Confession, Melanchthon reframes the Lutheran argument from a more anthropological perspective, moving from sin to grace. Article I states the traditional doctrine of the Trinity. But then Melanchthon immediately turns to sin and the human predicament in Article II. Article III declares the standard doctrine of the person of Christ, while Article IV asserts his justifying work. Article V then identifies the Holy Spirit's use of the means of grace to work faith; Article VI, the new obedience; Articles VII and VIII, the church. As in the catechism, God clearly claims ultimate responsibility in Melanchthon's formulations, but God's work is described in terms of an *ordo salutis* following from sin through grace to faith and the new obedience, which in Article VI becomes a command requiring obedience. This article is the first indication that Melanchthon's sequence has caused him difficulty, as Leif Grane points out in his definitive study of the Augsburg Confession.[6]

In Article IV of the Apology, the *locus classicus* in the confessional discussion of the doctrine of justification by faith, Melanchthon lays out the argument in the same sequence. Definitions of the law and sin provide the theological framework for focusing on the work of Christ, continuing in its forensic declaration, with faith and obedience following as consequences. The required human cooperation in the new obedience makes it necessary to separate the declaration of Christ's righteousness from its fruits, turning the doctrine more exclusively declaratory.

Authoritatively expressed in both the Augsburg Confession and the Apology, Melanchthon's sequence became the basis of subsequent discussion of justification in the Lutheran tradition. Both the Gnesio-Lutherans, so-called, and the Philippists took it over, ratifying it once more in the Formula of Concord by, among other things, eliminating Osiander's mystical alternative.

The last great generation of Luther scholarship, which included Althaus and Maurer, devoted a Luther Congress in 1960 to considering the differences between Luther and Melanchthon. Lauri Haikola, the outstanding Finnish Luther scholar, traced the difference to Melanchthon's closer relation to tradition; Wilhelm Pauck, doctor father at Union Seminary in New York to a generation of American Lutheran historians and theologians, traced it to Melanchthon's relationship with Erasmus and his biblically humanist moral reform.[7]

More recent Melanchthon scholarship has provided an important addition if not a correction. Timothy Wengert, James Kittelson, and Robert Kolb have pointed to Melanchthon's rhetorical theory.[8] Again, it is significant that Melanchthon was, above all, a teacher. He was not ordained and had no formal theological training. A recent doctoral dissertation by Christopher Croghan of Augustana College in Sioux Falls, SD (which was framed by James Kittelson before his death) has demonstrated the pervasive influence of Aristotle's rhetoric in Melanchthon's educational theory and theological work.[9]

His rhetoric is the apparent source of Melanchthon's sequence. Both to inform and persuade, he repackaged the theological argument of the Lutheran Reformation in an Aristotelian rhetorical form. In so doing, he may have assumed the theological neutrality of Aristotle's rhetoric. But either way, Melanchthon ran into difficulty at several critical points: the relationship of faith and good works, as noted, but also predestination, the bondage of the will, the real presence, and so forth. He was directly implicated in the controversies among his students that required the reconsiderations of the Formula of Concord, even as they used his theological methods to resolve their difficulties.

Luther recognized the problems with doing theology *ad modum aristoteles* early in his vocation. Written in 1518, the Heidelberg

Disputation opens with a sustained attack on traditional Greco-Roman assumptions shared by Aristotle, the freedom of the human will and the eternal law. Luther proposed a different method. Rather than beginning with the human situation and fitting Christ into such a presupposition, he began with the death and resurrection of Jesus Christ as the justifying act of God. Like the spokes of a wheel radiating out from a hub, both the assumptions necessary to declaring the justifying act of God in Christ and the relational consequences of it move out from this center.

This is the significance of Luther's eschatology, which Gerhard Forde regarded (along with the theology of the cross) as the driving forces of his reform. As Heiko Oberman, Robert Kolb, and Robin Barnes have argued, Luther was clearly an apocalypticist—not on the order of the book of Revelation or Daniel, but in the tradition of Isaiah and the Apostle Paul. Rather than beginning with the beginning, then, he begins at the end, with God's restoration of both creation and creature in Christ Jesus. He then, in effect, thinks backward to what must be assumed accordingly.

This explains an unusual feature of the catechism. If Luther had been following Melanchthon's conception of justification, the explanations of the Ten Commandments would have been followed by a discussion of sin. In fact, more orthodox expositions of the catechism have done exactly that, supplying what Luther did not. But in the Small Catechism itself, Luther does not refer to the power of sin until he has set out the work of Christ in the explanation of the Second Article. In the light of Christ's deliverance, the powers that oppose him, sin, death, and the devil, come into view. At the same time, faith in the promise of becoming Christ's own, stated at the end of the explanation of the Second Article, then flushes out the confession of unbelief at the beginning of the explanation of the Third Article. Similarly, the gift of baptism exposes the ongoing conflict in the life of the believer, the daily dying and rising. In all three cases, only when the gospel overlaps the law can the true reality of the believer's situation be stated. In effect, the solution exposes the problem. As Luther himself later put it in the Antinomian Disputations, the law can only become a teacher when it has been subordinated to the Holy Spirit's use of the gospel (WA 39, I: 445). Otherwise, as much as it drives, the law literally does not know where it is going.

This also clarifies the assumptions informing the overall order of the catechism. While he makes the Ten Commandments the starting point in the document, he does so for experiential rather than theological reasons. Beginning theologically with the justifying word takes the law out of the ultimate position. The gospel reduces the law to the penultimate, breaking any connection between the law and salvation. The logic is devastatingly simple. Because Christ saves, the law cannot—a deduction first drawn by the Apostle Paul (Gal 2:21). So as Luther wrote in the Antinomian Disputations, "The law was not given that it might justify or vivify or prescribe anything for righteousness" (WA 39, I: 347).

But just so, reduced to terms, the true force of the Ten Commandments gets established. They show what "must be done and left undone," as Luther put it, explaining the sequence. They set out the defining requirements of creaturely life in relation to both the Creator and other creatures. The Commandments explicitly formulate what is implicitly required of all people by life's conditions and limits. Not having life in themselves, creatures must be aligned with their Creator, the point of the first table. Receiving life through "hands" and "channels" provided by other people, terminology Luther uses in the Large Catechism, creatures can only obtain these gifts and services in continuing alignment with their neighbors, the second table, the remaining seven Commandments.

The Ten Commandments are placed first in the overall sequence of the catechism not for theological reasons, then, but because they come first in human experience. Human life takes shape amid creaturely limitations. The explanations describe earthly realities, moving from the ground up to analyze what is rather than from the top down to set out an ideal order.

This points to the original and true theological significance of the term justification. In Melanchthon's rhetoric, justification takes on a legal cast. Justification, as it is routinely pointed out, has to do with judgment; it is a declaration of where a person stands in relationship to the law.

But in Luther's understanding, the argument begins not with the law but with Christ Jesus. So, Luther could say, in some of his most famous statements, "In Christ, we become what Adam and Eve were meant to be, only better," the better being not a moral quality but faith itself. "In Christ, we are brought back to the point from which Adam and Eve fell" (WA 39, I: 354), that is, we become what we were created to be, people of faith.

Thus, for Luther, the original paradigm is not as much legal as relational. He can speak, as he sometimes does in the Antinomian Disputations, of an eternal significance of the law. It points beyond itself to what God intends for both creature and creation. But this significance can only be known in relationship to Christ Jesus. Then, the law's accusations, its characteristic office in this age, end in the forgiveness of sins. Thus freed, the believer joyfully turns to God in thanks and praise, simultaneously embracing other creatures and the creation. To put it another way, faith lives in alignment with God and the neighbor, glad and content to be a creature of the earth.

Thus, while the catechism begins experientially with the Commandments, it begins theologically with the last words of the explanation of the Second Article of the Creed in German, one sentence that has been called the most beautiful in the whole German language. In the previously most widely used English translation it reads, "All this he has done that I may be his own, live under him in his kingdom, and serve him in everlasting righteousness, innocence, and blessedness." Christ has taken on the forces that have distorted or misaligned humanity in relation to the Creator and other creatures, the triune God, and the neighbor, triumphing over sin, death, and the devil to realign, bringing creature and creation back into the relationships for which they were intended. This is justification by faith.

With this, then, the force of the progression through the last phrases of each of the three articles can be traced. Theologically, the promise of Christ's realignment reveals the original relationships for which humanity was intended. So, the explanation of the First Article concludes, "All this God has done out of sheer fatherly and divine goodness, though we do not deserve it. Therefore, surely we ought to thank and praise, serve and obey him." Receiving all of the gifts of creaturely life as sheer gift, the creature—every living human being—stands under the obligation of thanks and praise, God's original purpose in bestowing life. Turning towards God in thanks and praise, humanity then turns towards the neighbor in service and obedience, thereby joining the Creator in caring for creature and creation.

But as the Second Article makes clear, this is as far as the First Article can go. The obligations of creaturely life remain just that: fundamental, nonnegotiable, universal because they are rooted in the shape of life itself but external, beyond reach. Only in Christ Jesus do they become reality, beyond demand. As Luther wrote in the Antinomian Disputations, "Insofar as Christ is raised in us, so far are we without the law, sin, and death" (WA 39, I: 356).

Accordingly, in the explanation of the Second Article, the language of obligation disappears altogether just as the subject changes. The *ought* gets replaced with the *may*, understood as the creation of a new relationship. "All this he has done that I may be his own," and so live in the alignments for which the human creature was created, living under him in service and obedience—innocent because now properly aligned with him and so also blessed and righteous. The crucified and risen Christ, himself the way, the truth, and the life, literally "trues" his own, as in the end, he will true up the whole creation, bringing all things into cosmic balance.

But now, just as the promise of the gospel has moved back to reveal the true purpose of creaturely life, in the Third Article, it moves forward to expose the present reality of the believer under the sign of the simul. The gospel overlaps the law, so bringing into register what the law points to but cannot on its own confirm. Under the power of Christ's promise to create his own, the sinner can begin to see the grasping, clinging, residual struggles of the forces which, even in defeat, won't let go. Thus, the Third Article begins with what is surely one of the most powerful and deeply beloved confessions in the catechism, "I believe that I cannot . . ." The confession of such unbelief is a confession of sin in its most pernicious, radical form.

But having exposed and confirmed the power of sin, the gospel, having overlapped the law, continues past the overlap to elicit the second confession, this one of faith itself: The Spirit of the risen Christ "has called, has gathered, has enlightened, has sanctified, has kept." The creaturely self, which under the current conditions of the creation gets continually thrown out of balance by the forces of distortion, death, and destruction, now under the power of the Spirit at work in the word, comes into alignment with the Creator, creature, and creation through the oral and sacramental word of God in the community of faith. The *ought* set down in the conditions of creatureliness by the Creator, having yielded to the *may* in the justifying work of Christ, in the Third Article becomes the *has* of the present perfect tense, a continuing confession of both sin and faith.

So, like an alcoholic taking the first step in Alcoholics Anonymous, the believer can finally tell the truth about himself. He or she can finally begin to identify the immortality projects, all of the efforts to go it alone, the grasping desire to become self-creating. This is not, as so commonly misunderstood, mere preparation for the greater achievements of the transcendent self, in worship or in the ethics of pure tolerance. Rather, "the sacrifices of God are a broken spirit" (Ps 51:17). In the confession of sin opening the explanation, the sinner, aligned with Christ, joins in God's judgment of the rebellious self. This is true repentance, in which the Holy Spirit turns the self away from itself and all of the other powers of distortion to create anew. Such repentance, ending in faith, is genuine worship (Rom 12:1).

Just so, illusions broken, self-transcendence schemes shattered, dying with Christ, under the power of the Holy Spirit the sinner turns to the triune God in the expectation and hope of faith. Then, in the hiddenness of the every day, in the demands and joys of his vocations, the Spirit makes the believer some earthly good. Sometimes, the eye may even catch glimmers of service rendered, obedience in process, enough to confirm what faith knows: Since the Spirit of the risen Christ is at work, good is forthcoming - even amidst evidence that remains disputable.

Eschatologically conceived, apocalyptically oriented, relationally driven, this understanding of justification ends with a declaration of the now and the not yet. "In this Christian church, the Holy Spirit fully forgives my sins and the sins of all believers." The reality of the second confession, of faith in the Spirit's new creation, does not annul the truth of the first; the new being comes forth in contention with the old, and so there is no point where the believer progresses, in this life, beyond the absolution in either its proclaimed or its sacramental form. But the absolution, the present form of the resurrection of the dead, points ahead of itself to that day when "he will raise me and all the dead and give me and all believers in Christ everlasting life." Then the *simul* will be resolved; the old will have passed away in the arrival of the new.

Thus, Luther's doctrine of justification functions at two levels in the Small Catechism. On the first level, it functions as doctrine, informing Luther's proclamation without being the subject of it. On the second level, it shapes the progression from the "ought" of the First Article to "all this he has done that I may be his own" in the Second Article and the "has" of the Third Article. Apocalyptically driven, Luther's concept of justification does not fit into the rhetoric that shapes the Augsburg Confession and the Apology. Rather, beginning with Christ Jesus, it sets out the work of the triune God in justifying the godless by faith, apart from the works of the law.

Notes

1. Elizabeth L. Eisenstein, "The Advent of Printing and the Protestant Revolt: A New Approach to the Disruption of Western Christendom," in *Transition and Revolution: Problems and Issues of European Renaissance and Reformation History*, ed. Robert M. Kingdon (Minneapolis: Burgess, 1974), 250-257.

2. Paul Althaus, *The Theology of Martin Luther*, trans. Robert C. Schultz (Philadelphia: Fortress Press, 1966), 226.

3. Eric W. Gritsch and Robert W. Jenson, *Lutheranism: The Theological Movement and Its Confessional Writings* (Philadelphia: Fortress Press, 1976).

4. See Gerhard 0. Forde, *Theology is for Proclamation* (Minneapolis: Augsburg Fortress, 1990).

5. Wilhelm Maurer, *Historical Commentary on the Augsburg Confession*, trans. H. George Anderson (Philadelphia: Fortress Press, 1986), 23 ff.

6. Leif Grane, *The Augsburg Confession: A Commentary*, trans. John H. Rasmussen (Minneapolis: Augsburg Publishing House, 1987), 86 ff.

7. Lauri Haikola, "A Comparison of Melanchthon's and Luther's Doctrine of Justification," trans. Robert Schultz, *Dialog* 2 (1963): 32- 39; Wilhelm Pauck, "Luther and Melanchthon," in *Luther and Melanchthon in the History and Theology of the Reformation*, ed. Vilmos Vaita (Philadelphia: Fortress Press, 1961). The Vaita volume contains the major papers from the 1960 Luther Congress.

8. Timothy Wengert, "Beyond Stereotypes: The Real Philip Melanchthon," in *Philip Melanchthon Then and Now* (1497-1997), ed. Scott Hendrix and Timothy Wengert (Columbia, SC: Lutheran Theological Southern Seminary, 1999), 25-26; James Kittelson, "The Late Reformation in Germany," in *Reformation Europe: A Guide to Research*, ed. Steven Ozment (St. Louis: Center for Reformation Research, 1982), 368; Robert Kolb, *Bound Choice, Election, and Wittenberg Theological Method*, Lutheran Quarterly Books (Grand Rapids: Eerdmans, 2005), 3.

9. Christopher Croghan, *Melanchthon's* Der Ordinanden Examen and Examen Eorum: *A Case Study in Pedagogical Method* (Ph.D. diss., Luther Seminary, St. Paul, MN, 2007).

THE LORD'S PRAYER IN LUTHER'S CATECHISM

The Lord's Prayer is prayed on the battlefield between God and the devil, where faith is constantly under attack. To paraphrase Luther, the Lord's Prayer contains seven petitions of our wretchedness and seven promises of God's mercy. In this essay that first appeared in **Word & World** *(Winter 2002), Nestingen explores the cruciform shape of Jesus' prayer that God's children can pray with boldness and confidence. The focus is not on the one who prays but on the One to whom we pray, our Father in heaven. As Nestingen puts it, "Despair and heroism are two sides of the same coin: the self-seeking self." Prayer is not an assertion of autonomous spirituality but the cry for mercy born out of the promise of our Father. JTP+*

As commonly as it appears in personal devotion and the liturgical life of the church, the Lord's Prayer draws surprisingly little theological attention. Children raised in the Christian faith often learn it as the first full paragraph of their speech; if new Christians don't get a full treatment in adult instruction, they quickly come to know the prayer as generations have, by saying it with the congregation in services or with those standing with them at the close of a meeting. Yet, for all the prominence of the prayer, full theological treatments are not nearly as common as might be expected.

I. Recent Scholarship

This has not always been the case. The World War II generation of German theologians, perhaps just because of their experience, produced some classic studies, most all of them published in English translations. Joachim Jeremias and Ernst Lohmeyer did full-dress New Testament studies, Jeremias setting it in the context of first-century prayer, Lohmeyer paying particularly close attention to the eschatology.[1] Helmut Thielicke published a classic set of sermons on the Lord's Prayer that were preached when the city of Hamburg was being bombed.[2] Gerhard Ebeling, now often derided for his existentialism, shows some of the strength of Rudolf Bultmann's type of interpretation.[3]

With this scholarship, there have also been some masterful treatments of Martin Luther's interpretation of the Lord's Prayer. Herbert Girgensohn's two-volume *Teaching Luther's Catechism*, an invaluable work, contains a definitive treatment.[4] Girgensohn was also closely interested in the eschatology of the prayer. Though it has unfortunately not been translated, Albrecht Peters—a trenchant critic of Ebeling's existential treatment of Luther—did a five-volume treatment of the catechism that sets the current standard.[5]

For the generations that followed, however, it is as though the Lord's Prayer is merely piety or a liturgical construct of the early church that obtained a traditional textual standing. With rare exception, consideration of the prayer gets left for popular piety, with edifying treatments aimed for the religious bookstores stocked by publications of the Christian Booksellers Association.

The best antidote to such neglect of the Lord's Prayer is some close study of Luther's interpretation. He returned to it regularly, preaching and writing on the prayer, treating it as one of the keystones of the faith. At a preliminary level, Luther heard the Lord's Prayer as simple instruction in how to pray, writing of it this way in a letter to his barber, Peter. But as usual in Luther's catechisms, there is another level. As Luther heard it there, teaching the faithful to pray, the Lord Jesus is at the same time telling believers what to look for and expect in the crucible of everyday life, where the heart is contended for by the powers at work in this age—the devil, the world, and the sinful self—as well as the Spirit of the new age, released in Christ's death and resurrection. Thus, for Luther, the Lord's Prayer is a continuing lesson in the theology of the cross.

In order to see how this works, it is necessary to begin, first of all, with some examination of Luther's own situation in writing the catechism as well as his understanding of the situation of the believer. With that, secondly, it is possible to see more clearly the theology that shapes his exposition.

II. Luther's Situation

In the later 1520s, the Wittenberg reform—just gaining the pejorative nickname "Lutheran"—underwent a decisive change in perspective. To that point, a combination of external political forces had joined with Luther's own apocalyptically driven disinterest in structures to prevent the reform from developing organizational form. Though it had widespread sympathy and support, among the influential as well as popularly, the reform remained an *ad hoc* amalgam in which Luther functioned like a catalyst. At the first Diet of Speyer in 1526, however, supporting politicians gained what they interpreted as the power to effect reform in their own territories. Urged on by the elector of Saxony but also by their own concern for public witness, Luther and his Wittenberg colleagues began to think about bringing their movement home in the life of the congregations and the families—in a rudimentary way, organizationally; above all, in witness.

Forms of catechesis date back to the early church and beyond. One argument has it that 1 Peter, one of Luther's favorite books, was originally written as a catechism for new believers. Augustine himself wrote an *Enchiridion*, or handbook to the faith. The medieval church had produced a rich tradition. And in fact, the Wittenbergers had already been at work at this level. Several of Luther's friends had put their hand to it, including both Johann Agricola and Philip Melanchthon.[6] But the authority claimed after Speyer I and the results of the Saxon church visitation, which had been implemented to survey the circumstances of the local parishes, gave the project a new urgency. In 1528, Luther himself put his hand to it, writing the Small Catechism for families to use in the instruction of their children and the German or Large Catechism for the use of pastors and teachers.

The public character of the catechism can be observed above all in the basic outline Luther employed. Neither the Small Catechism nor the Large gives even a hint of indoctrinating a Lutheran gnosis; instead, they are organized on the basis of the Ten Commandments, the Creed, and the Lord's Prayer. For Luther himself, the three together formed "the catechism" in contradistinction to his own works, which have been "the catechism" for generations of Lutherans since. "The catechism" embodies the Catholic consensus of the faith as historically maintained by the church. In his own catechisms, Luther included the dominical sacraments, Holy Baptism, and the Lord's Supper, and shortly thereafter added a statement on absolution because all of these are perennially controverted in the life of the church.

Shaped by the ecumenical tradition of the church, the catechisms are novel for the order of the five, later six, chief parts. While other catechisms contained some of the same elements, Luther set a different precedent with his sequence, which he explained as following the order of experience:

> There are three things that everyone must know to be saved. First, he must know what we are to do and leave undone. Then, as he discovers that it is impossible for him to accomplish either with his own strength, he must know where to seek and find the power that will enable him to do his duty. And, in the third place, he must know where to seek and obtain that aid.[7]

The Ten Commandments set out the requirements of creaturely life, incumbent by creation; the Creed declares the gifts of the Triune God; the Lord's Prayer gives voice to the circumstances of the believer living in the world of the nomos (law) in the hope of the gospel.

While it explains the sequence, Luther's statement also indicates his method. Interpreting what he had received as defining statements of life in faith, he treats them experientially in light of their impact in the situation of the believer. Karl Barth is reputed to have said that the theologian should keep the Scripture in one hand and the daily newspaper in the other. Always pastorally inclined, Luther seeks a similar, if more proportional, combination, honoring both the historic texts and the way they register in everyday life.

Approaching the catechism in this way, Luther does not treat the Decalog either exegetically or as a particularly Christian ethic. Rather, he approaches the commandments analytically as a summary of the essential demands made in conditions of life where life is not a power possessed but a gift received in relationships with the Creator, other creatures, and, implicitly, the creation.[8] Into the web of such overlapping relationships, amidst all of the demands imposed by the shape of creaturely interdependence, the gospel comes as an alien word, declaring God's triune self-giving—in creation itself, in Christ, and in the work of the Holy Spirit.

In daily life, the law, codified in the Ten Commandments, and the gospel, declared by the Creed, place believers in a fundamental tension. Because the demands of the law arise out of the conditions of creaturely life, they are an inherent part of human experience—one way or another, they bear themselves out, if not in a codified form like the Decalog, in everyday limits and consequences. Further, compounding itself, the law becomes a power that attacks the person's sense of self, making league with sin, death, and the devil as powers of temptation. The gospel enters from outside of such pervasive experience, attacking the illusion that life can be obtained by the self through either obedience or withdrawal. It declares that the life sought in and by the law is bestowed as gift of grace by the Triune God. In this way, law and gospel contend against one another, the law claiming to bestow what only the gospel can give, the gospel undermining the law by declaring God's gracious self-giving. As Ernst Käsemann once remarked, life becomes a battleground, open to all comers.

Battered by the law's relentless demands, under the assault of the powers of this age, yet gripped by the gospel's overflowing promise, faith lives under the sign of the *simul—simul iustus et peccator* (simultaneously saint and sinner). Faith speaks two words that appear to be mutually exclusive but which are both required in relation to God. On the one hand, it says, "I believe that by my own reason or strength I cannot believe in Jesus Christ, my Lord, or come to him"—the *peccator*. This confession originates in a suspicion raised by the intractability of the law's conditions as the law continuously undermines the very certainty that it demands by requiring a selfless obedience of the self. The suspicion raised by the law is confirmed by the gospel, which declares, at the same time, the promise that elicits the rest of the phrase in Luther's explanation of the third article of the Apostles' Creed in the Small Catechism, "But the Holy Spirit has called me through the gospel, enlightened me with his gifts, and sanctified and preserved me in true faith"[9]—the *iustus*. What the law can only require, the gospel actually bestows, in repentance and faith.

There is both a death and a resurrection in this third-article confession. Acknowledging that faith and, thus, life itself is beyond the power of the self is the death of self. The illusion that shapes the life of the old Adam and Eve, that a death-defying wisdom or knowledge can be obtained from the law, dies here. Just so, to paraphrase one of Luther's best-known statements, Adam and Eve are here restored to the point from which they fell. Easter blossoms, full of the power of the resurrection, in that God's creatures are gripped by the grace bestowed by "the Lord and giver of life."

Luther's explanations of the Lord's Prayer arise from such an analysis of the situation of faith. Barraged by the relentless demands of the law, under assault by the powers of this age yet gripped in the hope of the gospel, the believer learns "where to seek and obtain that aid." So, while expositing the Lord's Prayer at its first level as instruction in how to pray, Luther is at the same time describing the contention in which faith lives, giving language for the rhythm of death and resurrection that is the hallmark of life in Christ. At this level, the Lord's Prayer is a cry wrung from the crucible, an exposition of the shape of life lived under the sign of the cross in the hope of the resurrection.

III. An Organizational Question

In the Small Catechism's explanations, Luther treats both the third and the seventh petitions as summaries. The explanation of the third, "your will be done, on earth as it is in heaven," refers back to both the hallowing of God's name and the coming of God's kingdom. The seventh, "deliver us from evil," is explicitly named a summary. This treatment, along with Luther's use of the traditional breaking of the Ten Commandments into two tables, suggests that the prayer might also be taken in two parts. Many have observed parallels between the first table of the commandments and the early petitions of the Lord's Prayer, as well, giving more credence to the idea.

If Luther did think about dividing the prayer into parts, however, he didn't develop the idea any further. While there are some intriguing possibilities, none of them quite work. One possibility would be to take the first three petitions as the crucifixion side and the remaining four as the resurrection. Calling out to God, praying for God's name, kingdom, and will, we are effectively praying against the old sinner in each of us, who would rather die than ask and whose defining efforts take place on behalf of our own good names, to build our own kingdoms, and to enforce our own wills. That is a death. By the same token, the new self raised in Christ is raised on the good graces of daily bread and forgiveness; it recognizes the power of temptation and calls out for deliverance. But such a division is a little too neat, attractive as it might be: each of the petitions has both a death and resurrection built right into it. So, for example, if asking is dying, God has nevertheless promised to hear; forgiveness frees, but by putting the resentful, revenge-seeking self to death.

Another way of organizing the Lord's Prayer into two parts would be to take the possible parallel to the commandments. Then, in the first part, we would be praying for ourselves in relation to God, asking for the word and faith and help in temptation; in the second, we would be praying for ourselves in relation to our neighbors, asking for the bread and forgiveness necessary to living in relationship, help with the self-enclosing temptations like despair, and, finally, deliverance from evil. But again, the idea fails. The Lord's Prayer sees all of life *coram deo*, in relation to God; the neighbor is intimately involved in the hearing of God's word, the coming of the kingdom, and the doing of God's will.

So, for whatever help a teacher or preacher might get from dividing the Lord's Prayer into parts, the best alternative appears to be the one that Luther took, working it through, petition by petition. Though they stand together in a single paragraph, they are rich enough individually for a lifetime's meditation. Luther's interpretations share the same character, particularly for the way in which they point to the *sub-contrario* (under the sign of the opposite) nature of life in faith.

IV. THE PETITIONS

In a classic study of Luther's theology of the cross, one of the definitive volumes of Luther research, Walter von Loewenich identifies five characteristics of such a way of thinking. It begins with the conviction that God is known not through speculation but revelation; regards this revelation as indirect or veiled; insists that such knowledge is gained not through active works but through passive suffering and is, therefore, a matter of faith; and, finally, is joined with a practical emphasis on suffering.[10] These themes are pervasive in Luther's work and can be taken as informing assumptions in explanations of the individual petitions.

It is important to note, however, as Gerhard Forde argues,[11] that the real subject of such a way of thinking is not so much theology as the theologian. Reducing life under the cross to a set of theological propositions has a way of becoming a theology of glory—a wisdom of suffering employed by the old Adam or Eve to transcend the reality of death in another futile attempt at self-deliverance. Then, the theology of the cross is just one more ideology, hawking itself in the marketplace as a breakfast of champions. In theology, as with any other enterprise, "whoever seeks his life will lose it; whoever loses her life for my sake will find it" (see Matt 10:39). One becomes a theologian of the cross not by enumerating theological themes but by dying with Christ in the crucible of everyday life and being raised with him under the sign of the cross.

Maybe this is why the theology of the cross comes to such poignant expression in the Lord's Prayer. Prayer takes place in a different posture—the self is not the active agent but a suppliant. Even in theologies that place a premium on personal participation, whether in knowledge or decision, prayer breaks through the religious pretense, undermining claims to autonomy and self-sufficiency. At bottom, to pray is to ask.

The introduction

Under such assumptions, the critical issue in the introduction to the Lord's Prayer—"Our Father in heaven"—is the relationship necessary to asking. In the Large Catechism, Luther addresses this matter head-on by spelling out the basis of prayer, beginning with the Second Commandment—"You shall not take God's name in vain"—as the command to pray,[12] then moving on to biblical promises in which God commits to hearing our prayers. Finally, he calls attention to the gift of having the words of the Lord's Prayer from Jesus' own mouth. In the Small Catechism, he takes up the same issue by spelling out the familial images Jesus invokes with the term "Father."[13]

Either way, whether in the more developed discussion in the Large Catechism or the compact summary of the Small, the problem is that living in the crucible of every day, we have to be encouraged to pray. The Holy Spirit has called, gathered, enlightened, sanctified, and kept, as the third article explains, but "the devil, along with the world and our flesh, resists our efforts with all of his power. Consequently, nothing is so necessary as to call upon God incessantly and drum into his ears our prayer that he may give, preserve, and increase in us faith and obedience to the Ten Commandments and remove all that stands in our way and hinders us from fulfilling them."[14] In the course of the discussion, spelling out the command and promise, Luther goes on to enumerate problems that beset prayer, such as convictions of unworthiness and the like.

Clearly, as the common objection has it, taken in isolation, the language of the Small Catechism's explanation is patriarchal. But the assumption guiding it is hardly the Norman Rockwellesque world of father-knows-best. Like a magnet's head, faith draws its opposite—a voracious unbelief that smells the aroma of death, particularly in asking, that has a whole list of compelling reasons for being discouraged about prayer and so reduces it to routine, refuses prayer altogether or turns it into pious self-demonstration. Prayer is only possible on the basis of God's self-disclosure in command and promise, finally in Christ Jesus.

The first petition

Luther interprets the first petition, "Holy be your name," in light of the biblical link between the name and the word. God's name, as indicated by the story of Moses' attempts to squeeze it out of him, discloses God's nature (Exod 3:13-15). By the same token, Jesus says, "Out of the treasure of the heart the mouth speaks" (Matt 12:34). On the basis of this connection, asking for the hallowing of God's name is a prayer for the faithful hearing of God's word, in its preached and sacramental form. At the same time, it is a prayer that God's word will do what it does, shaping faith and life within us. In this way, the petition recalls both the Second and Third Commandments, requesting that they be fulfilled in us.

One of the critical differences between Luther and some of his subsequent sixteenth- and seventeenth-century interpreters shows up here. Following Philip Melanchthon's later lead, the authors of the Formula of Concord defined the true speaking of God's word doctrinally. Interpreted in this way, the petition becomes a request for *reine lehre*, pure doctrine. While Luther was also concerned about proper theological definition, the measure of the truth of the word occurs as it bears out its proper effect in the faith and life of the believer. God's word is holy when, wielded by the Holy Spirit, it does what it is supposed to do, taking hold of the heart.

Opposition is assumed. God's word is not a possession that can be taken for granted in either public or personal life. Though word and sacrament have been entrusted to the church, the Holy Spirit "works faith, when and where he pleases, in those who hear the Gospel," as Article V of the Augsburg Confession states.[15] And because the means of grace takes the form of a human word, it has to contend with all of the other human words that lay their claims, inveigh, demand, and threaten. Because God's revelation is indirect or veiled, it is always vulnerable.

The second petition

The explanation of the second petition, "Your kingdom come," follows out of the first. Praying for the word and its proper effect in the believer already implies a request for the faith that goes with it. In the Large Catechism, Luther speaks of the coming of God's kingdom in two ways:

"first, it comes here, in time, through the Word and faith, and secondly, in eternity, it comes through the final revelation," in Christ's return.[16]

Lohmeyer and Girgensohn, emphasizing the original eschatological context of the Lord's Prayer, give particular attention to this petition.[17] It is closely related to Jesus' preaching of the coming kingdom, with an apocalyptic urgency that breaks out in the power of the gospel as well as in warnings of impending conflagration. In fact, the whole prayer has a forward lean, anticipating the end, each of the petitions being shaped by the expectation.

Luther was well aware of this urgency. Luther recovered not only the New Testament's theology of the cross but also its apocalyptic orientation, a critical factor in understanding his way of thinking. But his eschatology is more like Isaiah's or Paul's then it is like that of the book of Revelation. So the second manifestation of the kingdom, at the end, forms a horizon for the first, in which the Spirit of the risen Christ exercises dominion in the faith that relies on God for every good. The expectation of God's ultimate rule and faith in everyday life go hand in hand.

Hidden under the contrary factors of this age, however, God's dominion competes against all the other influences that seek the heart's allegiance. As Luther argued against Erasmus in *The Bondage of the Will*, the self is a beast meant to be ridden, with opposing riders in contention.[18] A seemingly endless array of loyalties and loves compete for the affections, drawing a person this way and that in a zigzag of confused longings. In and through them, the powers of this age are at work. Calling out, "Your kingdom come," is a prayer for God's sure hand on the rein.

The third petition

In the third petition, "Your will be done on earth as in heaven," the opposition that has attacked prayer, dishonored God's name, and undermined faith is identified explicitly—the devil, the world, and our sinful self, an array of powers linked by the conviction that death is in control and that, therefore, faith is illusory. To pray, "your will be done," is to pray against such powers in the hope of the resurrection, expecting that Christ Jesus has the last word.

With the opposition flushed out in the open, the Large Catechism speaks directly about the conflicts that characterize life in faith:

> [W]here God's Word is preached, accepted or believed, and bears fruit, there the blessed holy cross will not be far away. Let nobody think he will

> have peace; he must sacrifice all that he has on earth—possessions, honor, house and home, wife and children, body and life. Now, this grieves our flesh and the old Adam, for it means that we must remain steadfast, suffer patiently whatever befalls us, and let go whatever is taken from us.[19]

If such a statement is thought of as a command or appeal, the offense multiplies. The words fly right in the face of the bootstrap mentality of popular culture. This is not a prescription but a description: believers the world over face such circumstances daily, learning what it is to lose relationships and sinecures that have been defining. This is the context of the petition.

In the Small Catechism's explanation, Luther names the way God deals with the opposition: by hindering and defeating "every evil counsel" of the powers arrayed against us. In these terms, the prayer turns. To this point, we have been praying for the things of God, as Luther points out in the Large Catechism discussion—God's name, kingdom, and will. When we say "your will be done," however, the implicit over-againstness of the earlier petitions becomes explicit. "God's name is holy in itself"; "God's kingdom comes without our prayer," with no help from the pious. But now, when we ask that the "sinful self," along with the other powers, be hindered and defeated, we are explicitly praying against ourselves. There is a breach, a decisive discontinuity between God and the sinner that requires a break—the sinner must die.

Generally, in North American popular culture, repentance is thought of as an act of will, as a demand to be fulfilled by the self under the ministrations of the law. It is something sinners should do when apprehended. Luther speaks of repentance in a very different way. It is what happens to sinners as we get caught up in the maelstrom of daily demands and, not knowing where to turn, hear the word of Christ's promise. Then, there is a genuinely healthy self-rejection—a death. The self says, "I can't take this anymore. There is nothing left. I can't go on this way." As the promise takes hold once more, the litany of dread evoked by the hinderings and defeats of every day starts to take on overtones of hope and joy. There is death and resurrection, the peculiar hope of the gospel that thrives under the sign of the opposite, expecting good things of God in jail cells, by beds in intensive care units, at the graveside.

Two characteristic themes of the theology of the cross come to focus here. When von Loewenich speaks of a knowledge gained passively and the emphasis on suffering, he describes both the breach and its aftermath. The stories of faith that are told among believers have a dark background. They begin with self-loss—in a familial crisis, a lost job, a divorce, a move, the death of a parent—and continue with a description of confidence and hope given in just such loss. The faith that turns to Christ Jesus in hope gets generated in suffering by the power of the Spirit working through the word. As such, it knows itself to be broken, yet hopefully. When the illusions of a self-made autonomy end, suffering loses its terror. It is still suffering, surely, but now, with the Good Friday there is also Easter.

The fourth petition

In the petition on daily bread, the fourth, Luther invokes a biblical promise particularly dear to people who have known hunger. He sums up Psalms 34:10 and 37:19 by asserting, in the words of the Small Catechism, "God provides daily bread, even to the wicked."[20] In the Large Catechism, acknowledging the reality of disparate diets, Luther attributes the difference to problems of distribution—God provides for everyone, but the rich hoard at the expense of the poor.[21]

With this, the focus of the petition shifts to faith's gratitude. Living in the crucible, where the injustice of unequal distribution and the continuing power of want are manifest, the temptation is either outrage or, on the other side of the coin, a debilitating cynicism. Struggling against such self-indulgence, we pray in the fourth petition that we might realize that God does give daily bread in all of its forms to sinners and does so freely, graciously, without regard to merit or the lack of it. There is a death involved here, to be sure—the self-made, self-realizing, heaven-storming overachiever and the superior, withdrawing self-protector both meet their Waterloo. Just so, there is freedom and hope—there are gifts, and they are given in such abundance that the reality of injustice and inequality can be acknowledged in a confident expectation of good.

The fifth petition

For the pious, whether they be religious types bent on moral self-improvement or secular saints seeking above all to be well-adjusted, the fifth petition comes with a jolt: "Forgive us our sins, as we forgive those who sin against us." The petition takes for granted the reality of broken relationships in the family, the congregation, or the larger community and insists, in Luther's explanation, that such faults disqualify the possibility of remedy on a personally achievable basis. The petition is a request for a grace that will both restore the implicated self and overflow into other sustaining relationships.

Luther's analysis has been faulted by contemporary theologians arguing that people no longer feel guilt to the degree the reformer assumed and that, therefore, the word of forgiveness has lost its relevance. The multiplication of self-help publications, counseling agencies, and pharmaceutical therapies—along with the deluge in the media—might indicate a need to reconsider this modern objection. The measure of the gospel is not suburban sensitivities or the lack of them. In fact, an incapacity for guilt in a world so out of balance may be the real pathology.

From a theological point of view, it has to be assumed that giving forgiveness such a strategic place in this prayer, Jesus considered it a fundamental necessity, on the order of daily bread, for the pious and impious alike. At least, Luther begins with such an assumption, understanding forgiveness less as a therapeutic remedy for guilt and more as freedom to enter into relationship with Creator and creature on positive, gracious grounds. In his vocabulary, forgiveness, justification, and freedom are all synonyms. Only on such a basis can a person live in the crucible, with all of the contradictions, disappointments, and illusory quests.

The sixth petition

In the Small Catechism's explanations, Luther strikes a parallel between the third petition and the sixth, "lead us not into temptation." Both are prayers against the powers of this age that would "hinder us from hallowing his name and prevent the coming of his kingdom"[22] and "deceive or mislead us into unbelief, despair, and other great and shameful sins."[23]

Interpreted eschatologically, the original connotation of the "temptation," the "time of trial," or the "test," was the conflagration that Jesus speaks of in the little apocalypse of Mark 13. Convinced throughout the reformation that this time was approaching, Luther, in the later 1530s, attempted some calculations of the day and hour. But in the catechisms, he takes the cosmological imagery in its more immediate, personal connection.

In the crucible of everyday life, where "the law, sin, and death" or "the devil, the world, and our sinful self" decoy like so many hunters, despair and misplaced faith are ever-present threats, materializing out of what appear to be the only real possibilities of safety. Exposed, confronted, the self turns inward, seeking within itself the resources and plans necessary to cope. In the inevitable disappointments that follow, it conceives new plans and finds other resources, disappointment feeding on itself until all hope appears to be lost and despair sets its grip. Or the self turns outward, seeking by heroic effort to conquer the forces of the night, embroiling itself with "creatures, saints, and devils" to achieve what only the Creator can bestow. Despair and heroism are two sides of the same coin: the self-seeking self.

Freedom from despair and from the idolatrous cycle of misplaced trust happens only under the sign of Good Friday and Easter, in the death of the self-questing sinner and the resurrection of a new self in Christ's hands. This happens in the praying of the petition. In these words, the Lord Jesus takes on the powers of temptation to overcome them in faith.

The emphasis on faith that von Loewenich finds characteristic of the theology of the cross shows up particularly in this sixth petition, as also in the second. But it can't be isolated to just the two—the *sola fide* (faith alone) is like the clapper in a bell, sounding through each of the explanations and through all of Luther's work. Faith is the contemporary equivalent of the resurrection of the dead.

The seventh petition

The last petition, "Deliver us from evil," summarizes the whole prayer. As Luther interprets it, we have prayed for indispensable necessities of creaturely life: for the word, the faith to go with it, and for help against the powers of this age; for a gracious awareness of the sustaining gifts, freedom in relationship to God and our neighbors, and a sure grip on the shoulder in the face of temptation. With this, gathering up all of our hopes, we ask for deliverance from all of the evils that beset life.

In the original, apocalyptic context of the Lord's Prayer, evil includes all the powers that have made life in this age into a crucible. Using the method that he has followed throughout the prayer, Luther takes this prayer for the age to come, in which evil has been domesticated, in personal terms. He notes two evils, those that take hold of us now and those of "our last hour." In both circumstances, the Triune God is the one to whom faith turns, expecting that in Christ, the last word has already been spoken. It is the word of resurrection.

Amen

For this reason, Luther adds one more explanation, this one of the "amen." "'Amen, amen' means 'Yes, yes, it shall be so.'"[24] In the crucible, with the law's relentless demands and accusations, with powers loose compounding themselves in death, given over to forces beyond ourselves that nevertheless work themselves out within us, there can be no security. But there is the certainty bestowed by the one to whom the Lord's Prayer is addressed. So, sometimes tentatively, sometimes emphatically, faith says, "That's right; this is the way it's going to be." "If we are faithless, [God] is faithful—for he cannot deny himself" (2 Tim 2:13).

Notes

1. Joachim Jeremias, "The Lord's Prayer in Light of Recent Research," in *The Prayers of Jesus*, trans. John Reumann (London: SCM, 1967) 82-107; Ernest Lohmeyer, "Our Father"; *An Introduction to the Lord's Prayer*, trans. John Bowden (New York: Harper & Row, 1965).

2. Helmut Thielicke, *Our Heavenly Father: Sermons on the Lord's Prayer* (New York: Harper and Row, 1960).

3. Gerhard Ebeling, *On Prayer: Nine Sermons*, trans. James W. Leitch (Philadelphia: Fortress, 1966). The volume was reissued in 1978.

4. Herbert Girgensohn, *Teaching Luther's Catechism*, trans. John W. Doberstein, 2 vols. (Philadelphia: Muhlenberg, 1959) 1:199-306.

5. Albrecht Peters, *Kommentar zu Luthers Katechismen*, 5 vols. (Göttingen: Vandenhoeck & Ruprecht, 1990-94).

6. Timothy J. Wengert, *Law and Gospel: Philip Melanchthon's Debate with John Agricola of Eisleben over Poenitentia* (Grand Rapids: Baker, 1997) 47-76.

7. From Luther's "Eine kurze Form der zehn Gebote; eine kurze Form des Glaubens; eine kurze Form des Vaterunsers" (1520), *D. Martin Luthers Werke: Kritische Gesamtausgabe*, 60 vols. (Weimar: Hermann Böhlaus Nachfolger, 1883-1980) 7:204-205; English by J. Michael Reu, in *Luther's Small Catechism: A New English Translation Prepared by an Intersynodical Committee: A Jubilee Offering, 1529-1929* (Minneapolis: Augsburg, 1929) 15.

8. Still the best treatment of Luther's interpretation of the commandments is by Heinrich Bornkamm, *Luther and the Old Testament*, trans. Eric W. and Ruth Gritsch, ed. Victor I. Gruhn (Philadelphia: Fortress, 1969).

9. Martin Luther, *The Small Catechism*, in *The Book of Concord*, ed. Theodore Tappert (Philadelphia: Muhlenberg, 1959) 345. Hereafter, BC.

10. Walther von Loewenich, *Luther's Theology of the Cross*, trans. Herbert J. A. Bouman (Minneapolis: Augsburg, 1976) 19ff.

11. Gerhard O. Forde, On Being a Theologian of the Cross: Reflections on Luther's Heidelberg Disputations, 1518 (Grand Rapids: Eerdmans, 1997) 9.

12. BC, 420; Luther's exposition of the prayer in the Large Catechism is found in BC, 420-436.

13. BC, 346; Luther's exposition of the prayer in the Small Catechism is found in BC, 346-348.

14. BC, 420.

15. BC, 31.

16. BC, 427.

17. Lohmeyer, "Our Father," 88-110; Girgensohn, *Teaching Luther's Catechism*, 242-256.

18. Martin Luther on the Bondage of the Will. A New Translation of De Servo Arbitrio (1525), trans. J. I. Packer and O. R. Johnston (Westwood, NJ: Revell, 1957) 103.

19. BC, 429.

20. BC, 347.

21. BC, 430.

22. BC, 347 (third petition).

23. BC, 347-348 (sixth petition).

24. BC, 348.

LUTHER'S CULTURAL TRANSLATION OF THE CATECHISM

Nestingen was a missionary at heart as this article originally published in ***Lutheran Quarterly*** *(Winter 2001) demonstrates. Nestingen would have nothing to do with those who played off "confessional" against "missional" or vice versa. It is not one of the other but both. Drawing on the seminal work of Lamin Sanneh (1942-2019), a convert to Christianity from Islam whose prestigious career culminated with an appointment to the James D. Willis Chair of Missions and World Christianity at Yale Divinity School, Nestingen demonstrates that Luther was indeed a "creative translator" (Heinz Bluhm) rendering the truth of the ecumenical faith accessible in the "mother tongue" in the Small and Large Catechisms. In many ways, this article anticipates the 2023 book by Nestingen's friend, Gordon A. Jensen,* ***Experiencing the Gospel: The History and Creativity of Martin Luther's 1534 Bible Project*** *(Fortress Press). JTP+*

Translation takes place in two dimensions. The first is a linguistic exchange, roughly equivalent language being substituted for the original. The second is cultural, the new language inevitably giving that which is being translated another hue, colored with its own specific assumptions. Although Luther is remembered by the church primarily as a theologian, nowadays, most likely as one with some bad habits, cultural historians point to his translations. He translated the Old Testament in its entirety twice and the New Testament three times, letting Abraham and Sarah, Moses, the prophets, the Apostle Paul, and finally Jesus himself speak the Middle High German of Saxony. His Bible has the same place in the German language that the King James Version has in English.

But Luther was also keenly aware of the second dimension of translation. As eager as he was to find linguistic equivalents, he was just as intent on registering the historic witness of the faith in a culturally specific form. One of the best examples of Luther's achievement at this level is the Small Catechism. Along with the Bible translations, it was a key document in what became in Protestantism, a larger effort to move the altar from the church into the kitchen, bringing home the witness of the Christian faith at the family table.[1] This essay addresses Luther's accomplishment in cultural translation, first, by assessing the significance of the approach of the missiologist Lamen Sanneh to the analysis of the cultural level of translation. Secondly, we assess how Luther works with cultural translation in the Small Catechism's explanations of the Commandments, the Creed, and the Lord's Prayer. Thirdly, this assessment will be used to make suggestions for confessing the faith in the twenty-first century.

Lamen Sanneh's Cultural Level of Translation

One of the genuinely revolutionary books in recent years is Lamen Sanneh's *Translating the Message*.[2] Although perhaps not as well known as he should be, Sanneh is something of an academic superstar, having taught at St. Andrews, Harvard, and now Yale. He was born into a royal family in West Africa and was raised a Moslem before converting as a young man to the Christian faith. He is well versed in the history of Islam and has reconfigured treatment of the history of the Christian mission, particularly in Africa.

Sanneh begins with a striking contrast between Islam and Christianity. Islam has worked, he says, on the model of a quarantine. The unmediated Word of God revealed to Mohammed by the angel Gabriel has always to be protected from contamination. Thus, while there have been translations of the Koran into various languages, Islam has maintained a linguistic preserve, insisting on the primacy of Mohammed's eighth-century Arabic in its formal, religious usage. In contrast, the Christian faith was born at the meeting point of two cultures, Hebrew and Greek. The church came to be in translation. Although Jesus spoke Aramaic, with only a few exceptions, the Aramaic has given way completely so that we meet him first of all in Koine, the language of the Hellenists. Pentecost itself is a festival of translation, the Spirit of the Risen Christ breaking out in the mother tongues of all the nations represented in the markets of Jerusalem.

"Mother tongue" is a fertile phrase. As Sanneh carries on his argument, he notes how languages embody specific cultural assumptions. A biblical example supporting Sanneh's argument is Paul's use of the term *sarx* or flesh. In his biblically driven apocalyptic, the term describes the self bent on having itself, a drive that can express itself sexually but also religiously. Translated into the vernacular of the larger Mediterranean world, the term gets caught up in what Peter Brown has called "antiquity's strange embarrassment about the body."[3] Language learned in the home, on the street, in situations of intimacy and stress takes on its own connotations—in this case, for the whole of Mediterranean culture. Recognizing the assumptions and dealing with them effectively is the task of the second level of translation.

Whether or not it recognized this second level, then, Sanneh argues that by translating the message, the church effectively absorbed the cultural relations implicit in the new language into the biblical text. Here, as Paul Rajashekar, dean at the Lutheran Theological Seminary in Philadelphia, points out, Sanneh's analysis works better for Africa and parts of Europe than it does for Asia, where there were older cultures and written languages. But in Africa and the Western world, the church literally established the cultures it entered, providing not only grammar and syntax for the host language but, at the same time, implicitly, if not explicitly, ratifying the assumed relationships. Thus, in Sanneh's analysis, Christian mission has not been, as it is commonly portrayed, a history of imperial cultural subordination. Rather, while there is no doubt about sinners getting loose in the meeting of different cultures, the church's eagerness to translate has been a hallmark of an inherent openness to other forms of cultural expression. As Luke observes in the story of Pentecost, the hearers asked, "And how is it that we hear, each of us, in our own native language?" (Acts 2:7).

Although, to my knowledge, Sanneh does not apply his analysis to the Reformation, in fact it fits closely. As missionaries moved into Northern Europe in the later centuries of the first millennium, the papacy sought to establish a linguistic preserve, enforcing the use of Jerome's Vulgate and the Latin liturgy. Latin was part and parcel of other forms of Mediterranean domination in Northern Europe, economic, social, political, and otherwise. Significantly, when Charles V's troops broke into Wittenberg in 1547, they announced that they had come to teach the people to speak Spanish, thereby enforcing a further Mediterranean linguistic dominance.

Thus, Sanneh's analysis exposes the larger significance of the Lutheran Reformation. It was the first major attempt to translate the message of the gospel for German-speaking Europe. For this purpose, the reformers put the tradition of the church under a critical check, challenging the imposition of what was idiosyncratically Mediterranean, insisting on the priority of the biblical word proclaimed in Christ. Luther's goal was to speak the people's language in such a way as to engage the specific cultural assumptions that went with it.[4] Further, the Lutheran Reformation carried over in translation to the Scandinavian languages. Johannes Bugenhagen, Luther's pastor, helped with a translation into low German, laying a basis for translation into Danish and later Norwegian. The Petri brothers translated as the reform carried into Sweden. While Finnish comes from a different linguistic family, Michael Agricola—who studied with Luther in Wittenberg—is generally considered the founder of modern Finnish, just as Luther himself is considered the father of modern German. The Lutheran Reformation was, from beginning to end, above all, a matter of translation.

Luther's Cultural Translation

The Catechisms, Small and Large, were written at a turning point in the reform. From early on, Luther had been concerned about bringing home his re-interpretation of the faith to the lay people and had done so by preaching and popular pamphlets. But into the 1520s, the reform that gathered around him remained a loosely grouped, ad hoc movement focused primarily on improving the preaching. In the mid-1520s, this changed. The Lutheran reformers recognized that they needed to take some more formal steps. The two catechisms, the Small written for parents and families, the Large for pastors and teachers, were the first public results. In them we can see Luther carefully attempting to hand over the second level of translation, that is, to set out the faith in the language of the people.

Luther is generally regarded as a conservative reformer. This characterization grows out of his treatment of the mass, another cultural translation from the mid-1520s, as well as the structure of the catechism. In both cases, he uses standard catholic forms—the Latin Mass and in the catechisms, the Ten Commandments, the Apostles' Creed, and the Lord's Prayer.[5] The reform is, in this way, fully traditional and ecumenical, reflecting the self-understanding of Luther as well as his colleagues as loyal children of the church.

At the same time, using the traditional forms, Luther decisively reorients them. So the Latin Mass, shorn of its sacrificial elements, is reoriented sacramentally in terms of handing over God's down-toearth gifts. And while the catechism is built out of parts long considered standard in Latin Christianity, Luther tunes his explanations so that they will ring true to the heart of his immediate hearers, German families carrying the tradition into their kitchens on posterboards that could be hung on the wall for use while the family is at the table. This is the second level of Luther's translation, as becomes evident in his treatment of each of the first three chief parts, those elements that, in Luther's own mind comprised the catechism itself.

Traditionally, both Roman Catholic and Protestant accounts of the faith begin with the law, under the assumption that the law was originally given to save and that the Ten Commandments provide an eternal summary of its requirements. In fact, Luther was harshly critical of both assumptions. He insisted that from the be ginning, it was always God's intention to save in Christ Jesus and that the law had to be dealt with accordingly. "The law was not given that it might justify or vivify or prescribe anything for righteousness," he wrote in the later 1530s.[6] Similarly, in a characteristically colorful sermon of 1525, "How Christians Should Regard Moses," Luther personifies the commandments under Moses' name and says that, as such, they have no place among Christians.[7] In fact, he calls them the *Saxonspiegel*, or local code of laws, so culturally specific to Israel that they cannot be applied elsewhere. Clearly, when he explains the commandments in the Small Catechism as well as the Large, Luther is not proceeding exegetically or attempting a set of eternal standards.

Rather, Luther's explanations are much closer to hand. Given the fact that the law was not meant to save and cannot do so, he reasons the commandments must have some more proximate value. This can be seen in the way that they order everyday life, making explicit what is implicitly required of us in everyday relations with our Creator, other creatures, and the creation itself. Thus, explanations of the commandments in the Catechism offer a working analysis of how life works, of what is demanded of us in the working relations of the day.[8] Creatures have to get along with their creator; creatures have to get along with other creatures; this is what it takes.

Noticeable examples of this are Luther's treatment of the original second commandment and what, in the Roman Catholic numbering he took over, has been the third. Calvin restores the commandment against graven images on grounds of its biblical formulation—it is an eternal, unchanging standard for all of life. Luther argues that it was culturally specific, given to Israel alone and that the arts clearly can communicate the gospel.[9] Likewise, on the Third Commandment, he steps right around the extended biblical discussion of what constitutes work on the Sabbath, explaining that what the commandment really requires is defined by the relationship with God established in the First Commandment.[10] If there is going to be any faith in God's promise to be our God, we are going to have to hear the Word.

Luther's explanations of the commandments do have something timeless about them. Again and again, especially in the Large Catechism, people comment that it seems like the explanation was written just yesterday. But what makes them such is their gritty practicality. They are timeless because they are so timely, written out of close observation of the conditions that people are actually facing day to day.

As he turns to the Apostles' Creed, Luther follows the same method, setting out a translation into the mother tongue, the language of the heart. This is evident, to begin with, in what Luther does not do. If he had frozen a biblical metaphor, as critics have held, the two catechisms and particularly the second article of the creed would be the place for a treatment of justification by faith alone. In fact, as Paul Althaus noted a generation ago, both the language and the conceptuality of justification are completely missing in both catechisms.[11]

Rather, instead of moving conceptually, Luther works relationally, setting the gospel out in down-to-earth terms. He begins the explanations of the second article in both the Small Catechism and the Large by identifying the person of Jesus and then asserting what he has done: he has become our Lord. This is the non-negotiable, invariable center, reprised in the later phrase of the Small Catechism's explanation, "all this he has done that I may be his own, live under him and serve him." The rest of the second article, Luther says, explains how this has happened—namely, "he has bought and freed me, a lost and condemned person, not with silver and gold but with his holy and precious blood and his innocent suffering and death."[12] This is the first reference to the power of sin in the Small Catechism. What for later Lutheranism became a necessary precondition for the proclamation of the gospel, a sense of personal need, is for Luther as much a consequence of the gospel. The law drives, a defining characteristic, but it literally does not know where to go until it has been overtaken by the declaration of the gospel and placed under the direction of the Holy Spirit. Then words like "lost" and "condemned" become appropriate, but only in light of the promise: he "has saved me," "bought and freed me."

This points to the way Luther declares the gospel in his explanation. As Robert W. Jenson argued in *Lutheranism: The Theological Movement and Its Confessional Writings*, the doctrine of justification is, for Luther, a "meta-linguistic principle" or, better, a grammar for the declaration of the gospel.[13] While the doctrine is not a subject of the catechism, it nevertheless informs the proclamation. So, having declared the Lordship of Christ, Luther begins to preach. Christ claims every verb as subject: he has saved and redeemed, bought and freed. Because he is the worker, the work is whole and complete, utterly independent of my responses, an unconditional act: "all this he has done." The beneficiary of this work it is clearly identified: it is me, a lost and condemned person, a sinner. Although the action is past, it continues in the present all the way into the future as immediate gift and benefit: "that I may live under him and serve him in everlasting righteousness, innocence, and blessedness, just as he is risen from the dead and lives and rules eternally."

Declaring the gospel in such an immediate, down-to-earth way, in the explanation of the Third Article, Luther follows the movement of the heart. The promise of Christ's Lordship, that "I may be his own, live under and serve him," comes back against me, exposing the fundamental reality of my rebellion. In fact, hearing such a statement, in Luther's estimation, a person is driven to ex amine the self to see if it has actually happened and then to confess, "I believe that I cannot, by my own understanding or strength, believe in Jesus Christ my Lord or come to him." At the same time, the promise itself draws attention away from the self to the ongoing work of the Spirit, "calling, gathering, enlightening, sanctifying, keeping," not only me but the whole Christian church in the daily declaration of the absolution and the hope of the resurrection.

This dialectic, the *simul*, in which unbelief and faith, sin and righteousness coexist, lays the foundation for the closest thing to Elijah's unfailing jar of oil and bag of meal to be found in Luther's work, catechetical or otherwise: his explanations of the Lord's Prayer. Living in the world of the *nomos*, under conditions of life shaped by the seemingly unending demands of life in relationship, in a situation in which the law continuously gets away to turn in attack, believers are at the same time held under the power of the gospel, subject to the freeing work of the Holy Spirit.[14] So Luther argued, "To the extent that Christ is raised with us, so far are we without the law, sin, and death. To the extent that Christ is not raised in us, we are under the power of the law, sin, and death."[15]

Living in this tension, we are, in the words of Ernst Käsemann, territory contended for—a battleground open to all comers.[16] Thus, the shape of life in Christ is death and resurrection, the daily dying and rising noted by Paul in Romans 6 and by Luther in the Small Catechism's answer to the fourth question on baptism.

For this reason, the explanations of each of the petitions has the smell of death. If prayer is simply asking, so, too, we would rather die than ask—asking is a form of death. God's name is holy in itself; his kingdom comes without our prayer; his will is done with out our asking; he gives daily bread to all people, however sinful; although he tempts no one to sin, you can never be sure what the good Lord will do next as he "hinders and defeats every evil scheme and purpose of the devil, the world and the sinful self." There is no resurrection without death.

At the same time, putting us to death with Christ Jesus, God raises us to newness of life. So, if the explanations of the Lord's Prayer smell of the grave, they breathe with an eternal Spring: God encourages us to faith in a language of familial intimacy; speaks the word in its preached and sacramental forms; sends the Spirit upon us to keep us firm in the faith and in the word; softens us up to the gifts of everyday life; frees us in forgiveness; and promises deliverance.

So, as Luther explains it, the Lord's Prayer becomes, in effect, a table of contents to the Christian life, exposing the shape of the cross and, under it, the hope of the resurrection. While confirming the nature of life in faith as *sub contrario*, under the sign of the opposite, it at the same time points to the power of the gospel at work just there.

Thus, Luther's catechism is fundamentally a translation. Small or Large, it takes the defining elements of ecumenical faith to exposit them in the mother tongue. It not only speaks the language of the butcher shop and the tavern, the pew, and the kitchen but embodies that language at the second level of translation, where defining cultural relationships are expressed.

Confessing the Faith in the Twenty-First Century

Robert Kolb has made a critical contribution to confessional Lutheranism in our churches by turning from the noun to the continuing present tense of the verb: confession can only be such when it becomes confessing.[17] Thus, the critical and concluding question becomes the one posted: how does Luther's catechetics serve confessing in the twenty-first century?

To take up this question, we look at some contemporary implications for interpreting these three parts of the catechism.

W L. Morton, a great historian who taught at the University of Manitoba in Winnipeg, used to argue the academic form of a suspicion my Canadian grandfather also held: that a nation founded on the concept of personal rights fatally weakens the ability of the community to regulate questionable forms of behavior.[18] Public discourse over the last several decades especially, has compellingly illustrated this analysis. Repeatedly, the language of rights has been used to beat down historic standards long regarded as inviolate, the church often enough tagging along a couple of steps behind but making up for its tardiness with equally vehement renunciations. Now pastors teaching the commandments face the most ruthless of judges, one armed with an argument as efficient as a power flush: a hormonally handicapped adolescent slouched in a confirmation class drawling, "That's just where you're coming from, pastor."

The argument for the contextual nature of our knowledge is keyed to the second level of translation. If relationships of faith, hope, and love do not involve the language of the heart, they are not working. But in our own cultural context, the melting pot, this argument is used exclusively to disqualify particularly challenging ultimate claims to unchanging and eternal truths. It is not joined by an equal effort genuinely to qualify, that is, to contextualize at the second level, where we can speak to the heart of what is genuinely demanded as well as given. That is Luther's effort, an enterprise that needs to be continued in the twenty-first century. Luther argued, over and against the move commonly made in our culture, that simply dismissing the law is a "play put on in an empty theater."[19] Writing the law off verbally will only work if the theater is really empty. Real people, living in real situations, face real demands, whether they are codified or, even more dangerously, unspecified. Eliminating the word "should" from preaching does not eliminate the inevitable requirements of living in a world of sin and death. All that such verbal elimination accomplishes is driving the requirement temporarily underground, only to have it re surface to claim its pound of flesh, an experience readily observable in family conflicts, sexual misadventures, and so forth.

Thus, in this cultural context, amidst such verbal gamesmanship, one task of the confessing church is carefully tending the commanding word. We know that the law will not justify, that in spite of its ultimate claims, it can neither give life nor save, that at best, it is the rude schoolmaster who needs, above all, to be taught a set of manners. Just so, seeing through its claims to ultimacy, we need to tend its penultimate values. If we do not speak the legal word, our people, caught up in a fundamentally illusory language of personal rights, will hear it anyway and in a context where all alternatives have been taken away. Better us than Moses.

But finally, our calling is the gospel. The law is going to get through one way or another, if not by the ears, then through some other orifice. The gospel of Christ Jesus is an alien word antithetical to every human assumption. We do not possess it; it possesses us, coming, in Luther's beautiful image, like a place-shower, a hard-driving rain that moves through quickly on its way someplace else. To assume it is to deny it; to take it for granted is to see it moving off in another direction.

So, how do we speak it? It seems to me that it is very helpful to watch Luther's grammar, the grammar of justification. The risen Christ is not an idea but a person who is even now at work, through his Spirit, in the Word and the sacraments, to justify the godless, forgiving sin, delivering from the powers, raising the dead. To preach him is to identify his activity in the assigned text as continuing into the present for the hearers gathered so that they are numbered among those who are benefiting by his work, and so named without qualification or condition. It is to look the sinner full in the face and say, "In the name and the stead of Christ Jesus, I forgive you all your sin," to stand by an open grave and say, "This is one of Christ's own; death shall have no dominion."

Thus, while alien, the gospel is fundamentally a word in the mother tongue. Whether in its preached or its sacramental form, it comes home by being handed over in the dialect of the home, in the language of the heart. If it does not happen there, it does not happen—a reality that drives us to make every effort to speak it clearly even while recognizing, as Article V of the *Augustana* has it, that finally, only the Spirit makes faith and does so "when and where he pleases, in those who hear the gospel."

Finally, the Lord's Prayer. In *Lighten our Darkness*, his searing cultural critique, Douglas John Hall pointed out the intertwining of official optimism and private cynicism that afflicts genuine hope in our public life. The optimism denies the darkness, setting up impossible expectations; the cynicism, born of the original naivete, feeds its own continuous disappointments, corroding every effort.[20] "A theology of glory calls good evil and evil good," Luther argued; "a theology of the cross calls a thing what it is."[21] Christ's cross and resurrection together attack both of the false alternatives. The cross acknowledges the reality of discontinuity, dislocation, and loss of a world and a self at odds with themselves. The resurrection declares the new reality of life given under the sign of death, hope under despair, faith in the midst of unbelief.

In this way, the Lord's Prayer sets out an alternative vision, one that can be summed up in a passage from the prologue to John's Gospel (1:5): "The light shined in the darkness and the darkness comprehended it not." There is darkness. There is also light. In the end, the darkness will be broken by his dawning.

With this word of tempered hopes, there is a reality that incarnates them. In the growth of the early church, in the entrenchment of the Lutheran reform in Northern European culture, in the immigration of Lutheranism to North America, with the Word, there was always the reality of the congregation-that gathering, which gives a voice, hands, and feet to join the proclaimed word and the administered sacrament. There, the mother tongue is spoken, giving articulation to both the groaning and the delighted sighs of expectation. And there, as at Pentecost, the Spirit is at work to break open the reserve, to spread the Word to every tribe and nation.

Notes

1. See Elizabeth L. Eisenstein, "The Advent of Printing and the Protestant Revolt: A New Approach to the Disruption of Western Christendom," in Robert M. Kingdon, ed., *Transition and Revolution: Problems and Issues of European Renaissance and Reformation History* (Minneapolis: Burgess, 1974), 250-257.

2. Lamen O. Sanneh, *Translating the Message* (Maryknoll: Orbis, 1989).

3. Peter R.L. Brown, *The Body and Society: Men, Women and Sexual Renunciation in Early Christianity* (New York: Columbia University Press, 1988).

4. See Heinz Bluhm, *Luther: Translator of Paul: Studies in Romans and Galatians* (New York: Lang, 1984).

5. *Die Bekenntnisschriften der evangelische-lutherischen* Kirche 11th ed. (Göttingen: Vandenhoeck & Ruprecht, 1992), 507-515 [hereafter cited as BSLK]; *The Book of Concord: The Confessions of the Evangelical Lutheran Church*, Eds. Robert Kolb and Timothy J. Wengert (Minneapolis: Fortress Press, 2000), 351-358 [hereafter cited as BC]; The *Book of Concord: The Confessions of the Evangelical Lutheran Church*. Ed. Theodore G. Tappert (Philadelphia: Fortress Press, 1959), 342 [hereafter cited as BC-T]. When Luther himself refers to "the Catechism," for example on p. 348, he is generally not speaking of his own document but of the Commandments, the Creed and the Lord's Prayer together.

6. *Luthers Werke*, Kritische Gesamtausgabe, 57 vols. Eds. J.F.K. Knaake et al. (Weimar: Böhlau, 1883fr.), 39/1:347 [hereafter cited as WA].

7. WA 16:373-375; *Luther's Works* American Edition, 55 vols. Eds Pelikan and Lehmann (St. Louis and Philadelphia: Concordia and Fortress, 1955ff.) 35:165 [hereafter cited as LW].

8. The best available discussion of Luther's approach to the Commandments is in Heinrich Bornkamm, *Luther and the Old Testament*, trans. Eric W and Ruth Gritsch (Philadelphia: Fortress, 1969), 120-178.

9. *Calvin: Institutes of the Christian Religion*, ed. John T. McNeil, trans. Ford Lewis Battles (The Library of Christian Classics XX, Philadelphia: Westminster, i960), 112. For the larger issue in the Reformation see Sergiusz Michalski, *The Reformation and the Visual Arts: The Protestant Image Question in Western and Eastern Europe* (London: Routledge, 1993), 1-42.

10. The Small Catechism's explanation of the Third Commandment does not mention rest at all, but hearing and learning God's Word; the Large Catechism's explanation makes rest an occasion for the Word. BSLK 580-586; BC, 396-400; BC-T, 375-379.

11. Paul Althaus, *The Theology of Martin Luther*, tr. Robert C. Shultz (Philadelphia: Fortress, 1966), 225. In a lecture on Justification presented at Luther Seminary in St. Paul, March 20, 2001, Oswald Bayer has noted that the Small Catechism's explanation of the First Article does contain technical terminology characteristic of the medieval doctrine, in the language of merit and mercy. These references, however, are not further developed in the explanation of the Second Article, where a full treatment of justification by faith alone might be expected; Oswald Bayer, "Justification as the Basis and Boundary of Theology," *Lutheran Quarterly* 15 (2001): 275-77.

12. The citations to the Small Catechism are from the version still most commonly in use in Lutheran parishes, *The Small Catechism in Contemporary English* (Minneapolis, Philadelphia and St. Louis: Augsburg, the Board of Publication of the Lutheran Church in America, and Concordia, 1968).

13. Robert W. Jenson and Eric W. Gritsch, *Lutheranism: The Theological Movement and Its Confessional Writings* (Philadelphia: Fortress, 1976), 41-42.

14. The most helpful discussion of Luther's understanding of the relationship of the Commandments, the Creed and the Lord's Prayer in the life of the believer is Herbert Girgensohn's classic, *Teaching Luther's Catechism*, trans. John Doberstein (Philadelphia: Muhlenberg, 1959), 3-5. The explanations of the Lord's Prayer are clearly shaped by Luther's theology of the cross even though, as with Justification by faith in the Creed, there is no explicit reference. In both cases, his way of thinking theologically shapes the explanations without becoming the subject of them. The goal is not to inculcate ideology but to preach.

15. WA 39/I:352.

16. Ernst Käsemann, *Perspectives on Paul*, tr. Margaret Kohl (London: SCM Press, 1971), 9.

17. Robert Kolb, *Confessing the Faith: Reformers Define the Church, 1530-1580* (St. Louis: Concordia, 1991).

18. W.L. Morton, *The Canadian Identity*, 2nd ed. (Toronto: The University of Toronto Press, 1972). See also Charles Taylor, *Radical Tones. The Conservative Tradition in Canada* (Toronto: House of Anansi Press, 1982), 49-76. Paul Tillich, in his *Systematic Theology* (Chicago: The University of Chicago Press, 1951), I, 174-176, describes individuation and participation together as an "ontological polarity," an inherent tension of being. While both the United States and Canada have been shaped by a classically liberal tradition emphasizing the rights of the individual, Canada has retained an increasingly marginalized classical conservatism which has emphasized the priority of the community. Morton makes no reference to Tillich's formulation of the polarity, his criticism reflects a traditional Canadian conservative apprehension that by tipping toward individuation by entitling the individual, a system of rights undermines the community. Both the positive and the negative impact of upping the balance in this way is evident in American public life. While appeals to rights have served minorities and women facing communally imposed injustices, making the individual the ultimate standard reduces matters of law to personal preference or opinion, arbitrary values, and atomizes the community.

19. WA 39/1:358

20. Douglas John Hall, *Lighten Our Darkness: Toward an Indigenous Theology of the Cross* (Philadelphia: Westminster, 1976), 39-41.

21. WA 1:354. 21-22; LW 31:45.

GRAVEN IMAGES AND CHRISTIAN FREEDOM

In the Reformed numbering of the Ten Commandments, the prohibition of graven images became the second commandment, while Lutherans included it under the first commandment. As a careful historian, Nestingen traces the history of art and images in the pre-Reformation church and centers in on the debate occasioned by Karlstadt and other Enthusiasts in Luther's day. Always a pastor, Nestingen does not leave the matter of images in the sixteenth century but takes up the question anew in light of present-day addictions to virtual realities, noting that faith brings freedom and idols bring bondage. Virtual idols enslave, as can be seen with the widespread use of pornography. This essay is rich with Nestingen's pastoral wisdom. In this pastoral task, he is also a mentor on the use of the Decalogue in the Christian life as well as Luther's understanding of "flesh" and "spirit." Nestingen has packed much into this article, originally presented in Australia and published first in the ***Lutheran Theological Journal*** *(May 2015). JTP+*

Introduction

What is the second commandment? A Lutheran whose confirmation instruction has not faded away will promptly answer, "You shall not take God's name in vain." But someone who grew up in the legacy of the Church of England or one of the various Reformed traditions, looking quizzically at the Lutheran, will say with equal certainty, "You shall make no graven image."

The differing answers stem from some old historical battles that, even though long forgotten, still point to questions that arise in the life of the church. The oldest is a first-millennium controversy over the use of the arts among Christians, another a 16th-century Reformation conflict concerning the relation of the flesh and the spirit, and still a third, the place of the law in the Christian life. In front of these conflicts, another more contemporary issue clamors for attention: the binding power of virtual realities, which has silently become an enormous pastoral problem. The perennial nature of the older questions suggests that permanent answers may be elusive. But surveying them may help pastors and congregations as they grapple with the phenomenon.

Graven Images and the Bible

The original texts of the commandments in Exodus and Deuteronomy both forbid the use of graven images, the injunction following right out of the first commandment in Exodus 20:4 and Deuteronomy 5:8. The wording of the texts suggests that carved or cast statuary, like the golden calf, was the original problem. But, the prohibition has been expanded in various interpretations over the centuries to limit pictorial art and, in some cases, music as well.[1]

Given such a strong and strategically placed restriction of images in the Old Testament, exceptions to the rule come as a surprise. But they are common. The bronze serpent in Numbers 21:9, the cherubim carved over the ark of the covenant in Exodus 25:18-22 and the carvings in Solomon's temple (1 Kings 6:18-35) all indicate that images could gain prominence despite the prohibition.

The same situation prevails in the New Testament. The commandment against graven images did not generate enough disputes in the apostolic period to produce extensive comment. Most references come in passing. Still, there's enough to demonstrate that restrictions continued. So, Paul spoke out against the worship of images (Acts 17:29) and got into trouble with silversmiths for driving down the demand for their services (Acts 19:23-27). In Romans 1:23, Paul cites the misuse of images as a source of the deeper difficulty, exchanging faith in the Creator with worship of the creature. But there are still exceptions to the use of images, as well. In John 3, Jesus positively compares the bronze serpent Moses mounted on a pole to himself, being raised up for the redemption of the world.

The Use of the Arts in the Church: From the Patristic Period to the Middle Ages

In the patristic period, images took on increasing significance. The catacombs themselves show evidence of Christian art. As the church grew, pictures of Jesus, the Blessed Virgin Mary, and various saints were used extensively. They developed into icons, which are flat, stylized paintings that are said to participate in the reality they portray and, therefore, to communicate grace to the observer. The icons were honored and soon enough venerated, particularly in the Eastern church, where they have ever since been used in worship.

Veneration provoked a reaction, however, in both the East and the West. Despite the growing tendency to ignore the commandment against graven images, the prohibition still had enough authority to promote a challenge. The iconoclasm of Islam, a fierce and growing rival to the church in the East, may have been a contributing factor. The result was the iconoclastic controversy, which began in the eighth century and carried over to the ninth. It was settled by the bishops—they endorsed the continued use of icons. The conflict took its own form in the West, where the crucifix and other statuary had gained common usage. Gregory the Great supported the use of statuary as well as music. In the 13th century, Thomas Aquinas, the definitive theologian of Roman Catholicism, provided a theological rationale for the ongoing use of icons.

Some of the greatest paintings and statuary in Western history came out of the 15th-century Renaissance in southern Europe. Michelangelo complained constantly about the poor wages the papacy paid him for his work in the Sistine Chapel, but the quality of his work didn't suffer.

By the end of the Middle Ages, local parishes across Europe had become centers of the arts—the wealthy endowed paintings and statuary, building up collections in particular churches. Music flourished as well. In an age of limited literacy, the arts performed the vital function of telling the story through music and visual representation.[2] Opera began as performances of biblical narratives on the church steps. Choral composers from that time are still remembered and performed. Luther's favorite was Josquin des Prez.

The Relation of the Flesh and the Spirit: a Reformation Conflict

Several great painters were associated with the Reformation. Lucas Cranach earned his living as a pharmacist in Wittenberg. Even if his painting was an avocation, he became well known for his portraits, among others, his portraits of Luther himself. The best-known artist was Albrecht Durer, a printmaker whose woodcuts illustrated early editions of Luther's Small Catechism. Luther was a fine musician. He had a high tenor voice—sometimes he is described as an alto—and he was an accomplished lute player. But his real contribution was his hymns. It is not true, as seminarians have claimed for generations, that Luther took the hymn melodies from drinking songs. He had an ear for both the language and fine music of the time. Hymns like *A Mighty Fortress* and the Easter chorale 'Christ lay in death's strong bonds' carry the trademarks of the reform.[3]

But there were also iconoclasts in the 16th century Reformation. In fact, one of them—the first to claim international attention—was one of Luther's colleagues on the faculty at the University of Wittenberg. Though he didn't last long in the city after he led crowds in destroying some of the Elector's art, this man—Andreas Bodenstein von Karlstadt—spread his opposition to the use of images into the Rhine Valley in southwest Germany and then into Switzerland.[4] Regarded as one of the fathers of the left wing, or radical Reformation, Karlstadt was radical in the original sense of the term. Strictly speaking, he was a spiritualist. He believed that the church had been corrupted by its own structures and proposed that the true church was a fellowship of like-minded people joined in a spiritually disciplined quest. Whereas more conservative reformers, like Luther, sought reform within the structures of the church, Karlstadt, and his ilk believed that the church had lost contact with its origins and that, therefore, the only viable alternative was to go back to its roots in scripture, particularly the Old Testament and the Book of Acts, and begin all over again.

It was Karlstadt's spiritualism that led him to the commandment against graven images. An old intellectual tradition dating all the way back to the ancient Greeks and Romans marked a strict distinction between flesh and spirit. In its crude forms, like Gnosticism, this tradition held that the fleshy—matters of the body like sex and other physical functions—was inherently evil, marked by death, and that the way of salvation was found by transcending such bodily matters for more uplifted, spiritual matters like the mind and faith. In a book called *The Body*, one of the great historians of the early church, Peter Brown, has demonstrated how cultural apprehensions about physical life shaped the early church. It is the driving force behind monasticism, for instance, which grew into one of the most powerful institutions in both the East and the West, and also clerical celibacy. Origen and Augustine, the great biblical interpreters in the patristic period, were deeply imbued with this way of understanding the faith. Working from such assumptions, Karlstadt argued that the divine spirit cannot be portrayed in any physical form. This proscription includes not only art and statuary but also the sacraments—there can be no real presence because the Spirit, by its very nature, cannot take on physical form.[5]

To support his claims, Karlstadt appealed to the commandment against graven images. This injunction, he argued, has the same force as the commandments against murder and adultery. It cannot be suspended on any ground. To portray or present the divine in any physical way not only debases but effectively puts God to death. For this reason, it wasn't enough to condemn images—they had to be destroyed.

The trouble started when Luther was secreted away in the Wartburg. At the Diet of Worms in 1521, he stood before the crowned heads of Europe, refusing to back away from the biblical word. Unbeknown to him, Frederick the Wise-his own prince, the Elector of Saxony—had made arrangements to have him kidnapped on his way back to Wittenberg. At that point, Luther, an outlaw, spent the better part of a year hidden in the castle above Eisenach, a town he knew from his school days. Luther used this time to translate the New Testament from Greek into Middle High German, his dialect. While he was away, Karlstadt and a younger colleague, Philip Melanchthon, took over theological leadership of the Wittenberg reform, Karlstadt claiming his seniority.

During this time, Karlstadt's iconoclasm broke into the open. He not only preached and wrote against images, he encouraged the people of Wittenberg to join him in their destruction. Frederick the Wise had one of the most extensive collections of the time and displayed them in the churches. He had a lot to protect. For a while, it seemed that the balance of power that had sheltered and driven the Lutheran reform would break down. Frederick was reluctant to have Luther return to Wittenberg, but the uprising in the city became increasingly alarming. When Luther returned, he preached a series of eight sermons that restored his leadership. Karlstadt fled the city. In his travels, he spread his vision of the radical Reformation. In Zurich, in the eastern part of Switzerland, he got a sympathetic hearing. In 1525, he attempted a return to Wittenberg.

At that time, Luther wrote one of his most important statements concerning the conflict, *Against the heavenly prophets in the matter of images and sacraments.*[6] The reference to 'heavenly prophets' was sarcastic, like another term that Luther often used to describe Karlstadt and the radical Reformers, *Schwärmer*, people who manifested *Schwärmerei*. The word *Schwärmerei* refers to the swarming of bees during the season of the year when they leave the hive and fly around above it, forsaking the making of honey.

Schwärmer are like the bees who swarm about in such a way. The pejorative term points to a common assumption that Luther saw at work among these people, an implicit conviction that they had transcended earthly restraints and limitations so that they could use the law to impose their own visions of what was heavenly. Another common theological term for this kind of thinking is *enthusiasm*, from the Greek *en-theos*—a claim that God has taken up possession within a person.[7] One faction of the church at Corinth was the *Schwärmer*, or enthusiasts, in this sense. They believed that the power of the resurrection had taken them beyond earthly limits. So, the motto of some within the Corinthian church was "All things are lawful to me." Luther joked that Karlstadt and the enthusiasts of his day had "swallowed the Holy Spirit, feathers and all."

As usual with Luther, the polemical terms and the jokes are full of irony. Karlstadt appealed to the law to break the law. Insisting on his particular interpretation of the commandment against graven images, he defied the laws of electoral Saxony and appropriated to himself and his colleagues the authority to set aside requirements put in place by Frederick the Wise and the legal system of electoral Saxony. The result was chaos, people running loose in the street, overthrowing the earthly order. So, Luther wrote:

> Where God tells the community to do something and speaks to the people, he does not want it done by the masses without the authorities, but through the authorities with the people. Moreover, he does this so that dog does not learn to eat leather on the leash, that is, lest accustomed to rebellion in connection with the images, the people rebel against the authorities. Talk of the devil and his imps appear. (LW 40: 90)

This is, in fact, what happened at about the same time in the Peasants' Revolt. Thomas Munzer, one of Luther's students who also became an enthusiast, believed that the Reformation demanded the overthrow of the economic system that had oppressed the farmers. With some others, Munzer led an armed insurrection that severely disrupted Germany. When the authorities finally caught up with him, Munzer was hiding in an old woman's bed, wearing her nightie. His end wasn't so heavenly after all.

Luther disputed the dichotomy Karlstadt and other humanists drew between flesh and spirit. The difference can be described in a couple of contrasting Latin phrases. Karlstadt and his colleagues, with their heirs in Zurich and Geneva, argued *finitum non capax infiniti*—the finite, by its very nature, cannot contain the infinite. So, flesh and spirit are two entirely different realms. Taking the incarnation as definitive, Luther argued *finitum capax infiniti*; when God became flesh, the divine nature was found dwelling with the human nature. He is "true God and true man," as the Small Catechism says. Just so, God's word has become a human word, bearing all of its power and grace; likewise, Christ's body and blood take up residence in the bread and wine of the sacrament, dwelling in, with, and under the earthly forms. This is so not because a philosophical argument makes it possible but because of Christ's word and promise. After all, he said, "This is my body," or "This is my blood," not "this symbolizes or represents my body," or "this is a sign of my blood." It all comes down to this: Christ Jesus is as good as his word.

The Place of the Law in the Christian Life: a Perennial Question

A third issue that emerged from the debate over the commandment against graven images concerns the place of the law in the Christian life. As indicated, Karlstadt invoked the commandment against graven images to place it beyond dispute. Because God has said, "You shall make no graven image." Christians have no alternative but to submit to the law. The law demands obedience of all, without exception. Anything less is flat-out disobedience.

Luther went at the question in another way. Since the early days of the church fathers, theology had followed assumptions that can be summed up as follows: God gave the law so that we might be saved; sin entered the world to compromise obedience; Christ Jesus came to forgive sin against the law and enable new obedience; this new obedience confirms the reality of faith. Luther criticized these assumptions in several ways, describing this method as "doing theology in the manner of Aristotle." Instead, he proposed to begin theological reflection with Christ Jesus and his work. Because Christ is "the way, the truth and the life," the law can't be; it was never meant to save—the same reasoning Paul follows In Galatians 3. Instead, the law shows us our sins so that we learn of our need for our redeemer. Christ saves us from our sins through the forgiveness won on the cross and then goes to work in us to give us new hearts that delight in the service of God and the neighbor.

On this basis, Luther interpreted the Ten Commandments differently. He noticed, to begin with, that while the Old Testament strongly emphasized God's gift of the commandments to the Jews, the New

Testament identifies no such provisions for the Gentiles. Instead, for instance, in Romans and Galatians, the New Testament declares that Christians are free of the Mosaic law. The commandments apply to Christians not because they are Christians but in so far as we are creatures of the earth. So, Luther wrote in a famous sermon, "How Christians Should Regard Moses", that is, how Christians should think of the Ten Commandments. It is not enough to say God has commanded this or that. Instead, we have to ask, "To whom is God speaking?"[8] The commandments were given to Israel, not to the church. Christians use the commandments because they summarise what is required of us in creaturely relations.

In contrast to the creator, creatures are defined by the fact that we do not have life in ourselves as a possession. It comes into us from the outside, through our parents. At some point, life departs from us. That is death. Because we don't have life in ourselves, we have to be in a proper relationship with the God who gave it to us through our parents and who continues to sustain it through our neighbors. It follows that we have to know this God's name and use it properly; we have to take some time off every week to hear what this God has in mind for us.

Similarly, because we creatures don't have life in ourselves, we have to get along with our neighbors who help to nourish and protect life in us. So we have to honor our parents; killing is obviously out, and though the effects aren't always as immediately obvious, so is adultery. We need some property to make our way through the day, and, by the same token, language has to be protected from lies and distortions. Coveting in any form undermines neighborly life and trust—the tricks and traps used to dispossess create suspicions and reactions that destroy the community.

Thinking of the Decalogue this way, Luther saw an obvious problem with Karlstadt's appeal to the commandment against graven images. It doesn't have the support of natural law. Long before the Reformation, the Catholic tradition had identified the original second commandment as part of the ceremonial law of Israel—that is, a requirement for the practice of the faith that eventually became Judaism. The ceremonial law of the Old Testament, which includes all the provisions for sacrifice and worship, does not apply to Christians. On this basis, Catholicism dropped the commandment on graven images. To keep the number of the commandments at ten, the Catholic tradition divided the commandment against coveting into two: one concerning property, and the other concerning relationships. Luther accepted this arrangement, which had already held for several centuries. "Therefore Moses' legislation about images and the sabbath and what else goes beyond the natural law, since it is not supported by natural law, is free, null and void and is specifically given to the Jewish people alone."[9] Illustrating further, he says laws made in Germany don't necessarily apply in France. What God expects of the Jews, he doesn't necessarily expect of Gentiles.

With this, the proportions of Karlstad's enthusiasm become even clearer. Imagining himself in a heavenly position free and clear of all restraint, Karlstadt assumed that he could simply dismiss the Catholic tradition, jumping over long-established intervening Christian interpretation of the Ten Commandments. Then, on philosophical grounds that he imputed to scripture, Karlstadt took it for granted that he could help himself to what he found appealing in scripture and enforce its application on other Christians. The freedom of the gospel, the power of God's word to do what it says, and the real presence of Christ in the sacrament—with all of the comfort it bestows—can be arbitrarily written off in favor of legalism. It won't do. Christ Jesus loves sinners, real ones, and joins us in, with, and under the eating and drinking, freeing us through the gospel to portray him evangelically in images and music. Paul had taught Luther that as helpful as it is in some connections, the law couldn't have the last word. That belongs to Christ Jesus.

The Contemporary Problem

In the early church and at the time of the Reformation, the issue concerning graven images addressed relationships with God. In both cases, iconoclasts invoked the injunction to prevent what they considered idolatry, false worship. With recent advances in technology another dimension of the issue has emerged, this one in relationships among people. The difference can be summed up in a couple of Latin theological terms: *coram deo* (before God) and *coram hominibus* (before others). The logic is the same either way in this regard, but there is a question of what place the law should have in dealing with the human problem.

In Isaiah 46, the prophet exposes the logic of idolatry. The Babylonians had carved their gods, Bel and Nebo, out of large blocks of wood that had to be moved because of the rising waters. Isaiah has his tongue in his cheek, watching the rescue operation, but his criticism is deadly accurate. "Bel bows down, Nebo stoops, their idols are on beasts and cattle; these things you carry are loaded as burdens on weary animals. They stoop down, they bow down together; they cannot save the burden but themselves go into captivity" (Isa 46:1,2 NRSV). The God of

Abraham, Isaac, and Jacob doesn't bow or stoop; neither does the God of Israel have to be loaded and carried. In Christ, we know him as the one who forgives sinners, raises the dead, and brings faith out of unbelief. So, God can say, ". . . even to your old age, I am he, even when you turn gray I will carry you. I have made and I will bear; I will carry and I will save" (Isa 46:3b,4 NRSV).

This is the difference: An idol abstracts a characteristic of the living God, selecting one out of many, and freezes it in an image. Consequently, the idol doesn't give life but draws its life from the ones who worship it; it can't save but must be saved. So, to take Luther's example from his explanation of the first commandment in the Large Catechism, those who worship money have to accumulate it sufficiently to save themselves, a never-ending quest. Faith is freedom, idolatry bondage.

Images work the same way in human relationships. Taken out of a whole range of human characteristics, such as attractiveness or athleticism, they may appear to be freeing, but in the end, the burden falls on the image-maker, "Bel bows down, Nebo stoops." What promised an abstract freedom, significance, value, and a happy life requires continuous infusions of energy to make it work. In the end, compromised by human limitations, the idol necessarily fails. Illusory freedom becomes real bondage.

Church leaders in the USA report that two of the most common problems they face with their pastors are computer pornography and chat rooms. The abuse starts simply enough with images of nudity or risqué conversations carried on anonymously on the internet. But electronic images, like Bel and Nebo, soon require further infusions of energy to sustain interest. When nudity won't suffice, there must be some kind of activity supplementing the nudity that offers some more excitement. When flirtatious conversations that cross the usual boundaries between the sexes start losing their cache, greater levels of stimulus become necessary. Pastors who have gotten caught up in such inflationary cycles describe an ever-deepening plunge into degrading sexual portrayals or an insatiable hunger for ever dirtier talk. Virtual reality has become real bondage.

Can the law help? Iconoclasts in every age have been convinced that the only antidote against idolatry in relationship to God and now, putatively, against the multiplication of images in the electronic media, must involve a full-scale deployment of the commandment against graven images. Will it work? This much can surely be said: the apparent power and bondage inherent in the misuse of images needs to be exposed and critiqued. Additionally, in relation to computer porn and chatrooms, the sixth and the eighth commandments provide a clear word. Legal officials have proven notoriously averse to obscenity standards. But pastors and congregations who have had their consciences sensitized in matters of sex and conversation can set standards among themselves, particularly in relation to children. Recognizing the futility of idolatry, Christians can certainly help one another and their neighbors to stay out of the trap.

Should we go further?[10] Should Christians whose traditions have set the injunction against graven images aside attempt to recover it? It might be worthwhile for churches to talk over the possibility. In relation to God, idolatry is the root sin. In human relationships, the electronic exploitation of images has become an endemic characteristic of Western culture, working its bondage under claims to freedom. Popular music, too, when its language is closely examined, commonly conveys a view of life antithetical to faith. But this said, it also has to be observed that the commandment against graven images has never succeeded in eliminating them—not in the Old Testament or the New Testament and not in the history of the church either. When it has arisen, iconoclasm has proven destructive and fertile ground for legalism. As Paul points out in Romans 7, the law works in the opposite way in matters like this: forbidden fruit becomes all the more desirable.

Luther points in a different direction. Replying to Karlstadt in his famous statement against the heavenly prophets, he points to the real antidote. The law cannot, does not, and will not save. That is Christ's work. So, Luther wrote, "I approached the task of destroying images by first tearing them out of the heart through God's word and making them worthless and despised. This indeed took place before Dr. Karlstadt ever dreamed of destroying images. For when they are no longer in the heart, they can do no harm when seen with the eyes."[11] The word spoken, administered in the sacrament, and sung to the glory of God bestows a freedom that no image can compromise.

Notes

1. For an invaluable survey of the use of music in the history of the church, see Paul Westermeyer, *Te deum, the church and music*, (Minneapolis: Fortress Press, 1998). On the New Testament itself, see pages 39-58.
2. Carlos M. N. Eire, *The war against the idols: the reformation of worship from Erasmus to Calvin*, (Cambridge: Cambridge University Press, 1986), 13-23.
3. Westermeyer. 148.

4. Ulrich Zwingli. Martin Bucer and John Calvin also opposed the church's use of images to a greater or lesser extent.

5. For a full account of Karlstadt's iconoclasm, see Carl C. Chistensen, *Art and the Reformation in Germany*, (Athens, Ohio, and Detroit, Michigan: Ohio University Press and Wayne State University Press, 1979), 23-41; also Eire, 55-64.

6. LW 40: 65-223, tr. Bernhard Erling, Conrad Bergendoff.

7. Ronald Knox, *Enthusiasm: a chapter in the history of religion*, (New York: Oxford University Press, 1962).

8. LW 35: 168. See Paul Althaus, *The theology of Martin Luther*, tr. Robert C. Schulz, (Philadelphia: Fortress Press, 1966), 90-92.

9. LW 40: 97,98.

10. For helpful further discussion of this question see Kurt Hennig, *God's basic law: the ten commandments for the man of today*, (Philadelphia: Fortress Press, 1969).

11. LW 40: 84.

THE CATECHISM'S *SIMUL*

In this essay, Nestingen explores how Luther's simul justus et peccator is a confession of the work of the Holy Spirit, who is ever bringing sinners under the Lordship of Christ according to the Catechism's Explanation of the Third Article of Creed. Far from a resignation to the power of sin, the Simul is a bold confession of faith in the risen Lord who gives us the victory. JTP+

Luther's expression of the *simul iustus et peccator* in the Small Catechism strikes such a strange impression that it is in danger of becoming hackneyed. It is seized upon by some as evidence of Luther's disregard for moral improvement and taken by others as a watchword. Either way, the theological underpinnings of this great phrase at the beginning of the explanation of the third article—"I believe that I cannot by my own understanding or effort believe in Jesus Christ my Lord or come to him"—are in need of some further consideration.

I. The Lordship of the Crucified

In order to see the force of this "I cannot," it is necessary to begin with Luther's explanation of the second article in the catechism. In both the Small and the Large, he sums up his declaration of the person and work of Christ in terms of lordship. In the Small Catechism, this summary is the lead phrase: "I believe that Jesus Christ, true God, son of the Father from eternity, and also true man, born of the Virgin Mary, is my Lord."[1] In the Large Catechism, Luther is able to give a more developed presentation of how he is using this word:

> If you are asked, "What do you believe in the Second Article, concerning Jesus Christ?" answer briefly, "I believe that Jesus Christ, true Son of God, has become my Lord." What is it to "become a Lord?" It means that he

> has redeemed me from sin, from the devil, from death and from all evil. Before this I had no Lord and King but was captive under the power of the devil. I was condemned to death and entangled in sin and blindness.[2]

The word *Lord*, in Luther's usage as in the New Testament, is a power term. While the connection is generally lost in English, the Latin shows it clearly—the word for Lord is *dominus*, the root of our word to take dominion or dominate, to literally "lord it over" someone.

Not surprisingly, then, Luther's discussion of Christ's lordship in the Large Catechism is full of language of conflict. To become our Lord, Christ took on the powers of bondage and death to overcome them.

> Those tyrants and jailers have been routed, and their place has been taken by Jesus Christ, the Lord of life and righteousness and every good and blessing. He has snatched us, poor lost creatures, from the jaws of hell, won us, made us free, and restored us to the Father's favor and grace. He has taken us as his own, under his protection, in order that he may rule us by his righteousness, wisdom, power, life, and blessedness.[3]

Whatever might be said about Gustaf Aulén's methodology, here the "classical motif"—the Christus Victor—is unambiguously clear.[4]

It is the power of Christ's lordship that he transfers us from an alien field of force to his own, deposing the other powers which have held us to place us under his control. All the rest of the explanation of the second article is to be understood in these terms.

> Let this be the summary of this article, that the little word "Lord" simply means the same as Redeemer, that is, he who has brought us back from the devil to God, from death to life, from sin to righteousness, and now keeps us safe there. The remaining parts of this article simply serve to clarify and express how and by what means this redemption was accomplished—that is, how much it cost Christ and what he paid and risked in order to win us and bring us under his dominion.[5]

The force of this transfer of powers is evident in a seldom noticed but crucial transition in Luther's explanations of the first and second articles in the Small Catechism. The first article's explanation ends on an imperative: "All this he does out of pure, fatherly, and divine goodness and mercy, without any merit or worthiness on my part. For all of this I am *bound* [or in the contemporary version, "I ought"] to thank, praise, serve and obey him."[6]

Luther uses this imperative in a double sense. At one level, it describes the actual conditions of daily life. In order to obtain food and clothing, for example, a person must do something worthwhile for the neighbor—either render some service or, at minimum, pay the price. No matter how unwitting or begrudging, this benefit for the neighbor is a form of service to God.

But over and above the description level of the ought, there is a prescription. Gifted by God with the necessities of life, a person stands under obligation to be of service to God, the neighbor, and the earth. And this obligation holds for all, no matter what creed, or condition. The imperative is grounded in the creation itself as a constitutive requirement of life.

This *ought*, in both its senses, is at the same time the basis of indictment. In parallel to the First Commandment, Luther always considered the First Article the most difficult in the creed to believe.

> Much could be said if we were to describe in detail how few people believe this article. We all pass over it, hear and recite it, but we neither see nor consider what the words enjoin on us. For if we believed it with our whole heart, we would also act accordingly, and not swagger about and brag and boast as if we had life, riches, power, honor, and such things of ourselves, as if we ourselves were to be feared and served. This is the way the wretched and perverse world acts, drowned in its blindness, misusing all the blessings and gifts of God solely for its own pride and greed, pleasure and enjoyment, and never once turning to God to thank him or acknowledge him as Lord and Creator.[7]

It is so difficult because, in the First Article, as in the First Commandment, the godness of God is at stake—God's disposal of our lives and our futures, the control God exercises. God approaches us in the demands made upon us by our neighbors, in the conditions which shape each day, as well as in the overarching summons to service. Doing so, God exposes the rebellion against him at all levels—in the conviction that the neighbor's demands are baseless or exorbitant, in the desire to take control ourselves and reshape each day according to some personal standard, and finally, in the attempt to have the self on the self's own terms.

But as Luther turns from the first to the explanation of the second article, the ought—with both its demands and its accusations—disappears. For Luther, as for Paul, "Christ is the end of the law, that everyone who has faith may be justified" (Rom 10:4):

> when Paul says that through Christ we have been set free from the curse of the law (Gal. 3:13), he is certainly speaking about the entire law, and especially about the moral law. It alone actually accuses, curses, and condemns consciences. . ..

Therefore, we say that the law of the decalog has no right to accuse and terrify the conscience in which Christ reigns through grace, for Christ has made this right obsolete.[8]

The law is one of the spoils of Christ's victory. Becoming our Lord, he is the law's *terminus*, its stopping point! To put an ought at the end of the explanation of the second article would be to deny not only the purpose of his death and resurrection, but ultimately, his eschatological lordship over all things. If the *ought* is left, he literally died for nothing (Gal 2:21).

The *ought* does not simply evaporate, however. In Luther's explanation of the second article, it is transformed into something entirely different, a *may*. Jesus underwent his death and resurrection "in order that I may be his, live under him in his kingdom, and serve him in everlasting righteousness, innocence and blessedness, even as he is risen from the dead and lives and reigns to all eternity."[9]

The English word *may* carries connotations of capability, permission, or probability. Luther's German construction, a passive imperfect subjunctive, is more forceful. The subjunctive indicates purpose or result, the passive imperfect describing a new reality which has been created as the result of action completed by someone else in the past. The force of the *may* in the explanation of the second article, then, is to say that Christ died to make me his, to create a new situation in which I will be his, live under him in his kingdom, and actually serve him.

This is the effect of the transfer undertaken by Christ. In Luther's terms, Christ has broken into the realm ruled by sin, death, and the devil to recapture the rebels held there, thus reclaiming his own. In the cross and the resurrection, Jesus has taken the rebellion upon himself to put it to its end and establish his own rule.

For Luther, unlike some of his heirs, this is no mere theoretical transfer. It is a down-to-earth reality taking place in everyday life. Though the language and even the concept of justification by faith is completely missing in both the Small Catechism and the Large,[10] this is what is at stake in the doctrine of justification and this explanation: the work of Christ in the life of the believer and his creation.

The structure of Luther's thought at this point is evident in a set of theses written some years after the catechisms, the Antinomian Disputations. Arguing with Johann Agricola, a friend who had become an adversary, Luther speaks of a double effect of the transfer accomplished in Christ:

> For the law as it was before Christ, certainly accusing us, under Christ is placated through the remission of sins and therefore is to be fulfilled in the Spirit.
>
> Thus after Christ, in the future life, will then be fulfilled even that new creature which [the law] in the meantime demanded.
>
> Therefore the law in all eternity will never be abolished but will remain either to be fulfilled in the damned or already fulfilled in the blessed.[11]

The transfer occurs as a down-to-earth event in the forgiveness of sin. This is the fundamental force of the transfer. Christ reveals himself as Lord in the particular, by taking upon himself the consequences of our own rebellion and canceling out the accusation, the guilt engendered. He breaks into the *incurvatus in se*—the self-enclosed circle where guilt and fear preside—to turn it open. The accusing voice of the law, which attacks in the conscience, is silenced through the forgiveness he unconditionally grants. The law is then placated, not in some cosmological exchange or abstract compensation, but here and now, in the conscience. No matter how well based or just the accusation sounded by the law might be, the one against whom the rebellion is ultimately directed meets it in the word of release.

Another effect of the transfer can be distinguished, though it is inseparable from the event of forgiveness. The law which has been placated by Christ in the conscience is "to be fulfilled by the Spirit." In another section of the Antinomian Disputations, Luther speaks of how this happens:

But in truth, faith in Christ justifies, alone fulfills the law, alone does good works, without the law.

> It alone accepts the remission of sin and spontaneously does good works through love.
>
> Truly, it is after justification [that] good works follow spontaneously without the law, that is, without the help and coercion [of the law].
>
> In sum, the law is neither useful, nor necessary, not for justification or for good works, much less salvation. But on the other hand,

> justification, good works and wholeness are necessary to the fulfillment of the law. For Christ came to save that which was lost and to restore all things, as Peter says. Therefore, the law is not destroyed by Christ, but restored, so that Adam might be just as he was, and even better.[12]

The force of forgiveness follows through. As Christ attacks the power of sin by forgiving it, he also takes on the sinner. He silences the accusation to create a new person, a person who, in the freedom of release, spontaneously serves. It is the only obedience that is genuine, the obedience of freedom.

Thus, Luther sets out these words—"that I may be his own, live under him in his kingdom, and serve him in everlasting righteousness, innocence, and blessedness"—as a literal description of what happens in Christ. The transfer of powers is as real as sin and death, as forgiveness, as the love and gratitude of those who have been taken on by a Lord who refuses to accept the rebellion of his creatures as ultimately definitive of his creation's future.

II. Totally, Totally

This proclamation of the transfer effected by Christ—realized in forgiveness and the spontaneous service that follows—exposes another reality as well: the sheer intransigence of the old Adam or the Old Eve in either believing or serving. As Lennart Pinomaa writes in his classical introduction to Luther, as long as the word of Christ's work remains external, it is an attack upon the conscience.[13] The declaration of Christ's work stands in such conspicuous contrast to the shape of a person's life that he or she is brought to say, "Yes, but my life isn't like that." In this way, that statement, "I believe that I cannot by my own understanding or effort believe in Jesus Christ my Lord or come to him," is a direct response to the announcement of Christ's work which has been set out in the explanation of the second article. It is the acknowledgment of the other reality, the continuing force of sin and death.

Though it is not commonly recognized as such among Lutherans, this is a basic feature of Luther's understanding of law and gospel. The gospel has a cutting edge, a backflow or back-english, which draws it back in such a way that the sinner is exposed as sinner and so confesses the power that sin continues to hold.

There are a couple of biblical examples which illustrate this movement of the gospel: Peter's miraculous draught of fishes (Luke 5:1-11) and the story of Zacchaeus (Luke 19:1-9). In neither case does Jesus proclaim what would be considered, according to traditional Lutheran reckoning, a word of law. He tells Peter to cast his nets on the other side; Peter does so and brings in a tremendous haul. Jesus informs Zacchaeus in his sovereign way that he will be dining at Zacchaeus' house; he goes there, and they dine. In both cases, however, the result is the same: a confession of sin. "Depart from me, for I am a sinful man, O Lord," Peter says. "Behold, Lord, half of my goods 1 give to the poor; and if I have defrauded anyone of anything, I restore it fourfold."

In the casual and frequently self-serving cataloging that takes place in theological communities, references to this back-movement of the gospel are often considered evidence of a Barthianizing of Luther. For Luther, in fact, the confession of sin is a virtual trademark of the gospel—the closest one can come to *prima facie* evidence of the gospel's presence. This understanding is evident both early and late in his theological writings. Recent research into Luther's relationship with his father-confessor indicates, for example, that John Staupitz was Luther's teacher early on, showing him that repentance flows out of the gospel.[14] But a more systematic expression of this movement is found in the Antinomian Disputations, written late in the 1530s.

In his public dispute with Agricola, Luther discusses the relationship of the law and the gospel in repentance. He defines repentance briefly as "grief concerning sin joined with a resolve to a better life."[15] Whatever social and political value it may also have, it is the peculiar function of the law to bring about the grief. But it cannot bring about the acknowledgment of sin or create the good resolve. In fact, it endangers such a confession and the hope that goes with it.

> For a man, terrified by the form of sin, cannot intend the good by his own powers, since he can be neither quieted nor secured.
>
> But confused and ruined by the power of sin he falls into despair and hatred of God or he descends into hell, as Scripture says.[16]

Repentance produced by the law alone is a "halfway" repentance, the penitence of Cain, Saul, or Judas.[17]

But as the gospel is proclaimed, it takes hold of the grief produced by the law and completes it by turning it into confession and a new resolve. Through the gospel, the Holy Spirit becomes the agent of the law, putting it to work as a teacher. In the course of his discussion with Agricola, Luther digressed to address the law directly, as though it were another person present in the discussion. As he did so, he made this point:

> Although, moreover, we say that despair is useful, it is not so by virtue of the law, but of the Holy Spirit who does not make a robber or devil of the law, but a teacher. Thus whenever the law is dealt with, the nature and power and effect of the law is dealt with—that which it is able to do by itself. But when the law pretends that it follows or penetrates the gospel: Hear, quiet down, Law, see lest you jump your fences. You ought to be a teacher, not a robber, you can terrify, but beware, you may not entirely crush, as once you did to Cain, Saul, Judas; remember that you are a teacher. Here is your office, not of a devil or robber, but of a teacher. But these things are not by virtue of the law, but of the gospel and the Holy Spirit as interpreter of the law.[18]

Wielded by the Spirit, the gospel enters into the grief and confusion brought about by the law to bring the law to its end in Christ. It names what the law has exposed as sin by declaring the sin forgiven.

Taken together, then, the explanation of the second article and the opening "I cannot" of the third identify two realities—the reality of the transfer effected by Christ and the reality of the powers of sin and death. Christ's fidelity to the first commandment shows my infidelity; his love of his enemies exposes my self-protection; his self-giving illumines my desperate attempts to have myself.

This is the *simul*. It is a confession elicited by the gospel itself, a confession which acknowledges two apparently mutually exclusive realities—*iustus* or just and *peccator* or sinful—as totally co-existing in the believer. Theologically, it is reflection upon the declaration that Jesus loves sinners, not in the past tense but in the present, thus not sinners who have transcended themselves or resolved to transcend themselves but sinners—straight out, warm-blooded, garden variety sinners.

Theologically, the assertion of the *simul* can be kind of messy just because of the "totally"—how can a person be totally justified and totally sinful at the same time? Luther doesn't attempt to resolve the question. But as Kjell Ove Nilsson's researches indicate, already in the Romans commentary of 1515-16 Luther was using the Christological doctrine of the *communicatio idiomatum* to speak of how such opposites can hold together.[19] Through the sharing of the attributes, what characterizes the justified can be attributed to the sinner; what characterizes the sinner can be attributed to the justified.

III. Partly, Partly

Having spoken of the reality of both Christ's work and the force of sin and death, Luther continues his explanation of the third article: "But the Holy Spirit has called me through the gospel, enlightened me with his gifts, and sanctified and preserved me in true faith, just as he calls, gathers, enlightens, and sanctifies the whole Christian church on earth and preserves it in union with Jesus Christ in the one true faith."

In one sense, Luther is simply carrying over into the third article the *totally* that has already been established in the explanation of the second with his discussion of the transfer. His text appears to be the farewell discourses in the Gospel of John, which speak of the Spirit as carrying the work of Christ on into the present, "And when he comes, he will convince the world concerning sin and righteousness and judgment" (John 16:8). That the transfer happens here and now and to me is the work of the Spirit of the risen Christ.

But there is something else in the rest of the explanation of the third article. Implicit in the Small Catechism, it becomes explicit in the Large—a notion of growth or development, of progress in holiness.

> Meanwhile, since holiness has begun and is growing daily, we await the time when our flesh will be put to death, will be buried with all its uncleanness, and will come forth gloriously and arise to complete and perfect holiness in a new, eternal life. Now we are only halfway pure and holy. The Holy Spirit must continue to work in us through the Word, daily granting forgiveness until we attain to that life where there will be no more forgiveness. In that life are only perfectly pure and holy people, full of goodness and righteousness, completely freed from sin, death, and all evil, living in new, immortal and glorified bodies.[20]

If a set of paradoxes isn't enough, Luther will satisfy the desires of any theological bureaucrat by turning them out in triplicate—not only *iustus* and *peccator* at one and the same time but totally *iustus*, totally *peccator* and now partially *iustus* and partially *peccator* as well!

The trouble with statements such as this citation from the Large Catechism, and they are to be found scattered throughout Luther's writings,[21] is that they seem to break down everything that has so far been established. Images of growth and development do not fit with a metaphor of transfer—growth and development take place over time as a process, while transfer is a completed action, a moving or being moved from one situation to another. What's worse, totally and partially are another pair of mutually exclusive terms—something can't be complete and incomplete at the same time.

But the logical problems aren't nearly as troublesome as the pastoral. Such statements make it appear that Luther has dropped back to the old notion of justification and sanctification as a moral rehabilitation process, which measures its effectiveness in the ethical earnestness of its products. Then, the law, instead of ending, is ratified in Christ, becoming the final test of whether sanctification is genuine. And the effectiveness of Christ's work, as well as a person's certainty of the promise, hinges on visible evidence of moral progress. It would be the late medieval "doing what it is within you to do," now empowered with a little more grace.

Whatever the language might imply, Luther has an entirely different purpose in speaking of this "partially." Once again, it is the down-to-earthness—the daily reality—of the gospel that is being contended for, the actual effectiveness of the Spirit's work.

The key to the combinations—*simul iustus et peccator*, both totally and partially—is eschatological. It is the hope expressed in Luther's statement in the Antinomian Disputations that since "Christ came to save what is lost and to restore all things," he will make "Adam [and Eve] such as [they were] and even better."[22] The same hope is set out in the statement from the Large Catechism, which speaks of the eschatological victory—the new day.

This is not a moralistic vision but a Christological assertion of hope—the confidence that as Christ has effected the transfer, the Spirit is even now reshaping the lives of Christ's own according to what was originally intended and thus extending Christ's lordship over his creatures. As in Paul's letters, the restoration of the individual is then of a piece with the restoration of the whole creation, when Christ will be revealed as Lord of all. The believer is partially just, partially sinful because the Spirit's work is not yet complete—the ultimate restoration of all things is still a hope.

It is Wilfried Joest who has done the basic analysis of this "partially." Understanding it eschatologically, as Luther does, in effect, turns all notions of development and progress on their head.[23] It is not the movement of an individual toward a pre-determined goal which has been set by the law; rather, it is the movement of the Spirit of the risen Christ to the creature and the creation to recreate and restore, both now and in the future.

So, in the explanation of the third article of the creed, the Spirit has all the verbs. The Spirit has called, enlightened, sanctified, and preserved, just as he calls, gathers, enlightens, sanctifies, and preserves the whole church. The ought of the first article, which is anchored in the creation itself and becomes a *may* through the work of Christ described in the second article, is here, in the third, spoken of as an accomplished fact, a *has*—the Spirit *has* enlightened, *has* sanctified. Sanctification is not a summons tacked on to the end—it is the work of the Spirit of the one who justifies the godless, thus the work of the Holy Spirit who will not rest until his mission is accomplished.

But now, just as the declaration of Christ's work in the second article elicits the confession that opens the explanation of the third, this declaration of the Spirit's work brings a matching acknowledgment of the necessity of forgiveness. As the remaining portion of the explanation declares, the fact that the Spirit has sanctified does not eliminate the need for forgiveness. Rather, it identifies the pronouncement of forgiveness as the continuing work of the Spirit in a community that lives in the hiddenness of eschatological hope. Therefore "in this Christian church he daily and abundantly forgives all my sins, and the sins of all believers, and on the last day he will raise me and all the dead and grant eternal life to me and all who believe in Christ."[24]

In the Small Catechism, then, *simul iustus et peccator* is, first of all, a confession of faith in the one who loves sinners; theologically, it is a reflection on the faith that the ones he loves are genuinely sinners; eschatologically, it is a statement of hope that one day this friend of sinners will be manifest as Lord of all by putting sin itself to flight.

Notes

1. *The Book of Concord: The Confessional Writings of the Evangelical Lutheran Church*, Theodore G. Tappert, ed. (Philadelphia: Fortress, 1959) 345.
2. Ibid., 414.
3. Ibid., 414.
4. Gustaf Aulén, *Christus Victor* (London: SPCK, 1950).
5. BC 414.
6. Ibid., 345.
7. Ibid., 413.
8. Martin Luther, "Lectures on Galatians (1535)," *Luther's Works* (55 vols.; St. Louis: Concordia; Philadelphia: Fortress, 1955-76) 26.413.
9. BC 345.
10. This absence is noted by Paul Althaus, *The Theology of Martin Luther* (Philadelphia: Fortress, 1966) 226.

11. *Martin Luthers Werke* (Weimar: Herman Bohlaus Nachfolger, 1883) 39/1.349f.; hereafter cited as WA. At the time of this essay's original publication, the Antinomian Disputations were not translated into English. They are now available in English in LW 73.

12. WA 39/1.354.

13. Lennart Pinomaa, *Faith Victorious: An Introduction to Luther's Theology* (Philadelphia: Fortress, 1963) 66.

14. David C. Steinmetz, *Luther and Staupitz: An Essay in the Intellectual Origins of the Protestant Reformation* (Durham: Duke University, 1980) 124.

15. WA 39/1.345.

16. Ibid.

17. Ibid., 346.

18. WA 39/1.445.

19. Kjell Ove Nilsson, *Simul: Das Miteinander van Göttlichem und Menschlichem in Luthers Theologie*, (Göttingen: Vandenhoeck & Ruprecht, 1966) 315.

20. BC 418.

21. Wilfried Joest, *Gesetz und Freiheit*, (Göttingen: Vandenhoeck & Ruprecht, 1951) 60ff.

22. WA 39/1.354.

23. W. Joest, *Gesetz und Freiheit*, 93. See also Gerhard Forde, "The Exodus from Virtue to Grace: Justification by Faith Today," *Interpretation* 34 (1980), 38ff.

24. BC 345.

III

STUDIES IN LUTHER AND THE LUTHERAN CONFESSIONS

BIBLICAL CLARITY AND AMBIGUITY IN *THE BONDAGE OF THE WILL*

This essay brings to mind Sasse's class treatise from 1968, "Erasmus, Luther, and Modern Christendom" (in ***The Lonely Way, Vol. 2*** *edited by Matthew Harrison, Concordia Publishing House, 2002, pp.373-385), where Sasse argues that Luther "saw behind Erasmus's concept of an undogmatic Christianity the coming neo-paganism of the modern world" (381). Nestingen notes how contemporary ecumenists and church functionaries speak of the "ambiguity" of Scripture, thus repeating Erasmus' claim. So to paraphrase Steven Paulson, Erasmus thought that the Scriptures were a dark book, so we need the magisterium of the church to tell us what it means, while today, modern theologians have simply substituted the academy of higher-critical scholars for the magisterium (see the excellent chapter by Paulson, "Internal Clarity of Scripture and the Modern World. Luther and Erasmus Revisited" in* ***Hermenuetica Sacra: Studies in the Interpretation of Scripture in the Sixteenth and Seventeenth Centuries*** *ed. Torbjörn Johansson, Robert Kolb, and Johann Anselm Steiger, De Gruyter, 2010, pp. 85-110). Noting the debates over homosexuality in contemporary denominations that are built on the twin pillars of an unclear text and a free interpreter, Nestingen argues, "If freedom is an innate human characteristic, the death of Jesus counts for nothing." JTP+*

Though it has been overshadowed by the engagement on the will, an additional major issue in Luther's *Bondage of the Will* concerns the clarity of Scripture. Erasmus, seeking to protect the integrity and power of human choice, had claimed in his *Diatribe* that the Bible is ambiguous on key matters. In reply, Luther asserted its clarity. "For what solemn truth can the Scripture be concealing, now that the seals have been broken, the stone rolled away from the door of the tomb, and that greatest of all mysteries brought to light—that Christ is God's Son become man, that God is three in one, that Christ suffered for us and will reign forever?" A sentence later, he puts the question more poignantly, "Take Christ from the Scriptures and what will you find in them?"[1]

Several mainline denominations, including some Lutherans, are dealing with this issue once again. On the basis of allegations of biblical ambiguity, these churches have set aside standards that have held for millennia to take historic legal restraints off personal, generally sexual, behavior. Given such claims, it makes sense to look once more at Luther's treatment of the clarity of Scripture in *De Servo Arbitrio* to discuss this issue further and see how this clarity and the bondage of the will relates to justification by faith, the article of the standing or falling church.

Luther on the Clarity of Scripture

In writing his reply to Erasmus's *Diatribe*, Luther followed a late medieval method of disputation that involved careful and extensive restatement of the opponent's argument before refutation of it. In effect, the proponent sets the groundwork for the debate, the opponent following point by point to undermine or overturn the claims made. Because of Erasmus's standing as the leading intellectual light of Western Europe, Luther followed this method closely to the point that he sometimes may seem pedantic. But the overall impact is massive. As Gerhard Forde observed, even Luther's jokes are calculated for their effect on his case. Thus, before moving to the clarity of Scripture, Luther takes up two preliminary arguments, both of them instructive.

First, in his attack on Luther, Erasmus had avowed that he would "readily take up the skeptic's position wherever the inviolable authority of Holy Scripture and the church's decision permit."[2] Second, he held that "some things are of such a kind that, even if they were true and could be known, it would be imprudent to expose them to everyone's hearing."[3] Herewith, Erasmus sets his terms to claim ambiguity in the Scripture concerning the role of the will in faith and salvation and to argue further that claims about such matters are offensive to the ears of the pious and should, therefore, be silenced.

Luther makes short work of both arguments. "To take no pleasure in assertions is not the mark of a Christian heart," for, as he develops his claim, asserting involves "staunchly holding your ground, stating your position, confessing it, defending it and preserving it unvanquished."[4]

Assertions of the Christian faith are a form of proclamation. On the second point, in which Erasmus had worried openly about the peasants' abuse of theological conclusions, Luther rejoined, "A good theologian teaches that people should be restrained by external power of the sword when they do evil, as Paul teaches. . . . But their consciences must not be ensnared by false laws, and thereby tormented for sins where according to God's law there is no sin."[5]

With this, it quickly becomes clear that Erasmus was spoiling for bigger game. While in passing, tarring Luther with the unrest of the peasants, a major concern in 1524, his real target was Luther's unqualified proclamation of the gospel. Erasmus wondered famously about who would be good upon hearing that God simply gives himself away in Christ Jesus. Luther answers by declaring the gospel even more unreservedly:

> "*Who*" (you say) "*will try to reform his life*?" I reply, Nobody! Nobody can! God has no time for your practitioners of self-reformation, for they are hypocrites. The elect, who fear God, will be reformed by the Holy Spirit; the rest will perish unreformed . . . "*Who will believe*" (you say) "*that God loves him*?" I reply, Nobody! Nobody can! But the elect shall believe it; and the rest will perish without believing it, raging and blaspheming, as you describe them. So there will be some who believe it.[6]

Then, having replied in similar terms to Erasmus's question concerning faith, Luther clinches his argument:

> You say that a floodgate of iniquity will be opened by our doctrines. So be it. Ungodly men are a part of the leprosy . . . which we must endure. Nevertheless, these are the very doctrines which throw open to the elect, who fear God, a gateway to righteousness, an entrance to heaven, and a road to God.[7]

The gospel is nonnegotiable.

With this engagement of the opening issue, Luther turns to the second: the overall clarity of Scripture. Though tangential to it at several other points, in this matter Erasmus had solid support in the Roman Catholic tradition. The papacy had long invoked the purported ambiguity of Scripture in support of its office. The possibility of interpreting the Scripture in a variety of ways demands a teaching authority that can arbitrate its interpretations and thereby hold the church in unity.

While acknowledging that some passages of Scripture remain obscure, Luther proclaims its overwhelming clarity in Christ Jesus. He is the subject of the Scripture both as the one acting through it by his Spirit and as its continuing topic. In him, the Scripture interprets itself—it requires no additional office or document to guarantee its message.

Any obscurity concerning the message of Scripture can be assigned to one of two causes, Luther writes. It is either due "to our own linguistic and grammatical ignorance" or to "blindness and dullness," which makes "no effort to see truth which, in itself, could not be made plainer."[8] Later, Luther develops his treatment of the second source more fully.

> Man's failure to grasp God's word does not spring from weakness of understanding. . . . No, the cause is the wickedness of Satan, who is enthroned and reigns over our weakness, and who himself resists the Word of God. If Satan did not do so, the whole world would be converted by a single word of God, heard once.[9]

In contrast to the two sources of obscurity stands a twofold clarity of Scripture: one external, the other internal.

The "external perspicuity" of the word is Christological. "Nothing whatever is left obscure or ambiguous, but all that is in the Scripture is through the Word brought forth into the clearest light and proclaimed to the whole world."[10] Christ Jesus, as the subject of Scripture in both senses, is the Bible's ultimate interpreter—the light of his incarnation, death, and resurrection clarifies all. At the same time, when obscurities appear, there is readily available recourse. Those passages that are grammatically or linguistically unclear can be tested by comparison.

> If words are obscure in one place, they are clear in another. What God has so plainly declared to the world is in some parts of Scripture stated in plain words, while in other parts it still lies hidden under obscure words.[11]

The second level of clarity in the Bible pertains to the "knowledge of the heart. If you speak of the internal perspicuity, the truth is that nobody who has not the Spirit of God sees a jot of what is in the Scriptures." Because of the power of sin, "all men have their hearts darkened, so that even when they can discuss and quote all that is in Scripture, they do not understand or really know any of it." Thus, "the Spirit is needed for the under standing of all Scripture and every part of Scripture."[12]

Further Discussion

It has commonly been observed that while Luther won the theological battle with Erasmus, he lost the war. By implication, Erasmus himself appears to have accepted the former judgment. Something of a sixteenth-century Henry Kissinger, combining a celebrated erudition with easy access to the halls of power, the widely feted scholar from Rotterdam spent the rest of his life attempting to recover his ground against Luther. The result was a volume of over eight hundred pages.

Harry McSorley, who wrote one of the major volumes on the conflict, claims to have been one of the only people in the twentieth century actually to have read it.[13] But even if Erasmus's subsequent response to Luther lingers in obscurity, the assumptions of the arguments he employed against the reformer have become so dominant in public culture that they seem inescapable. So, searching out the implications of Luther's replies concerning the clarity of Scripture has to proceed at two levels: one in relation to the historical conflict itself, the other in relation to the victorious heritage of humanism in these times.

To begin with, Luther's preliminary arguments expose the assumptions that drive Erasmus's argument. From the start, Erasmus assumes sufficient detachment from Scripture and the authoritative traditions of the church to choose skepticism as an available alternative. He is the agent, surveying the range of claims before him, discerning their relative value. Having taken such a position for granted, Erasmus's goal is to preserve his options. Just as he picks and chooses among truths presented to him, in his own mind, he will preserve his alternatives before God.

Thus, Erasmus, in illusion if not in reality, remains sovereign. Untouched by (if at all aware of) the claims and promises God makes against, and for him, he stands aloof as arbiter of Scripture, the faith of the church, and what falls most appropriately on the ears of the peasants. The major premise of the argument controls the conclusion. From the beginning, Erasmus is the acting subject.

Further, the preliminary argument demonstrates Erasmus's appraisal of authority. It is essentially negative, setting limits without offering anything significantly positive—the authority of law as opposed to gospel. So, it limits and confines without any acknowledged promise or benefit. The gifts of the gospel—in Luther's summary, forgiveness of sins, deliverance from death and the devil, and everlasting salvation—have no place in Erasmus's construct beyond the remedial.

Thus, finally, Erasmus's freedom is negative. It is an innate quality of the will that asserts itself over and against the authorities that encompass and seek to limit it. It is not a positive gift or bestowal granted in a life-determining relationship with its saving Lord. Consequently, the self has no alternative but to seize on ambiguity as though it were liberty. No wonder Luther later described Erasmus as "Christless, Spiritless and cold as ice."[14]

Luther begins from the assumption of an attachment so definitive that any alternative would be inconceivable. Both assertion and proclamation follow out of the relationship that God has established and maintains through the work of the Holy Spirit. Thus, in contrast to Erasmus, while Luther clearly acknowledged the authority of the law and its necessity, he recognized, on the other hand, a deeper authority that gives what it requires and bestows what it demands. This authority exercises itself positively in the power of the gospel. It defines freedom positively, not simply as freedom from, but as the liberty grant ed deep in relationship to God and the neighbor.[15]

Forde sometimes sets out the contrast between Erasmus and Luther as the difference between a playboy and a lover. The playboy assumes distance, seeking opportunity for the self that preserves the detachment. The lover seeks the beloved, hoping to be so comprehended or grasped by the relationship that any possible alternative would be transcended.

In the arguments concerning the clarity of Scripture, at the first level—the external—Luther's argument sets footings for dealing with the problem of ambiguity. He does not appeal to the origins of the biblical word, to divine inspiration, to eliminate the challenge. Instead, as he defines external clarity and suggests a method for addressing questions raised by the text, the appropriate tool is reason.

Texts can be compared and contrasted, similarities weighed and measured so that obscurities are explained. Such methods are common to Bible studies, are accessible to anyone interested, and have produced a treasury of insight. Testing Paul's use of the word *flesh*, for example, demonstrates that he is not using the word as a reference to the body but to describe the rebellious, self-seeking desire of the heart. With this, comparisons among Paul's various references to the flesh can isolate further nuances of the term. External clarity is just that and available to all—even historical critics.

This is particularly important in dealing with the law. Because times and circumstances change, law requires interpretation. So, the Ten Commandments in Judaism became 613. The single-volume Mishnah became the Babylonian Talmud, all 30 volumes' worth. As Luther put it, "Every house needs its own Moses"; someone who measures circumstances and states the demands of the law accordingly.[16] While requiring registration in a process of reason, however, circumstances do not eliminate but refocus the demands of the law. Changing public sexual mores does not eliminate historic standards. They require continued scrutiny in light of the Sixth Commandment as well as, among believers, Jesus' exposure of lust in the Sermon on the Mount (Matt 5:27-28).

In contrast, the internal perspicuity of Scripture is not a matter of reason but of faith that has been worked by the Holy Spirit through the proclaimed word and administered sacraments. As Luther indicates in the fourth question concerning baptism in the Small Catechism, this begins with a death, and it continues in a daily dying and rising. This death eliminates the self as actor. Lazarus did not in any way help, cooperate, or do when Christ Jesus called him out of his grave; neither did he somehow become worthy of it in the aftermath. The gospel is Christ's unaided work now carried through by his Spirit, bringing the faithful into the rhythm of dying and rising with him. Faith has ears for the gospel, hearing in Scripture the movement and power of Christ Jesus.

Thus, internal clarification of the gospel involves continued proclamation and administration. Words of love, having been spoken, both demand and elicit more such declarations. As the gospel creates faith, faith returns to the word daily and afresh. Ambiguity in this context becomes intolerable, threatening to undermine what has become life-defining. This clarification in faith is not merely remedial; it is a joyous renewal in the promises and gifts of the gospel. "This is what makes our theology certain," as Luther wrote in the Galatians commentary, "it takes us outside of ourselves and brings us to rest in Christ Jesus" (AE 26: 387).

This exposes Erasmus's objection. The problem for him is not the ambiguity of the text but the clarity of Luther's proclamation. Erasmus hadn't died yet. Consequently, confronted by the word of Christ's unqualified self-giving, the Dutchman ran for cover, trying to hide his unbelief under a theological objection. Should by some stretch of the imagination his objection be met in Erasmus's mind, it would morph into another. His will is bound. He cannot accept the gospel but, tied up inextricably in himself, can only provide more emphatic illustrations of his captivation. As Luther wrote late in *De Servo Arbitrio*,

> The Scripture sets before us a man who is not only bound, wretched, captive, sick and dead, but who, through the operations of Satan his lord,

> adds to his miseries that of blindness so that he believes himself to be free, happy, possessed of liberty and ability, whole and alive.[17]

Contemporary uses of Erasmus's argument for ambiguity follow a similar pattern. There are some important differences, however. As Leo Strauss and later Wayne Booth, both from the University of Chicago, pointed out, contemporary standards of evidence have taken over from the sciences a hard definition of truth. Only the measurable, quantifiable, and repeatable can be considered factual or truthful. Everything else that is unable to meet such standards falls into the category of values or personal opinion.[18] In effect, what Charles Sanders Peirce called "the argument from personal tenacity" has become normative. There literally is no law regarding personal and interpersonal relations; there are just choices.

In this context, by such standards, the claim that biblical law is ambiguous goes without saying. Ancient, it is, by definition, out of touch with contemporary realities. Patriarchal, it was conditioned by an age in which male-female relationships were by definition inappropriate. With these and similar objections, the assertion of ambiguity requires no further explanation or defense. It is an assumption that needs no further investigation and brooks no challenge.

For this reason, in the mainline churches where the argument for ambiguity has been deployed, the next step has not been the one a reasonable person—Luther or anyone else—would suggest. Because by contemporary definition, the self cannot move beyond the self-assertion evident in the use of any form of standard, there is no point in further examination of the arguments. Bondage to the self represents a given, an a priori that makes further examination pointless. In fact, Erasmus, for all of his vaunted cultural significance, has become something of an antique. Only theologians talk about free will anymore. In a cynical reversal, while the heirs of Erasmus reduce the gospel to an appeal—speaking of faith as one alternative among many—the culture describes what the law has condemned as predestined and so beyond any choice.

Luther called this kind of thinking, which he saw in Agricola, a "play put on in an empty theater" (WA 39, I: 358). Denied access to the ear by what amounts to an intellectual trick, the law goes underground, playing itself out anonymously. A more appropriate standard of truthfulness in interpersonal relationships would bring the law back to the surface, demonstrating the consequences of disobedience to both the first and the second table of the commandments. As it stands, the casual antinomianism of contemporary American life has made the old Adam the one acceptable ethical standard—desire equals identity and so entitlement. As usual, the escape from illusionary bondage has run straight into the arms of one profoundly more real.

For the church, appeals to the supposed ambiguity of the biblical text bring an end to any further conversation. Students of Scripture can cite any number of passages that, at the level of external clarity, require further study. Such investigation is the logical next step, and entirely reasonable. But when a church body invokes ambiguity to legislate a particular reading of passages, the possibility of any other reading has been officially eliminated. The authority of the Scripture has been taken over by its interpreters to enforce their commitments. Imperially silenced, those who disagree, who hold to the biblical priority set by the Formula of Concord, have been effectively excluded, literally unchurched.

Correlating Clarity, Bondage of the Will, and Justification by Faith

The force of this exclusion is seen even more clearly in light of the correlation between Luther's arguments in *De Servo Arbitrio* and justification by faith. The centrality of justification in Luther's theology shows itself, particularly in the way he places it in his theological considerations. Instead of reasoning sequentially *ad modum* Aristotelis, as he called it, to arrive at Christ's justifying act as a conclusion, he reasons more circularly. He moves from justification to what it assumes or implies. Christ is always the center, the first premise in the theological argument. Every other theological point goes out from or returns to the center.[19]

This is very much like Paul's argument in his letter to the Galatians: "If justification were by the law, Christ died for nothing" (2:21). To be sure, the frustrations, disappointments, and standing indictments leveled by the law further illustrate, as they must, the necessity of Christ's work; but there is also a backward movement theologically from Christ's death and resurrection to what we can now see of ourselves in its light.

So, in his great commentary on Psalm 51, Luther writes, "Thus the First Commandment denounces sin by its very promise" and argues that "if God promises life, it follows that we are under death. If he promises forgiveness of sins, it follows that sins dominate and possess us" (AE 12: 340). This is the backward movement. Originally from law to gospel, to be certain, but following the gospel's declaration, theologically from gospel to law. Thus, an external clarity shows itself in the correlation between the perspicuity of the word, the bondage of the will, and justification. "How can they hear without a preacher?" Paul asks in Romans.

Without the clarity of the word, the justifying act does not come home to the justified. By the same token, contemporary literature provides virtually endless examples of the self's inability to manage its own destiny. The law drives, even if it doesn't necessarily drive to the gospel without the power of the Holy Spirit putting it in harness for this purpose. The theological correlation between the justification, the word, and the bondage of the will can, in this way, be seen and reasoned out.

But, the deepest correlation appears at the level of internal clarity. It is because the crucified and risen Christ justifies by the word that the word, both law and gospel, makes its ultimate claim. Here, ambiguity is not freedom at all but an enemy to be overcome. The freedom of the gospel, as positive as Christ himself, grounds faith by the word in the everyday relationships with God and the neighbor. So also, by justifying, Christ's death and resurrection expose claims to the freedom of the will as an impossible illusion. This is why Luther asked who would ever want such a thing. Faith clings to its Lord, seeing choice not as freedom but as evidence of disintegration of the will, as compelling evidence of slavery in which even the word of life, Christ's gift, becomes mere alternative.

Given such correlations, making ambiguity a legislatively enforced hermeneutical principle sets the church adrift. Justification, the article of the standing and falling church, goes down with the clarity of the word. If freedom is an innate human characteristic, Christ's death counts for nothing. Institutions that surrender such certainties are no longer the people of God gathered together to hear the word and receive the sacraments, but "the ecclesiola," as an old friend called it—empty pretense.

Notes

1. Both quotations from Martin Luther, *De Servo Arbitrio*, trans. J. I. Packer and 0. R. Johnston, in *Martin Luther on the Bondage of the Will: A New Translation of De Servo Arbitrio (1525), Martin Luther's Reply to Erasmus of Rotterdam* (Edinburgh: James Clarke, 1957), 71.
2. Luther, *De Servo Arbitrio*, 62.
3. Luther, *De Servo Arbitrio*, 86.
4. Luther, *De Servo Arbitrio*, 66.
5. Luther, *De Servo Arbitrio*, 89.
6. Luther, *De Servo Arbitrio*, 99.
7. Luther, *De Servo Arbitrio*, 99.

8. Luther, *De Servo Arbitrio*, 71-72.

9. Luther, *De Servo Arbitrio*, 133-34.

10. Luther, *De Servo Arbitrio*, 74.

11. Luther, *De Servo Arbitrio*, 71-72.

12. Luther, *De Servo Arbitrio*, 74.

13. Harry McSorley, *Luther: Right or Wrong?* (Minneapolis: Augsburg Publishing House, 1967). The title, which McSorley considered unfortunate, was provided by the publisher.

14. Luther, *De Servo Arbitrio*, 75.

15. Martin Luther, "The Freedom of the Christian," in *Martin Luther's Basic Theological Writings*, ed. Timothy Lull (Minneapolis: Augsburg Fortress, 1989), 595-630.

16. Luther, "How Christians Should Regard Moses," in Lull, 142-46.

17. Luther, *De Servo Arbitrio*, 162.

18. Leo Strauss, *Natural Right and History* (Chicago: University of Chicago Press, 1950), 5.

19. Leif Grane, *Modus Loquendi Theologicus: Luthers Kampf um die Erneuerung der Theologie (1515-1518)* (Leiden: E. J. Brill, 1975).

CHANGING DEFINITIONS: THE LAW IN FORMULA VI

Debates over the "third use of the Law" are not new to Lutheranism, even though, recently, they seem to generate more heat than light. On the one side, there are those who attempt to reject the Law altogether. On the other side, there are those who make of the Law, the governing premise of theology. With this side, the Law dominates, and the Gospel is the means of divine assistance in keeping the Law. Here, the "third use" becomes the primary use. Not so with Luther as he insists on the exclusivity of Christ alone. If Christ is the only way, the Law cannot be the way. In this essay, Nestingen becomes something of a detective tracing the shift from Luther's dialectical definition of the Law to the later Melanchthon and from there to the debates over to the "third use" in the 1550s that led to Article VI of the Formula. The Law remains, and it is to be preached also to Christians insofar as they remain in sin, but it can never be reduced to friendly coach whose encouragement will create the good performance it demands. Nestingen presented this paper at the annual Symposium on the Lutheran Confessions on the campus of Concordia Theological Seminary in Fort Wayne. It was then published in the seminary's journal, ***Concordia Theological Quarterly*** *(October 2005). JTP+*

There are a couple of key theological issues percolating through the dispute over the third use of the law. When they are isolated, they illustrate some of the key historical differences between Luther and Melanchthon and, beyond them, between Luther and the theologians who drafted Article VI of the Formula of Concord.

The first issue is the end of the law, an assertion that emerged early in the Reformation out of Luther and Melanchthon's consideration of Roman 10:4, where Paul states that "Christ is the end [τέλος] of the law, that all who believe may be justified." Luther and Melanchthon both picked up what had generally been either passed over or minimized by the tradition, the sense of termination that is also included in τέλος. In fact, from 1520 to 1530, this became a theme of the Lutheran reformers to the point that in the later Galatians commentary, "the end of the law" in the sense of termination became a virtual christological title. Christ is the end of the law just as he is Savior and Lord.

For Luther, the original force of the argument is as much theological as it is exegetical, very much along the lines of Paul's argument in Galatians 2:21, ". . . if justification comes through the law, then Christ died for nothing." The logic is devastatingly simple. Christ Jesus' justification of the godless is the first and, therefore, the controlling premise in the theological argument. So, if Christ saves, the law cannot. If Christ is "the way, the truth, and the life," the law cannot be; if Christ has the last word, the law must fall silent before him. Christ's death and resurrection are, in effect, the first premises in every theological argument.

Characteristically, once the logic of the gospel has set this theme, Luther expands on it voluminously. For example, in one of his great sermons, "How Christians Should Regard Moses", Luther personifies the law in Moses' name to declare, "Moses is dead."[1] Not one iota of Moses concerns us. "We would rather not preach again for the rest of our life than to let Moses return and have Christ be tom out of our hearts. We will not have Moses as ruler or lawgiver any longer."[2] Similarly, in the great Galatians commentary, he can argue that the whole goal of the Christian life is to become ignorant of the law.

But for all of his expansiveness on this pole of the dialectic, Luther, at the same time, carefully set out the other pole: as Christ ends the law, he also establishes it. Christ Jesus stops the law by bringing to an end its characteristic functions in this age, besieged as the fallen world is by the powers of sin, death, and the devil. By the absolution, the oral or sacramental declaration of the forgiveness of sin, Christ silences the law's badgering and accusing. Then, freed from the relentless hounding of the law, the believer has a new sense of self in relation to God, the neighbor, and the earth—a free and merry conscience.

At this point, on the other pole of the dialectic, the law is reduced to terms. While it has lost its ultimate standing, it nevertheless retains its penultimate value. While it cannot justify, bestow life, or "contribute anything to righteousness," the law can clear some order in the chaos and, however tenuously, point the way toward justice and peace; it can also, when the Holy Spirit takes hold of it through the gospel, become useful in driving a person to the repentance that accompanies faith.

Thus, for Luther, the way from law to gospel is marked by breach, a fundamental discontinuity, death, and resurrection. Left to itself, the law can only kill, showing the self to its end in death. But as the Holy Spirit takes hold of the law under the power of the gospel, joining the believer to Christ in a death like his, the faith which he creates shares in a resurrection like his. The gospel can never be confined to mere knowledge or a bit of assistance for the continuous self: it is the power of the resurrection itself breaking out where it always does, tearing open graves.

One of the most powerful statements of the end of the law in the early Reformation was set out by Melanchthon in the 1521 *Loci Communes*. The bulk of one whole chapter is devoted to what he calls "the Abrogation of the Law," the argument proceeding along the same lines as Luther's. So, Melanchthon explicitly states that ". . . that part of the law called the Decalogue has been abrogated by the New Testament" and then follows with further explanation: "But our freedom consists in this, that every right of accusing and condemning us has been taken away from the law" and "Christ took away the curse of the law and the right it had so that even though you have sinned, even though you now have sin . . . yet you are saved. Our Samson has shattered the power of death, the power of sin, the gates of hell."[3] What was later termed "the new obedience" properly follows: "Those who have been renewed by the Spirit of Christ now conform voluntarily even without the law to what the law used to command."[4]

Against this background, developments later in the Lutheran Reformation stand out in bold relief. Antinomianism, the argument that the law had ended temporally and was therefore of no further significance to Christians, surfaced for the first time in 1527 and again between 1536 and 1539. Both times, the source was Johann Agricola. Though the initial conflict was between Agricola and Melanchthon, Luther took responsibility for dealing with the matter. While Luther was confronting Agricola, Melanchthon, on the other hand, began to move off in other directions.

Though he dismissed the 1527 conflict as a *pugnam verborum*, a "war of words," in the 1530s, Luther recognized that the situation had changed. As he once said, "The world is like a drunken peasant. If you lift him into the saddle on one side, he will fall off on the other side."[5] In his analysis early on, the problem was that the conscience was oppressed by the law. But now he said, writing in the early 1530s, "they have mastered the fine art of abusing their liberty," having moved from legalism to license.[6] Thus, without compromising the assertion of the termination of the law, Luther took even greater care in spelling out the law's establishment. This concern appears already in the careful exposition of the Ten Commandments in the Small and Large Catechisms but in a fully developed theological form in the Antinomian Disputations.

Asserting the end of the law in the Disputations, Luther argues that it can only happen when, in faith, the sinner dies with Christ. "Indeed, in Christ the law is fulfilled, sin abolished and death destroyed. That is, when through faith we are crucified and have died in Christ, such things are also true in us" and "To one raised in Christ there is certainly no more sin, no death, no law -things to which he was subject while living" and finally, "Now in so far as Christ is raised in us, so far are we without law, sin, and death."[7]

The correlation of the law with sin and death as the powers of this age makes it impossible simply to write the law off conceptually or theologically, exposing such an effort as a play put on in an empty theater.

> Necessarily, therefore, in so far as they are under death, they are still under the law and sin. They are altogether ignorant and deceivers of souls who endeavor to abolish the law from the church. For that is not only stupid and impious, but absolutely impossible. For if you want to remove the law, it is necessary at the same time to remove sin and death.[8]

But with this, there is an important difference in Luther's argument in the Antinomian Disputations. While he still says, as earlier in the Reformation, that the law terminates in the conscience of the believer when it no longer accuses, now he also asserts that the law remains for all eternity.

> For the law as it was before Christ did indeed accuse us; but under Christ it is placated through the forgiveness of sin and thereafter it is to be fulfilled in the Spirit. Accordingly after Christ, in the future [the law] will remain, having been fulfilled, and then the new creature himself will be what [the law] in the meantime demanded. Therefore the law will never in all eternity be abolished, but will remain either to be fulfilled by the damned, or already fulfilled in the blessed.[9]

Thus, even though in this age, the law is defined by its essential functions or offices, it cannot be reduced to the function. It points beyond itself, signifying what is to come eschatologically when Christ has put all of his enemies under his feet.

This eschatological sense is rooted in the original Hebrew, in which the Commandments are set out in the future tense. Now, in a world under the siege of sin, death, and the devil, the future turns to imperative and so to indictment. But as Christ reclaims both creature and creation, there is coming a time when the Commandments will be fulfilled in the believer. It happens now proleptically, in bits and snatches. Then, when Christ has finally overcome all of his enemies, what we can only anticipate in hope will be the reality: the faithful will have no other gods before him, will exalt in his name, and enter into the final Sabbath rest of eternity with every human relationship restored in the forgiveness of sins. In this way, the gospel turns the law itself into promise, where the law signifies the shape of the life to come. On the other hand, to those stuck in their own self-absorption, the gates of hell have already opened—the law's accusation continues relentlessly and for all eternity.

While Luther confronted the antinomian strife by further clarifying the dialectic, Melanchthon set off in another direction. His changes can be measured fairly closely by comparing the various editions of the Loci Communes. He put this volume through a whole series of revisions, substantially between 1525 and 1535 and even more dramatically, between 1535 and 1555.[10] In the 1533 edition, the chapter on "the Abrogation of the Law," which claimed such prominence in 1521, has been reformulated as a chapter on Christian freedom with the language of abrogation carefully qualified to pertain only to the curse of the law.[11] In the 1555 edition, Melanchthon limits abrogation to "freedom from two parts of the law of Moses, ceremonial and civil law," and then asks why the same term could not be used for the Decalogue. He answers that the Christian is free from the Ten Commandments ". . . so far as the meriting of forgiveness and of sins and justification by God are concerned . . ." but that ". . . the law, which is called the Ten Commandments, or *legam moralem*, is the eternal, unchangeable wisdom and righteousness in God, which he has imparted to us. As he created us to be like him in eternity, the law cannot be effaced, as writing on the wall, for the order that the rational creatures should be obedient to God stands forever."[12]

The form of Melanchthon's later argument retains familiar characteristics, but the proportions have changed. The end of the law as termination remains in a strictly qualified form, but the emphasis has shifted to qualities of the law that place it beyond any real end—it is "the eternal, unchangeable wisdom and righteousness of God." With this, two other differences become evident. The term *eternal* is not used eschatologically, as with Luther, but structurally and ontologically to describe God's will in creation. Reduced to the penultimate by the gospel in the earlier argument as a provisional necessity in a fallen world, its true significance is to be found only in Christ's fulfillment of it; the law has, in the later argument, once again emerged to claim ultimate status. It is "eternal" in and of itself. At the same time, there has been a change of method. In Melanchthon's later work, the gospel is no longer the first premise in the theological argument, with the law defined accordingly; rather, the law as God's eternal and unchangeable righteousness has taken the theological priority, and the gospel is defined accordingly.

These changes—the qualification of termination, the redefinition of the law's eternal character, and the methodological shift—are reflected in a couple of other contemporaneous developments in Melanchthon's overall treatment of the law. One appeared in the 1535 edition of the *Loci Communes*. This is the explicit introduction of the third use. There are earlier instances where Melanchthon uses the imperative to describe the good works that follow faith, even in Article VI of the Augustana. Now, however, the third use follows the developing redefinition: since the law is eternal, there must, by the very term, be a use specifically directed to the believer. The third use did not generate controversy until the 1550s, when it came under the attack of a group of parish pastors, among them Andreas Poach of Erfurt and Agricola's brother-in-law, Andreas Musculus.

The other development followed in 1536. It was a proposal, originally floated through Casper Cruciger, to describe obedience to the law as necessary to salvation. The language was carefully qualified to indicate that good works were not a cause of salvation but effectively a catalyst. Yet the impact of Melanchthon's developing redefinition of the law is manifest: when the law takes priority over the gospel as the all-cohesive structure of God's will in creation—"the eternal" and "unchangeable wisdom and righteousness of God"—it is impossible to conceive of salvation apart from obedience to the law.

Not surprisingly, given the differences emerging between Luther and Melanchthon, the new proposal came under direct attack. When he took up the ensuing conflict, Luther called the proposed phrase "the very theology of Erasmus" and said, "Nothing could be more contrary to our doctrine."[13] By this time, it had become evident that Melanchthon was behind Cruciger's experiment. The two of them agreed to withdraw the phrase—Melanchthon after several conversations at Luther's table. But, the force of the revised definition of the law remained unabated. With Luther gone, however, Melanchthon brought the argument for the law's necessity to salvation back once more in the Majoristic strife of the 1550s.

Luther's comment suggests one possible source of Melanchthon's movement on the doctrine of law. When Erasmus was dying in 1536, Melanchthon wrote him a letter saying that he "had attempted to follow him [Erasmus] in all that he had taught." In another comment, which Wilhelm Pauck took as programmatic, Melanchthon, toward the end of his own life, told his first biographer that he had striven, in everything that he had done, to contribute to the actual improvement of public life. The increased emphasis on the significance and value of the law may then reflect Melanchthon's humanism.

But there is an additional possibility. In the later 1530s and early 1540s, just as the most dramatic changes in the *Loci Communes* were underway, Melanchthon had undertaken a sweeping reappraisal of Aristotle. That by itself could account for the shift to a more structural understanding of the law, putting a premium on its eternal and all-cohesive qualities.

With this consideration of the end of the law, there is a second theological issue that bears on the dispute over the third use: the *simul*. Again, there is a strategic difference, especially between Luther and Formula VI. Luther's concept of *simul iustus et peccator* is worked out, like all of his theology, christologically. His goal, as the Apostle Paul put it, was literally to "take every thought captive to serve Christ" (2 Cor 10:5). So, as Luther proclaims him, Christ Jesus is not an idea or an ideologue but the living presence at work in his word to justify the godless and raise the dead.

The Small Catechism provides one of the best examples. Christ's work is not a distant abstraction but a concrete, accomplished reality: "he has saved me, a lost and condemned person, bought and freed me . . ." (SC II, ii, 4). In the same way, the verbs that give the explanation of the third article of the Creed such movement are all cast in the present perfect: the Holy Spirit "has called . . . has enlightened . . . has sanctified . . . and has kept me in the true faith" (SC II, iii, 6). Since all of this is the work of the triune God who justifies his enemies, the work is complete in itself even as it is now continuing.

Yet at the same time, what is now realized goes on into the future. So the explanation of the second article concludes with the words, "All this he has done that I may be his own" (SC II, ii, 4). And the use of the present perfect in the third article explanation indicates that what has begun continues in a way that, as justified, the believer remains a sinner who confesses: "I believe that I cannot by my own understanding or effort believe in Jesus Christ my Lord or come to him" and who therefore depends on the ministry of the church, in which "day after day, he fully forgives all my sins" until the last day, "when he will raise me and all the dead" (SC II, iii, 6).

Thus, for Luther, the *simul* is both totally complete (*totius*, *totius*) and partial and awaiting completion (*partim*, *partim*). But the incompleteness does not, therefore, devolve to us as though sanctification were something to be sought and achieved. Rather, as in the statement on the eternal character of the law in the Antinomian Disputations, what is now begun will be completed eschatologically by the work of the Holy Spirit. Thus, in the Large Catechism, Luther writes: "Now we are only halfway pure or holy. The Holy Spirit must continue to work in us through the Word, daily granting forgiveness until we attain to that life where there will be no more forgiveness. In that life we are only perfectly pure and holy people, full of goodness and righteousness, completely freed, from sin, death and all evil, living new, immortal and glorified bodies" (LC II, iii, 58).[14]

In the Antinomian Disputations, Luther summarizes the whole christological argument in a pair of theses: "Insofar as Christ is now raised in us, so far are we without the law, sin and death. Insofar as he truly is not yet raised in us, so far are we under the law, sin and death."[15] Here is the *simul* in a nutshell. The argument is worked out of Christ's justifying work, not from the law or observations about the current state of human sinfulness. Christ Jesus, at one and the same time, establishes the totality and exposes the partiality, taking responsibility through his Spirit for both.

Against this background, the differences in Article VI of the Formula of Concord are striking. As the work of a committee, the article reflects a number of hands. Jakob Andreae, with the Swabian Concord, provided the first fourteen paragraphs of the Solid Declaration, Andreas Musculus, who had been involved in the later antinomian conflict, provided the substance of paragraphs fifteen to nineteen, and David Chytraeus the last paragraphs, twenty to twenty-five. Though the hands are individual, there is nevertheless a clear consensus among them concerning the law that reflects the shaping influence of Melanchthon. As Willard Dow Allbeck observed long ago, while the Formula attempts to recover Luther's theological conclusions, the method employed is Melanchthon's. This is nowhere more evident than in Article VI.

So, the language of the end or abrogation of the law, so important to Luther and the earlier Melanchthon, is conspicuously absent. The law has claimed priority as the controlling assumption in the argument and so cannot be spoken of as having been abrogated. Thus, Andreae, in paragraph four, acknowledges the justifying work of Christ but immediately sets it in the context of the law: ". . . although Christians who believe faithfully have been truly converted to God, and have been justified are indeed freed and liberated from the curse of the law, they should daily practice the law of the Lord as it is written in Psalms 1 and 119, 'Blessed are those . . . whose delight is in the law of the Lord, and on his law they meditate day and night.' For the law is a mirror that accurately depicts the will of God and what pleases him" (SD VI,4). Musculus uses similar terms in paragraph fifteen, ". . . the word 'law' has one single meaning, namely, the unchanging will of God, according to which human beings are to conduct themselves in this life" (SD VI,15). Chytraeus brings this back in paragraph twenty-one: "the law of God prescribes good works for believers, so that it may at the same time show and indicate, as if in a mirror, that they are still imperfect and impure in this life" (SD VI,21).

These references to the law as a mirror of God's will bring forward into Article VI the definition of law provided in Article V, which closely parallels Melanchthon's later definition: "We therefore unanimously believe, teach and confess that in its strict sense the law is a divine teaching in which the righteous, unchanging will of God revealed how human beings were created in their nature, thoughts, words and deeds to be pleasing and acceptable to God" (SD V,17). The law is no longer defined functionally in light of the gospel but structurally and cohesively as the definitive expression of God's will.

In effect, law and gospel have traded places. Whereas in the earlier Lutheran argument, the gospel as the ultimate word rendered the law penultimate, now in the Formula, the law is set forward as the ultimate expression of God's will, and the gospel becomes effectively penultimate in that context—it provides what the law demanded but could not affect. Just as in Melanchthon's later work, an eternal law, by the very definition ascribed to it, cannot end but must necessarily continue in its claims.

The third use follows as a necessary consequence of the way the law has been redefined.

A similar shift occurs with the *simul*. Of the three authors, Musculus comes the closest to Luther's original language of an accomplished reality in paragraph seventeen: "However, when people are born again through the Spirit of God and set free from the law (that is, liberated from its driving powers and driven by the Spirit of Christ), they live according to the unchanging will of God, as comprehended in the law, and do everything, insofar as they are reborn from a free and merry spirit" (SD VI, 17). This, however, is really, as Robert Kolb notes in the new edition of the Book of Concord, Musculus' interpolation of his own theology into the text.[16]

For, in fact, the *totius, totius* of Luther's *simul isutus et peccator* has, in the overall argument of Article VI, for all practical purposes, dissolved into the *partim, partim*. Thus, in paragraph six, Andreae treats the totality as a hypothetical possibility: "Indeed, if the faithful and elect children of God were perfectly renewed in this life . . . they would need no law . . ." and then continues to state emphatically the partiality in paragraph seven: "Since, however, believers in this life are not perfectly, wholly *completetive vel consummative* [completely or entirely] renewed—even though their sin is completely covered by the perfect obedience of Christ so that this sin is not reckoned to them as damning, and even though the killing of the old creature and the renewal of their minds has begun—nonetheless, the old creature continues to hang on their nature and all of its inward and outward powers" (SD Vl,6-7).

Of the other two, Musculus preserves a little more tension in the dialectic, as in paragraph eighteen. Since the Spirit and the flesh continue to battle it out, believers live in contention: ". . . they are never without the law, but at the same time they are not under the law but in the law; they live and walk in the law of the Lord and yet do nothing because of the compulsion of the law" (SD VI,18). Chytraeus resolves the tension completely: "For the old creature, like a stubborn, recalcitrant donkey, is also still a part of them, and it needs to be forced into obedience to Christ not only through the law's teaching, admonition, compulsion and threat but also often with the cudgel of punishments and tribulations until the sinful flesh is stripped away and people are perfectly renewed in the resurrection" (SD VI,24).

Not surprisingly, as the totality dissolves into partiality in the simul, the verbs shift accordingly. In the older Lutheran argument, as in the Small Catechism's explanation, God is the subject of every verb.

Both Andreae and Musculus take some pains to maintain this priority. Acknowledging the law cannot create what it requires, Andreae describes the Spirit's use of law and gospel to effect the new life in paragraphs ten and eleven. Similarly, Musculus repeatedly comes back to the work of the Spirit of God (SD VI,17). With that said, the purpose of the law in its third use is to instruct and engage the self in the process.

In fact, the sequences of uses, from the external discipline of the political use to the accusation and exposure of the second use and then from the gospel to the third use, has the character of a process of moral rehabilitation, from the partial toward the complete, or to pick up Gerhard Forde's colorful phrase, an exodus from vice to virtue. Consequently, the whole argument requires the kind of distinction Musculus makes when he speaks of "the difference between two different kinds of people," those who are not reborn who remain under the law alone and "the people who are born again" (SD VI,16-17) and who are therefore on the way.

A couple of conclusions can be drawn from this analysis. First, the changes in Melanchthon's definition of the law, whether they are attributed to Erasmus or to his developing Aristotelianism, result in a decisive recasting of the dialectic of law and gospel. Christ's termination of the law, so central to the earlier Lutheran witness, has been reduced to a theoretical end in which the law continues as unrequited demand. Second, the totality of Luther's *simul* resolves into a partiality in which the believer strives, with the assistance of the Spirit, to achieve further what has been begun. The discontinuity of law and gospel has been ironed out into a continuous process of moral rehabilitation.

These conclusions call for a careful reconsideration of Article VI of the Formula. There can be no doubt about the necessity of continued faithful proclamation of both law and gospel to all and sundry. The contemporary experience of the church, whether in the antinomian reduction of the law to mere relative value or in the church growth movement's unease with the absolution, manifests the aimless drift that sets in when the law's voice is silenced. Article VI can under no circumstance be simply set aside. At the same time, however, the faithful proclamation of the law calls for the continuing critical theological reflection on the distinction of law and gospel in our own time and situation. This is the enterprise the Formula began, carefully reassessing Melanchthon's later conclusions. Faithful subscription to the Formula now involves continuing the project, extending it to Melanchthon's theological method, and then moving in the same direction as the authors of the Formula, going back to Luther and, with him, to the biblical text.

Luther himself points the way in a thesis from the Antinomian Disputations quoted in the Formula: "Therefore the law (and likewise the gospel) is to be taught without distinction to the pious just as to the wicked."[17] Instead of sorting the congregation out into those who require first, second, or third use, the preacher is called to declare the biblical text and to proclaim both law and gospel in their fullness: the law in its requirements and accusations as the text demands; the gospel in its power to actually forgive and raise to newness of life. In such proclamation, under the power of the Holy Spirit, the law comes to its one, true, and only end: Christ Jesus himself.

Notes

1. Martin Luther, "How Christians Should Regard Moses," in *Luther's Works*, Vol. 35: Word and Sacrament I, American Edition, ed. Jaroslav Jan Pelikan, Hilton C. Oswald, and Helmut T. Lehmann (Philadelphia: Fortress Press, 1960), 165; hereafter LW 35:165.

2. LW 35:164.

3. Philip Melanchthon, *Loci Communes*, tr. J. A. 0. Preus (St. Louis: Concordia Publishing House, 1992), 15,120,122.

4. Melanchthon, *Loci Communes*, 123.

5. Martin Luther, *Luther's Works*, Vol. 54: *Table Talk*, American Edition, ed. Jaroslav Jan Pelikan, Hilton C. Oswald, and Helmut T. Lehmann (Philadelphia: Fortress Press, 1967), 111, n. 630; hereafter LW54:111.

6. Theodore G. Tappert, ed., *The Book of Concord: The Confessions of the Evangelical Lutheran Church* (Philadelphia: Fortress Press, 1959), 338.

7. Martin Luther, *Luthers Werke: Kritische Gesamtausgabe*, Vol. 39, Part I (Weimar: H. Bohlau, 1926), 354-356, Numbers 10-11, 36, 40; hereafter WA 35.I:354-356, 10-11, 36, 40.

8. WA 35.l:354, 14-17.

9. WA 35.1:356, 45-47.

10. See Hans Engelland, "Introduction," in *Melanchthon on Christian Doctrine: Loci Communes, 1555*, ed and tr. Clyde L. Manschreck (New York: Oxford University Press, 1965), xxiii.

11. *Corpus Reformatorum: Philippi Melanthonis Opera Quae Supersunt Omnia*, Vol. 21 (Halle and Brunswick: C. A. Schwetschke), 458ff.; hereafter CR 21:458ff.

12. CR 21:198.

13. Friedrich Bente, *Historical Introductions to the Lutheran Confessions* (St. Louis: Concordia Publishing House, 1965), 113.

14. Tappert, *The Book of Concord*, 418.

15. WA 35.I:356,40-41.

16. Robert Kolb and Timothy J. Wengert, eds., *The Book of Concord: The Confessions of the Evangelical Lutheran Church*, tr. Charles Arand, Eric Gritsch, Robert Kolb, William Russell, James Schaaf, Jane Strohl, and Timothy J. Wengert (Minneapolis: Fortress Press, 2000), 590, n. 169.

17. WA 35.1:356,42.

LUTHER ON PSALM 51

Luther said of Psalm 51, "This is the teaching of this Psalm and our perpetual school, from which we never graduate as perfect masters" (LW 12:331). In this article, first published in ***Lutheran Theological Journal*** *(December 2016), Nestingen guides readers through Luther's radical confession of repentance not merely as a "moral overhaul" shaped by the second table of the Law but death to the old Adam brought about by the first table of the Law. Adultery and murder were the results of David's misplacing the true God in favor of himself. Further, Nestingen demonstrates how both Law and Gospel function in repentance drawing out connections with the Reformer's Antinomian Disputations. JTP+*

What is the correlation between the gospel properly defined and repentance? As simply as the question can be stated, this has been a neuralgic point in Lutheran dialectics, occasioning one major controversy and sparking apprehensions ever since.

According to standard Lutheran doctrine, repentance is a corollary of the law. In its second use, the law accuses the sinner, exposing what has been hidden to the sinful heart and thereby creating a crisis. Smitten by a guilty conscience, the sinner begins a process of self-examination that involves remorse over the offense or condition and some form of hope for better. The gospel follows, declaring Christ's gracious forgiveness, thereby silencing the accusation and creating the faith to go on in daily life and vocation.

The controversy over associating the gospel with repentance was settled in the fifth article of the Formula of Concord of 1577. The controversy had erupted in the heated theological atmosphere that followed the military defeat suffered by the Lutherans in 1548. Melanchthon, suspected of compromise with the Roman Catholic authorities, had made some statements that included the gospel in the doctrine of repentance.

His nemesis, Matthias Flacius Illyricus, who suffered much from an anguished conscience, suspected that Melanchthon was confusing law and gospel, making the gospel conditional on further repentance.

The fifth article of the Formula of Concord sets out a terminological settlement. The term gospel was clearly being employed in two different senses in the conflict, one to speak of the whole doctrine of the gospel, which includes repentance and faith, and the other to speak of the specific declaration of forgiveness. Both parties accepted this clarification, and unlike several of the other controversies between the Philippists and Flacius' party, the Gnesio-Lutherans, this one ended.

But an issue remains. The problem is that Luther himself makes several statements, especially in his Commentary on Psalm 51, but also in the Antinomian Disputations, asserting that the power of the gospel is necessary to repentance. The commentary is based on notes from lectures that Luther gave in 1532; it was published in 1538. The Antinomian Disputations, six sets of theses for disputes with Johann Agricola, were written between 1536 and 1539. These publications provide an opportunity to examine Luther's argument for the function of the gospel in repentance, specifically at a point where matters of law and gospel were in dispute in the Lutheran community. That is the purpose of this paper, offered in tribute to Jeffrey Silcock, a fine Australian friend who did his doctoral studies with Norman Nagel in St. Louis and has spent much of his academic life working with the Antinomian Disputations.

Psalm 51

Numbered as one of the seven penitential psalms, historically, Psalm 51 has been associated with King David's adultery with Bathsheba and the murder of her husband, Uriah the Hittite. David himself has, until the advent of historical criticism, been considered the author. Thus, as Luther read it, the Psalm offers a first-hand insight into David's repentance. But he is concerned from the beginning to make sure that the repentance is not confined to the specific event or to David himself—a mistake he ascribes to the scholastics. "We must not concentrate on those external signs, but go further and look at the whole nature, source and origin of sin. The Psalm talks about the whole of sin, about the root of sin, not merely about the outward work, which springs like fruit from the root and tree of sin."[1] Thus, the presenting issue for Luther is original sin, "all that is born of father and mother, before a man is old enough to say, do or think anything."[2]

On this basis, he argues, "two kinds of sin can be distinguished. There is, first, the whole nature corrupted by sin and subject to eternal death. There is, second, a kind of sin which a man who has the Law can recognize when such things as theft, murder and adultery are committed. Even the civil laws talk about this latter kind, though not very precisely." Luther's topic is the first kind. Reason and willpower have some purchase on matters of the second table of the Ten Commandments, commandments four to ten. He discusses these matters elsewhere, for instance, in the Large Catechism, and passes over them here.

These definitions of sin set the terms for the whole commentary. The fundamental issue is the First Commandment. While David's sin against both Bathsheba and Uriah is important, David's defining sin is directly against God, whom he has displaced in favor of himself. "We say that the natural powers are corrupt in the extreme. When he was created, Adam had a right will and understanding. He could hear and see perfectly, and he took care of earthly things perfectly, with praise and faith in God. Through the Fall his will, understanding, and all natural powers were so corrupted that man was no longer whole, but was diverted by sin, lost his correct judgment before God and thought everything perversely against the will and Law of God. He has no longer an adequate understanding of the love of God but fled from him and hated him."[3] Thus, David's specific sins, including the breach of the First Commandment, are fruits of the root of original sin.

Luther's definition of repentance in Psalm 51 is keyed to faith. It is direct and traditional, but its grounding in the first table of the commandments makes it much more sweeping. "There are two elements in true repentance: recognition of sin and recognition of grace; or, to use more familiar terms, the fear of God and trust in mercy."[4]

In the Antinomian Disputations, later in the 1530s, Luther uses slightly different language. The first element is still sorrow over sin. But this time the second element is what he calls in Latin the *bonitum propositum*, which can be translated as a good resolve or a desire to do better. The precise definition of this resolve has mystified Luther interpreters, including some of the best of them. It is problematic because it implies a more active, participatory self.

Both the Commentary on Psalm 51 and the Antinomian Disputations, along with the Genesis Commentary, were edited and published by associates of Melanchthon. Along with political officials in Wittenberg, they were concerned about emerging differences between the two reformers, especially in issues where Melanchthon was making his own offerings. Generally, these proposals involve correlative matters of law and will. In 1533, Melanchthon began speaking of a third use of the law to provide guidance in the Christian life. This would presumably require greater emphasis on willpower. Luther neither explicitly endorsed nor repudiated a third use. But when it was suggested, more likely by Melanchthon's students than by Melanchthon himself, that the will is a third force in conversion, Luther exploded, dismissing it as evidence of the theology of Erasmus.

Evidence of later editorial work has been isolated in both the commentary on Psalm 51 and the Antinomian Disputation. Jaroslav Pelikan, the translator and editor of the commentary, notes an interpolation inserted by Veit Dietrich that includes a carefully qualified contribution of the will in conversion.[5] More famously, Werner Elert found an interpolation of the third use of the law in the Antinomian Disputations, dismissing it as a forgery.[6]

The documented exposure of such editorial revisions might be suggested as an explanation of the difference in the definition of repentance in the Antinomian Disputations. A "good resolve" implies, if subtly, the involvement of the will. The assertion of universal Christian usage to support the addition to the definition can also raise suspicions, especially since in the Psalm commentary Luther uses different language.

But when the "good resolve" is considered in light of Theses 17, 18, and 22 in the First Disputations, the apprehension resolves. Thesis 17 argues that the "good resolve" is not a "resolution chosen by human powers regarding the avoiding of sin in the future."[7] Thesis 18 asserts that the good resolve "is an impetus from the Holy Spirit that immediately detests sin out of love," even while sin continues to rebel in the flesh.[8] Thesis 22 sums up the argument: "But those who repent ought to entertain hope, and in this way, out of love of God, hate sin, which is really what the good intention means."[9]

Understood in this way, even if the language is somewhat different, the definition in the Antinomian Disputations closely parallels the definition in Psalm 51. Repentance is not a moral overhaul shaped by the second table but a matter of the first table and so of faith. As Luther writes in the commentary, "The psalm talks about the whole of sin, about the root of sin, not merely about the outward work, which springs like fruit from the root and tree of sin."[10] Repentance is a correlate of faith, a reorientation of the self, driven by both law and gospel, in which the falsely attaching self is broken loose to be sunk ever deeper into Christ Jesus and his promises.

Thus, as Luther insists throughout his commentary on Psalm 51, repentance requires both law and gospel. The law initiates repentance. As Luther reconstructs the original circumstance, God had established David in a position of prominence both spiritually and politically. "Yet such a man fell, not into some peccadillo, but at one time into the whole mass of sins. What is even worse, he fell into impenitence and deep smugness, so that If Nathan had not come, David might have sinned against the Holy Spirit."[11] Nathan's little story of the poor man's lamb broke through the delusion and started David's reconsiderations.

Through the law comes knowledge of sin. This is much more than simple recollection or awareness, Luther writes. "It is a true feeling, a true experience, and a very serious struggle of the heart. It means to feel and experience the intolerable burden of the wrath of God. . . . The sinful man is the one who is oppressed by his conscience and tossed to and fro, not knowing where to turn."[12]

Later in the commentary, he compares the straitened conscience to birds being hunted. "Troubled consciences are like geese;' he jokes wryly. "When the hawk pursues them, they try to escape by flying, though they could do better by running. On the other hand, when the wolves threaten them, they try to escape by running, though they could do better by flying. So when their consciences are oppressed, men run first here, then there; they try first this work, then that work, not knowing where to turn."[13] Critically, as effectively as it drives, the law doesn't know where it is going. Like the unspecified accusation that relentlessly pursues Mr. K in Franz Kafka's *The Trial*, the law just hammers away insatiably. In this connection, Luther frequently mentions Saul, Cain, and Judas, the biblical suicides.

In the Antinomian Disputations, Luther gives much more consideration to the specific connections in the law's work on the conscience. He sets out a broad definition. "Whatever shows sin, wrath, or death exercises the office of the law. For to reveal sin is nothing else nor can be nothing else than law, or the most proper effect and power of the law."[14] The law is not confined to a specific grammatical form. It can function just as well, if not better, in words that are grammatically promissory—the Lord's Prayer, for example.[15] There are innumerable sources besides proclamation. Threat and afflictions are the work of the law; so is being given up to death. In fact, even the falling of the leaf—as in the Garden of Eden—can become the voice of the law in the conscience.[16]

Defined in this way, the law is one of the forces of the fallen creation. It is linked with sin and death and, as such, a power that is let loose in the sinner's life. It does not know its own end but chronically "ascends into the conscience, seeking to rule there" by making ultimate claims for itself.

In this way, instead of driving to repentance, the law actually undermines itself. So, in the first of the Disputations, Luther argues that "a man, terrified by the form of sin, cannot intend the good by his own powers, since he can be neither quieted nor secured. But confused and ruined by the power of sin, he falls into despair and hatred of God, or he descends into hell, as Scripture says."[17] This renders a halfway repentance produced by the law alone, for it cannot be anything more than sorrow, remorse, or worse.[18]

This is where the gospel comes into play. In fact, at several points in the Commentary on Psalm 51, Luther speaks of the law and the gospel working together to produce the proper knowledge of God. This is the issue, he asserts, "that theological knowledge in the Spirit by which we pronounce and judge that we are sinners but that God is righteous."[19] Because this knowledge is hidden to a sinner, "it has to be divinely revealed. This revelation of sin takes place through the Law and through the Gospel, or promise. Both teachings denounce sin."[20] In a parallel argument in the Antinomian Disputations, Luther insists that the law can only drive to the Gospel, its proper destination when the Holy Spirit takes it under control by becoming its interpreter.

In the Psalm 51 commentary, he further defines the role of the gospel in bringing repentance with reference to the First Commandment, which, he says, "denounces sin by its very promise. God promises: 'I am the Lord, your God; that is, I am He through whom salvation will come to you against death and sin.' This itself argues that our whole nature is punishable by death and sin. Why else should He promise that He will be God to us? Thus, the Word of God—that is, both the Law and the Gospel, or promise—proves with clear and certain arguments that we are sinners and are saved by grace alone. If God promises life, it follows that we are under death. If he promises the forgiveness of sins, it follows that sins dominate and possess us. Now the wages of sin is death (Rom. 6:23). Both the threats and the promises all show the same thing."[21]

Further on, Luther applies that same argument to the doctrine of original sin. Reason does not know this doctrine, he writes. Rather, it "is learned from the Law and the promises of God." and it is handed down by tradition. "Moses and David, and after them the Apostle Paul, set it down in writing. Undoubtedly, they drew this wisdom from the

First Commandment and from the promises given to Abraham and to Adam. Since these promise a blessing, they make it clear that this nature is under a curse and under the kingdom of the devil, in which there is darkness, hate of God and mistrust."[22]

In fact, Luther can say that since "sin remains hidden in our nature and cannot be fully recognized, it had to be divinely revealed. This revelation of sin takes place through the Law and through the Gospel, or promise. Both teachings denounce sin which we can neither know nor feel nor believe to be sins unless we are admonished by the Word of God."[23] This is a dimension of the law-gospel distinction that commonly goes unobserved. When the Holy Spirit brings the law into the service of the gospel by pointing forward to its true end in Christ Jesus, the gospel, in effect, turns around to establish the law by fulfilling what it demands. The usual sequence is problem-solution; in this dimension, the direction reverses to become solution-problem. The gospel effectively overlaps the law to both confirm the indictment and declare its full satisfaction in Christ's death and resurrection. This dimension of the distinction is especially prominent in the Commentary on Psalm 51—so the references (above) to the doctrine of original sin and the First Commandment. As Luther observes along the way, the gospel creates an appetite for itself, "the taste provokes a greater thirst."[24]

Along the same line, Luther notes what experienced pastors also observe. "The godly always talk as though they were sinners, as indeed they are." "Though they have the forgiveness of sins, they still pray and sigh for the forgiveness of sins. On the other hand, smug sinners say, 'I thank Thee that I am not like other men,' as that man in Luke (18:11) did."[25]

Because repentance is the work of both law and gospel, the Christian is always marked as *simul iustus et peccator*. There is a double knowledge of the self as sinner and of the new self as justified by faith in Christ Jesus.

> The theologian is concerned that man becomes aware of this nature of his, corrupted by sins. When this happens, despair follows, casting him into hell. In the face of the righteous God, what shall a man do who knows that his whole nature has been crushed by sin and that there is nothing left on which he can rely, but that his righteousness has been reduced to exactly nothing? When the mind has felt this much, the other part of this knowledge should follow. This is not a matter of speculation either, but completely of practice and feeling. A man hears and learns what grace and justification are, what God's plan is for the man who has fallen into hell, namely, that he has decided to restore man through Christ. Here the

> dejected mind cheers up, and on the basis of grace it joyfully declares: "Though I am a sinner in myself, I am not a sinner in Christ, who has been made righteousness for us (1 Cor. 1:30). I am righteous and justified through Christ, the Righteous and Justifier because he belongs to sinners and was sent for sinners."[26]

As he develops the argument, Luther points out that "this is really what they call the conjunction of two things that are incompatible." It is "an art and a wisdom that is above the wisdom of the Decalogue, a truly heavenly wisdom, which is not taught by the law or imagined or understood by reason without the Holy Spirit!'[27] The incompatibility falls between sin and righteousness, opposites that, by definition, exclude one another. According to the law and reason, it is one or the other, not both, and at the same time. So, apart from the gospel, the sinner believes the self to be condemned. Apart from the law, the self imagines itself free of condemnation. Thus, the "theology of this Psalm is unknown to the schools of the papists,"[28] for sinfulness and righteousness cannot co-exist or inhere in the same person. Luther writes:

> But look at David here. With his mouth wide open he breaks out in the words "have mercy on me, O God." Thus he combines things that by nature are dissimilar, God and himself the sinner, the Righteous and the unrighteous. That gigantic mountain of divine wrath that so separates God and David, he crosses by trust in mercy and joins himself to God. This is really what our theology adds to the law. To call on God and to say, "Have mercy," is not a great deal of work. But to add the article "on me"—this is really what the Gospel inculcates so earnestly, and yet we experience how hard it is for us to do it. This "on me" hinders all our prayers, when it ought to be the only reason and highest occasion for praying.

Luther's seemingly offhand comment, "this is what our theology adds to the law," points to a dramatically important difference between his way of thinking and more traditional formulations. Usually, the traditions—both Roman Catholic and Protestant—are worked out in relation to the law. So, as Gerhard Forde wrote some years ago in a brilliant essay, the usual formulations of the Christian faith are set up as "an exodus from vice to virtue!"[29] Sin, generally defined in moral terms that give prominence to the second table, is set out as the problem to be solved. Grace, in its various forms, atones for the sin and enlists the sinner's will to cooperate in a process of conversion that overcomes vices to achieve virtue. This framework disallows the *simul iustus et peccator* because it undermines claims to progress. By this confession, the sinner confesses to remaining just exactly that. Luther thinks in a different frame of reference, involving both law and gospel. The believer is on an exodus not from vice to virtue, with all of the accompanying self-absorption, but from "virtue to the grace of God." The *simul* worked in the hearing of both law and gospel, theologically describes not progressive development but the death of the old man, who is always intent on creating himself, and the birth of the new, who lives by the promise.

Thus, as Luther argues throughout the Commentary on Psalm 51, both law and gospel are required for the preaching of genuine repentance. The law must be preached to faithfully expose the bondage of original sin, to confront the pious, and to dislodge the smug. But the best it can produce, by itself, is cynicism, despair, and finally death. The gospel brings the law to its proper goal in Christ, who is "the end of the law that all who believe may be justified" (Rom. 10:4). It enables the good resolve, or better yet, it creates the faith that makes it possible for the sinner to tell the truth about the self in faith and hope.

Some Further Consideration

In the course of his argument for both the law and the gospel in the preaching of repentance, Luther makes three additional points that should be noted here for further understanding of the preacher's task. One concerns "the God clothed in his promise," the second, the alien character of repentance and faith, and the third, the creation of the new being.

First of all, from the beginning and throughout the argument in the Commentary of Psalm 51, Luther asserts that in these considerations, we are not dealing with the "absolute God," God as God is in God's own being, but the God who is dressed in his word. In the course of his writings, Luther describes this distinction in different terms. Sometimes, he distinguishes between *deus absconditus* and *deus revelatus*, the hidden and the revealed God; sometimes, between *deus nudus* and *deus indutus*, the naked and the clothed God. In *The Bondage of the Will*, the distinction is made between the unpreached and the preached God.

Though there are differences that might be noted in scholarship, each of these distinctions effectively serves the same purpose, that is, to focus on the God who has become known to us in his Word, in Christ Jesus.

It is, to some extent, conceivable theologically to speak of God apart from his revelation. This is the "absolute God," the term Luther uses in this commentary. There is some vague sense in the human heart of a God out there, on the loose, God in his potential *absoluta*, or absolute power, to use the term Luther himself learned from his studies with the nominalists. This is the hidden God who lurks on the edge of the revelation, who cannot be known, and who, therefore, is always threatening. One way or another, speculation that seeks to penetrate God's hiddenness always encounters wrath that dissolves both law and gospel.

"From this absolute God everyone should flee who does not want to perish," Luther writes in the opening pages of the commentary, "because human nature and the absolute God—for the sake of teaching we use the familiar term—are the bitterest of enemies."[30] Further on in the same paragraph, he states,

> Let no one, therefore, interpret David as speaking of the absolute God. He is speaking with God as he is dressed and clothed in His Word and promises so that from the name God, we cannot exclude Christ, whom God promised to Adam and the other patriarchs. We must take hold of this God, not naked but clothed and revealed in his Word; otherwise certain despair will crush us.[31]

In contrast, God, clothed in his Word, is "clothed in a kind appearance and, so to speak, in such a pleasant mask, that is, dressed in his promises—this God we can grasp and look at with joy and trust."[32] Later in the commentary, Luther returns to the same distinction. "This God is not a vague God, like the Turks worship. He is God revealed and, so to speak, sealed. He has circumscribed himself with a certain place, Word, and signs, so that he might be acknowledged and grasped."[33]

It is already clear from this distinction that by setting aside speculation and proceeding on the basis of what God has revealed, Luther is going to work with both law and gospel. The promises, set out in both the Old and the New Testament, came to fulfillment in Christ's death and resurrection and so, with the law, inform faith and understanding.

Secondly, in the course of his commentary on Psalm 51, Luther repeatedly uses language familiar from his much earlier sermon on two kinds of righteousness to describe the alien character of the righteousness of faith. It is alien as opposed to proper, to begin with, because it is worked from outside of the self by the power of another, namely, the Holy Spirit. The Christian "is righteous and holy by an alien or foreign holiness—I call it this for the sake of instruction—that is, he is righteous by the mercy and grace of God. This mercy and grace is not something human; it is not some sort of disposition or quality of the heart. It is a divine blessing, given through the true knowledge of the gospel, when we know and believe that our sin has been forgiven us through the grace and merit of Christ and when we hope for steadfast love and mercy for Christ's sake."[34] Because it comes from outside of the self as opposed to developing within, "we still need the gift of the Holy Spirit to clean out the remnants of sin in us or at least to help lest we succumb to sin and to the lusts of the flesh."[35]

This is critically important because repentance is not an external or political act that can be achieved by the will and measured accordingly. A Christian "is not righteous according to substance or quality—I use these terms for instruction's sake. He is righteous according to his relation to something; namely, only in respect to divine grace and the free forgiveness of sins," Luther argues. To use the language of the older sermon, the righteousness of Christ is always just that, arising from outside of its beneficiary, and it only becomes proper or appropriate to the self to the extent that the Holy Spirit works it in the believer through the Word.[36]

Later in the commentary, Luther picks up the same argument in relation to grace. "Grace means the favor by which God accepts us, forgiving sins and justifying freely through Christ. It belongs to the category of relationship, which the dialecticians say has a minimum of entity and a maximum of power. So you should not think of it as a quality, as the scholastics dreamed. The forgiveness of sins depends simply on the promise which faith accepts—not our works or merits."[37] The same can be said of repentance and faith. Since they are worked from outside of the self by the Holy Spirit, they do not become any more observable to the self than the love of the beloved or joy. The impact is evident but the substance is hidden in the one who bestows such gifts.

Thirdly and finally, in the course of the commentary of Psalm 51, particularly in regard to the last verses, Luther carefully describes how the new person is shaped in Christ Jesus. It is possible, shopping for them, to pick out passages in this discussion where Luther appears to be appealing to the self to join in the struggle against sin and for the new obedience. He writes, for example, that "once a Christian is righteous by faith and has accepted the forgiveness of sins, he should not be smug, as though he were pure of all sins. For only then does he face the constant battle with the remnants of sin."[38] Or later, he speaks of sanctification in something of the same manner. "Let us take care to be washed daily, to become purer day by day, so that daily the new man may arise and the old man crushed, not only for his death but our sanctification.[39] When such statements are taken out of context, as they nearly always are, Luther starts to sound like he has read John Wesley's critique of himself and is self-correcting accordingly.

But when the passages are taken in the context of the overall argument, as they must be, it quickly becomes clear that Luther is right on track with his earlier work, like the Sermon on two kinds of righteousness. To the extent that any proper or personal righteousness becomes viable, it is the fruit of the alien righteousness of Christ Jesus worked in the believer by the Holy Spirit. The basic assumption of Luther's argument in the 1532 commentary is set down in his comments on Psalm 51:10, "Create in me a clean heart, O God, and renew a right Spirit within me." "Thus the true Spirit dwells in the believers not merely according to his gifts, but according to his own substance. He does not give his gifts (the charismata) in such a way that he is somewhere else or asleep, but he is present with his gifts and creatures by preserving, ruling and strengthening them."[40] With this, Luther discounts appeals to free will, arguing that "grace is the continuous and perpetual operation or action through which we are grasped and moved by the Spirit of God so that we do not disbelieve his promises and that we think and do what is favorable and pleasing to God. The Spirit is something living, not dead. Just as life is never idle, but as long as it is present is doing something, so the Holy Spirit is never idle in the pious but is always doing something that pertains to the kingdom of God."[41] Luther is even more explicit in the following statement:

> It is well known that in the new obedience the Spirit in the justified brings with it daily growth of the heart in the Spirit, who sanctifies us, namely, that after the battles against the remnants of false opinions about God and against doubt the Spirit goes on to govern the action of the body so that lust is cast out and the mind becomes accustomed to patience and other moral virtues.[42]

The new life in Christ is not a matter of either the human will, bound to itself in original sin, nor the law. It is the new creation, wrought by the spirit of the Risen Christ, who justifies the godless.

Throughout the argument, Luther returns to the word "create," as in "create in me." Like the old creation, the new creation is the work of the Creator, not the creature ever seeking rebelliously to become its own creator. With this, as is to be expected from the date of the commentary and its authorship, the apparatus of the third-use argument is entirely missing. The conceptuality is also missing. The bound will, like stony soil, does not respond productively to appeals or specially modified forms of the law. It is like preaching to the dead.

Because of the way the Lutheran community divided over these issues after Luther's death, from the late 1540s into the 1560s and early 1570s, they were taken up in the Formula of Concord. Article II slams the door and throws away the key against the experimentation with the free will argument that had shown up in edits attributed to Luther in the earlier commentaries. "The free will by its own natural powers can do nothing for man's conversion, righteousness, peace and salvation, cannot cooperate and cannot obey, believe and give assent when the Holy Spirit offers the grace of God and salvation through the Gospel."[43] There are no degrees in death—a person dead in sin is exactly that.

Given such strong medicine concerning the will, it is to be expected that the doctrine of the third use will also be contained. By this time, the language had become a standard feature of Lutheran dialectics. There was just one small group of students of Luther who held out against it, the so-called later Antinomians. They held that the Holy Spirit's work in the creation of the new life makes the preaching of the law for that purpose superfluous.

Part of the problem in the discussion is the attempt to distinguish among classes of people: the impious or wanton sinners on the one side and the pious or the faithful on the other. It may be possible to make such distinctions *coram hominibus*, politically or in public behavior. But *coram deo*, before God, Luther's *simul* obscures the line. The saints are always and, at the same time, sinners. As Jesus' parables and the stories of the Gospels demonstrate clearly, the sinners may very well be among the saints. Though Luther himself occasionally distinguishes between the kinds of preaching appropriate to the pious and the impious, the *simul* itself clearly makes it impossible to separate weeds and wheat in this life. Given the inseparable presence of both, the preacher—as Luther insisted throughout his life—must preach both law and gospel in their fullness.

With this, it can be noted that all three of the voices discernable in Article VI of the Formula—James Andreae, who provided the basic form of the language, Andreas Musculus, who has been associated with the later Antinomians, and David Chytraeus, one of the early Lutheran orthodox theologians—share two essential arguments. They are convinced, first of all, that the law provides instruction for all. They are equally convinced, in Chytraeus's words, that "the Old Adam, like an unmanageable and recalcitrant donkey" continues to afflict believers and unbelievers alike until death and therefore requires the ministry of Moses, that is the law, until Christ takes the last and ultimate word.[44]

It might be asked what the third use, as so defined in the Formula, adds to Luther's understanding of the first (political) use and the second (theological) use of the law. It might be further wondered if the third use, in distinction from the first two, can actually be brought off in preaching and, if so, whether it is actually effective. The law is the law, after all. But such questions noted, it is emphatically clear in any Lutheran consideration that the law must be preached. Luther's Small Catechism, with its careful explanations of the Ten Commandments, offers a particularly good place to start. But the *viva vox evangelii* finally puts Moses in his place.

Notes

1. LW 12, 305-306.
2. LW 12,307.
3. LW 12, 308-309,
4. LW 12, 305.
5. Note 10, LW 12,332.
6. Werner Elert, "Eine theologische Falschung zur Lehre vom tertius usus legis," in Zeitschrift fur Religions-und Geistesgeschicte, ed. H.J. Schoeps I (1948), 168-70.
7. Helger Sonntag, tr. and ed., *Only the Decalogue is eternal: Martin Luther's complete Antinomian Theses and Disputations* (Minneapolis: Lutheran Press, 2008), 35.
8. Sonntag, 35.
9. Sonntag, 35.
10. LW 12, 305.
11. LW 12,336.
12. LW 12,310.
13. LW 12,368.
14. WA39.1,351.
15. WA39.1,351.
16. WA 39.1, 357,355, 571-74.
17. WA 39.1, 574
18. WA 39.1, 574.
19. LW 12, 339.
20. LW 12, 339.
21. LW 12, 340.
22. LW 12, 350.
23. LW 15, 339-40.

24. LW 12, 359.
25. LW 12, 358, 359.
26. LW 12, 310.
27. LW 12, 314.
28. LW 12,317.
29. Gerhard O Forde, "The exodus from virtue to grace: justification by faith today," *Interpretation*, vol. 23, no. 1 (Winter, 1980) 32-44.
30. LW 12, 312.
31. LW 12, 312.
32. LW 12, 312.
33. LW 12, 352.
34. LW 12, 328.
35. LW 12, 329.
36. LW 12, 329.
37. LW 12, 376-77.
38. LW 12, 328.
39. LW 12, 330.
40. LW 12, 377.
41. LW 12, 377-78.
42. LW 12, 381.
43. BC, Tappert, 524.
44. BC, Tappert, 564.4; 565.7 (Andreae); 566.15; 567.18 (Musculus); 567.21; 568.24 (Chytraeus).

THE END OF THE END: THE ROLE OF APOCALYPTIC IN THE LUTHERAN REFORM

Nestingen revisits Luther's reading of Romans 10:4 drawing on Luther's sermon Galatians 3:23-29, his greater Galatians lectures, and the Antinomian Disputations. In this essay, Nestingen unpacks the apocalyptic character of Luther's understanding of proclamation. In the preached and sacramental words, the future guaranteed by Christ's death and resurrection breaks in on this old world of sin and death declaring Christ not in the form of an explanation but a promise. Christ comes to those who are dead in sin and incapable of resurrecting themselves. His word does what it says. It forgives sin and raises the dead. This essay was published in ***Word & World*** *(Spring 1995). JTP+*

One of the perplexing questions of Lutheran confessional scholarship is the relation between Luther and Melanchthon. For all their friendship and theological agreement, they could come to deep conflict at both levels.[1] In fact, in Luther's last years, Melanchthon was attempting a theological overhaul of the Lutheran witness which subsequently divided the church into contending parties and necessitated the *Formula of Concord*.

Most of the Lutheran confessions, all but the *Formula*, were complete before Melanchthon's proposed theological revisions came to light. Questions have been raised about some of Melanchthon's formulations in the prior confessions; there is evidence of some shifting assumptions as early as 1528.[2] But well into the 1530s, the differences were more a matter of nuance than genuine alternatives. The 1539 *Variata*, or altered edition of the *Augsburg Confession*, was the first published evidence that the differences were becoming substantial—at that point, on the nature of Christ's presence in the sacrament.[3]

In the later 1540s and '50s, following Luther's death and the defeat of the Lutheran forces in the Smalcald War, Melanchthon's alternatives became a matter of open conflict. The disputes concerned matters at the very center of the Lutheran witness: sin and grace, law and gospel, repentance and faith, Christ's presence in the sacrament, the limits of civil obedience, and so forth. Some of Melanchthon's students, the "Philippists," stayed with him, sometimes fronting, usually defending his proposed revisions. Others of his students appealed over Melanchthon's shoulder to Luther, seeking to restore what they considered original or pure Lutheranism. They have subsequently been called the "Gnesio-Lutherans."

What happened? How did a movement like Lutheranism, with such an historical reputation for "pure doctrine," come to disagree over such definitive issues? No doubt, there were a whole host of causes—personal, social, and economic as well as theological. This paper proposes that one of the critical factors commonly overlooked is a shift from Luther's apocalyptic interpretation to Melanchthon's later substantialist ontology, taken over from Aristotle.

One way this shift can be demonstrated is by comparing interpretations of a controversial aspect of the Lutheran reform: the "end of the law," as the Apostle Paul originally speaks of it in Rom 10:4. Luther took the passage apocalyptically, linking Christ's victory over the law in the "end" to an actual cessation of law in the conscience of the contemporary believer.

While Melanchthon interpreted the end of the law in the same way in the earliest edition of his theological textbook, the *Loci Communes*, in later editions, he backed away from the apocalyptic perspective, proposing a more structural view. When the law loses its end, there are theological consequences throughout traditional Lutheran dialectics, including the very topics over which the Philippists and the Gnesio-Lutherans fought so disastrously.

I. Luther: The End of the Law

Luther speaks of the end of the law in three of his commonly recognized works: the treatise on *The Freedom of a Christian* of 1520, a sermon in the *Church Postil* written in 1522, and the great *Galatians* of 1535. His Antinomian disputations, written between 1536 and 1539, show the apocalyptic basis of his interpretation.

1. In The Freedom of a Christian

In *The Freedom of a Christian*, features characteristic of Luther's interpretation of the end of the law immediately appear: a christological heightening and an emphasis on the reality of faith's participation in Christ.

> To preach Christ means to feed the soul, make it righteous, set it free, and save it, provided it believes the preaching. Faith alone is the saving and efficacious use of the Word of God, according to Rom. 10[:9]. . . . Furthermore, "Christ is the end of the law, that everyone who has faith may be justified" [Rom. 10:4].[4]

The christological heightening appears in the immediacy of the preaching. Declaring Christ is not a conceptual act, such as an explanation, but the actual bestowal of Christ's benefits on the hearer. When Christ is preached, the soul is actually fed, made righteous, and freed. The word is the power of Christ functioning in the act of speaking to effect that which is being said. Though it is the preacher's mouth, the actor in the word is God, using the common event of human communication to carry out the divine purpose.

The believer participates in these benefits by faith, which is the product of the word, as Luther makes clear in the sentences that follow. "The Word of God cannot be received and cherished by any works whatever but only by faith. Therefore, it is clear that, as the soul needs only the Word of God for its life and righteousness, so it is justified by faith alone and not any works."[5] Hearing the word places the hearer *coram deo*, before God, where there are no alternatives: the new creation, like the old, is *ex nihilo*.

2. In a Sermon on Galatians 3:23-29

Written while Luther was in hiding following his appearance before the emperor at Worms, the *Postil* is a series of sermons on the texts of the church year. While preaching on Galatians 3:23-29, Luther quotes Romans 10:4, saying that it implies that "all believers in Christ are justified and receive his Spirit and his grace, through faith. Here the Law ends for them because they are no longer under it. This is the final meaning of the Law; for it follows: 'But now that faith is come, we are no longer under a tutor.'"[6] One of the benefits of Christ is that the law loses its power. The word and faith take the hearer beyond the law, so that it can be spoken of as ending, as "no longer" being in force.

In the same sermon, Luther defines this assertion further, using the example of a person being freed from prison. Such freedom could come in either of two ways, he suggests: either physically, through release; or spiritually, so that even though still held, the prisoner felt at home, gladly accepting the conditions imposed.

> Thus, mark you, has Christ given us spiritual freedom from the Law. He did not abrogate, did not destroy, the Law. But he changed the heart which before was unwillingly under the Law. He so benefited it and made the Law so desirable that the heart has no greater delight and joy than in the Law. The heart would not willingly have the Law fail in one tittle.[7]

The end of the law is an event of faith. Externally, in conditions of everyday life, the demands that grow out of creaturely limits and obligations continue in effect. But to faith, the demands are no longer demands—caught up in relation to God and the neighbor, the requirements of relationship are no longer impositions but simply strophes in the rhythms of love.

3. In the Lectures on Galatians

In the Galatians commentary, based on lectures given in 1531 but not published until 1535, the end of the law becomes a major theme. Consequently, Romans 10:4 appears again and again throughout the discussion.

Only one of the many references to the end of the law and the Romans text is a developed exposition. Summarizing the argument in Galatians in his own introduction, Luther argues that in faith the believer is no longer under the law but is under grace.

> How not under Law? According to the new man, to whom the Law does not apply. For the Law had its limits until Christ, as Paul says below (Gal. 3:24): "The Law, until Christ." When He came, Moses and the Law stopped. So did circumcision, sacrifices, and the Sabbath. So did all the prophets.[8]

He goes on to develop the contrast between two kinds of righteousness: the righteousness of the law, an imposed conformity, and the righteousness of faith, the spontaneous consequence of being held in relation to Christ.

The remaining references to the end of the law and Romans 10:4 in the Galatians commentary are formulaic invocations of Christ, to the point that "end of the law" becomes a virtual christological title. For example, in Luther's comments on Galatians 4:8, he answers those who invoke the presence of demands in scripture to support the law's unbroken continuance:

> All right, but it does not follow: "God has commanded; therefore we do so". . . In the corruption of their nature men neither do nor can produce this. Therefore the Law, "You shall love the Lord," does not justify but accuses and damns all men, in accordance with the statement (Rom. 4:15): "The Law brings wrath." But "Christ is the end of the Law, that everyone who has faith may be justified" (Rom. 10:4).[9]

There is the sense in these formulaic references of a sequence being completed. Christ is the end of the law in that he is the last step, relieving the suffering that the law imposes as its completion or finish. But the use of the verse itself is titular, on the order of the so-called "I am" sayings of John's Gospel. Christ is the end of the law just as he is the Good Shepherd, exclusively, exhaustively, as the only one in whom the law is terminated, completed, and fulfilled.

Another difference in the *Galatians* commentary is that, given Paul's polemics and his own situation, Luther freely uses language he sometimes elsewhere disavows, as in the sermon quoted above: the "abrogation" or "abolition" of the law. From the beginning, where he says the whole purpose of Christian theology is to learn to ignore the law,[10] Luther repeatedly insists that the law has no place in the life of the believer. In another connection, he puts it even more dramatically: "Moses is dead." "Not one little period in Moses [that is, the decalog] pertains to us" as Christians.[11]

It is more than polemics. Luther is convinced, over and against the medieval tradition, that the whole law has come to a terminus in Christ. He explicitly rejects the tradition which excepted the moral law, confining termination to the ceremonial and judicial law of Israel. The theologians who made this distinction, Luther argues, "do not know what they are saying . . . For when Paul says that through Christ we have been set free from the curse of the Law (Gal. 3:13), he is certainly speaking about the entire Law, and especially about the Moral Law. It alone actually accuses, curses, and condemns consciences."[12]

Insisting on it, driving it home again and again, Luther uses the language of abolition quite carefully. The curse of the law, its continual accusation, has been abolished or abrogated. Because Christ is at work in the word to affect faith, the end of the law is a reality in the conscience: the believer experiences an actual termination of the law's defining characteristic, its constant accusation. So, Luther writes:

> Now if our sin has been forgiven through Christ Himself, the Lord of the Law—and forgiven by His having given Himself for it—the Law, that slave, no longer has a right to accuse and condemn us because of our sin; for this has been forgiven, and we have become free by the deliverance of the Son. Therefore the entire Law has been abrogated for believers in Christ.[13]

When the law loses its essential quality among sinners, it is no longer law—under the power of the word which creates faith in Christ, the law has literally, historically, come to an end in the conscience of the faithful. Under such circumstances, the language of abolition or abrogation, exhortations to ignorance of the law, and death notices for Moses are entirely appropriate to Luther: the enemy is vanquished.

4. In the Antinomian Disputations

At the same time, there is another dimension to the law: what it signifies for the constitutive relationships of life with God, the neighbor, or the earth itself, both now and in the world to come. The law terminates in the conscience in that it loses its defining function in the life of sinners, but as long as relationships remain, the law will continue to have this significative function. At this level, it can only be abolished when it is also completed and fulfilled.

This other dimension of the law's end comes into closer focus in Luther's Antinomian disputations, which were written over several years in an extended dispute with Johann Agricola, an early friend of both Luther and Melanchthon who became the antinomian of the Lutheran reform. Agricola objectified Luther's understanding of the end of the law, presenting it as an external event beyond faith and the conscience, and therefore argued that the law should no longer be preached in the church. The controversy required Luther to break down the argument concerning the end of the law to its basic premises. In the course of this analysis, the apocalyptic frame of reference becomes clear.

Luther never backed away from his earlier argument that the end of the law was an actual termination. Rather, he defined it more fully. Christ puts an end to the law's idiosyncratic function in this age, its accusation, through the forgiveness of sin and in the creation of the new self that gladly goes about the keeping of the law. Thus, Luther argues, "Insofar as Christ is now raised in us, so far are we without the law, sin, and death."[14] Faith participates in the gifts of Christ's resurrection.

Participation in the resurrection is, at the same time, participation in Christ's death, however. So, freedom from the law occurs in being crucified with Christ.[15] When the believer is taken up with Christ in his death and resurrection, the law is "quieted" or "emptied"[16] so that its accusation is silenced. The law remains *in vacuo*, without function.

But having defined his sense of the end more closely, Luther went on to fill in the other side of the dialectic in even more detail. Even as it is silenced, the law can quickly recover its voice, whether to accuse or, more passively, to signify the relationships of restoration.

One source of the law's continuance is its linkage with sin and death. Like Paul before him, Luther speaks of the law as a power working in cooperation with the other forces that contend against Christ. So he follows the earlier statement, "insofar as Christ is raised in us . . .," with the converse: "Insofar as he is not yet truly raised in us, so far are we under the law, sin, and death."[17] Silenced in the conscience, the law regains its voice whenever sin and death return.[18] Consequently, the law requires a public voice for believers and unbelievers alike.

But the other, quieter dimension of the law's continuance grows out of its capacity to signify. As is evident in the statement on the end of the law in *The Freedom of a Christian*, Luther rejects the notion of *significatio* in relation to the gospel. The gospel doesn't mean anything; it gives everything. It is an active force, a power, through which the Spirit of the risen Christ works to affect what it says, the end of the law. But the law, in contrast, does signify. It points beyond itself to what it requires but can never, in and of itself, either create or give.

The law signifies the restoration of the defining relationships of life: the first commandment, with the second and the third, in relation to God; the remaining commandments, in relation to the neighbor and the earth. These are the relationships of redemption, the hope of faith. Consequently, Luther insists, they are eternal: they can never end. "The decalog is eternal, in its reality, however, not as law, because in the future those things which the law demands will be realized."[19] Here, the apocalyptic character of Luther's argument is plain. Though the characteristic imagery and terminology of such literature are missing, the frame of reference and the driving force of Luther's language is clearly shaped by this hope: the conviction of a creation-wide end, secured in Christ's death and resurrection, is the basis of the discussion of an end to the law in the conscience of the individual. Christ's victory has brought the powers of this age which contend against him—sin, death, and the law—to submission; he establishes by its fulfillment what the law could, at best, implicitly promise but never deliver.

II. Melanchthon: The End of the End of the Law

When Melanchthon arrived in Wittenberg in 1518, he and Luther quickly became close friends. Regarded as a prodigy, Melanchthon promptly established himself with Luther as another leading spokesman in the movement that was spreading through Germany and into adjoining areas. His *Loci Communes* of 1521, his editorial work with the *Augsburg Confession*, and his *Apology of the Augsburg Confession* are compelling demonstrations of his contribution to Lutheranism.

But, the relationship between Luther and Melanchthon was considerably more complicated than commonly conceived. Luther's continued prominence in theological discussion has put his younger colleague into an unhistorical subservience: Melanchthon was at least Luther's equal at the time, if not in some ways his superior. Such partnerships were no easier in the sixteenth century than they are in the late twentieth.

The first sign of trouble was in 1522 when Melanchthon's difficulties maintaining a firmly consistent hand in leadership prompted Luther's return from the Wartburg. Relations between them were broken off for five years. During these years, Melanchthon was additionally offended both by Luther's marriage and his reply to Erasmus in *The Bondage of the Will*.

As strongly impressed as Melanchthon had been by Luther's theology, he nevertheless retained deep loyalties to Erasmus and the program of renaissance humanism that he had learned, as a younger scholar, at Heidelberg and Tübingen. In 1535, when Erasmus was dying, Melanchthon wrote to him, saying that he had sought to be faithful to Erasmus in everything that he had taught.[20] A particular point of the loyalty was a practical bent characteristic of this type of humanism. Toward the end of his life, Melanchthon wrote to his biographer Joachim Camerarius that he had sought in everything that he had written to contribute to the actual betterment of community life, a statement Wilhelm Pauck takes as programmatic for Melanchthon.[21]

Though the personal conflict between Luther and Melanchthon ended in 1527, it soon became clear to the Wittenberg reformers that Melanchthon was moving in a different direction. His *Articles of Visitation*, calling for full-scale use of the law in restoring the moral order of the congregations in Saxony, provoked the first stage of what was to become the antinomian controversy,[22] which erupted in the summer of 1528.

Melanchthon's theological development can be traced by examining his interpretations of the end of the law in reference to Romans 10:4. The *Loci*, intended for use as a theological textbook, went through several editions as Melanchthon revised it. The revisions give firsthand evidence of the changes in his theological reflection.

The first edition presents a chapter entitled "The Difference between the Old and the New Testaments and the Abrogation of the Law." It is a systematic presentation of what is spread over several documents in Luther's work, including a ten-page statement on abrogation.[23] The arguments are identical to Luther's: abolishing the accusation of the law, Christ brings a halt to the law's definitive function in the conscience, thereby freeing the faithful to tend, in the liberty of faith, to what the law signifies. "Christ took away the curse of the law and the right it had so that even though you have sinned, even though you now have sin . . . yet you are saved. Our Samson has shattered the power of death, the power of sin, the gates of hell."[24] "Freedom does not consist in this, that we do not observe the law, but that we will and desire spontaneously and from the heart what the law demands."[25]

Significant changes began to appear in the various editions of the *Loci Communes* after 1525. Taking the 1533 edition as representative,[26] Melanchthon's movement on the doctrine of law is immediately evident. The discussion of the law has been rewritten under the title "On Christian Freedom," with the language of abrogation toned down in careful qualification. It applies not to the impenitent but only to those who faithfully participate in the benefits of Christ. "To be free from the law is not to be free from obedience to the moral law but from the curse of the law."[27]

The most dramatic changes among the various editions of the *Loci Communes* occur for the most part after 1540. The 1555 edition, which has been translated, shows the transformation. This time in the chapter on Christian freedom, Melanchthon goes back to the original medieval limits on abrogation and then, after some further discussion, acknowledges the question: "Here we might ask why freedom from law is only from the ceremonial and civil law of Moses and not also from the Ten Commandments," and while implicitly acknowledging a more carefully qualified abrogation of the moral law, quickly blunts even that: "But the law, which is called the Ten Commandments, or *legem moralem*, is the eternal unchangeable wisdom and righteousness of God . . . It cannot be effaced . . . for the order that the rational creature should be obedient to God stands forever."[28]

That Melanchthon himself sensed the change and had trouble dealing with it is evident in the question that immediately follows this discussion in the 1555 edition: "If the law is eternal, how could Adam have been received again?" Having emphasized the eternal requirement of the law, Melanchthon was apprehensive that forgiveness had been endangered—eternal requirements that cannot be effaced cannot simply be dropped! Beginning by invoking mystery, he finds the answer, predictably, in Christ's eternal satisfaction of the law, finally insisting that we are free from the law in the matter of justification and condemnation but not in obedience.[29]

When the 1521 and 1555 editions of the *Loci* are put side by side, it is clear that the poles of the argument have been reversed. In his earlier work, as in Luther's work throughout, the first premise is implicitly apocalyptic: by his death and resurrection, Christ has brought the powers to submission and is even now doing the same for the individual by abrogating the law in the conscience to enable its spontaneous fulfillment in faith. The abrogation of the law is the focus of the whole argument. In Melanchthon's later work, the controlling assumption is the law as an eternal structure of life that, above all, demands to be satisfied. The apocalyptic is gone.

III. The Role of the Apocalyptic

Some years ago, Ernst Käsemann called apocalyptic "the mother of Christian theology," asking whether it is possible to think faithfully without it. He was quickly challenged by Gerhard Ebeling, pressing for what has proven very difficult for biblical scholars to achieve: a common definition.[30]

Whatever the status of apocalyptic for Christian theology overall, if it is defined as the cosmological dimension of Easter hope, the expectation of Christ's imminent return and his present restoration of both creature and creation in light of his coming, this much is certain: Luther's way of thinking theologically cannot be understood without it. His recovery of the eschatology of the New Testament, in its apocalyptic form, has to be counted with the theology of the cross as constitutive of his theology.[31]

In fact, the whole framework of the Lutheran reform was apocalyptic. A variety of forces had combined to heighten the expectations of late fifteenth and early sixteenth-century people;[32] caught up in the eschatology of Paul, Luther, like the apostle before him, was carried from obscurity to stand before the emperor; he was understood and came to understand himself as a prophet on the order of Elijah and John the Baptist, called to faithful confession at the end of time.[33] Given such circumstances, it can hardly be considered surprising that Luther would find apocalyptic so persuasive.

It is a different kind of apocalyptic than commonly conceived, however. Luther had changing views of books like Daniel and Revelation, with their imagery and calculations.[34] But the structure of his thinking, like Isaiah's or Paul's, is shaped by the assumptions evident in his treatment of the end of the law.

Luther's dialectics move accordingly, generally working backward from the apocalyptic conviction to its predicates. For example, the argument for the bound will begins with a conclusion drawn from the gospel: if Christ has overcome the power of sin, we must be sinners; if Christ's death and resurrection were the necessary condition of such release, humanity must be incapable of freeing itself any other way. There is a descriptive quality to Luther's reasoning; beginning with assumptions about human sinfulness, it is not difficult to find evidence. But the force of the argument theologically is shaped by the gospel.

The same must be said for Luther's understanding of law. It is certainly true, as he argued experientially, that the law must come before the gospel. As commonly observed, people don't change without a reason. But it is just as certain that theologically, Luther's understanding of law is predicated on his prior conviction about the gospel: if Christ saves, the law must not be capable of redeeming; if God saves apart from the law, he must always have intended to come to us in Christ; if there is no salvation in the law, it must have some other essential but ancillary functions.

Lutherans who work in the traditional categories run into trouble as soon as this apocalyptic drive is lost. That is what happened to Melanchthon. Holding to his renaissance humanist convictions concerning moral betterment or transformation, anxious about the alarming disorder he perceived in the congregations, he turned in the later 1520s to the law as a force for renewal; throughout the 1530s, he attempted to develop a theological superstructure that would bear the law's weight.

But the most important change took place in the early 1540s. After his experiments of the '30s, Melanchthon was convinced that more basic steps were needed. He began a programmatic rethinking of the Lutheran witness, using Aristotelian metaphysical categories for this purpose.[35] In such a way of thinking, the law is an eternal structure guaranteeing the cohesiveness of the universe, and freedom of the will is an essential human characteristic necessary to speak of obedience to the law.

The result was a disaster, for Melanchthon as well as his students. Luther's apocalyptically driven, experientially oriented dialectics just wouldn't fit in a structural world dominated by law and the human will. Apart from the gospel, the doctrine of the bound will quickly degenerates into an abstract knowledge to be contended for as part of a theological system; in the context of a Greco-Roman, Aristotelian definition, the law simply cannot end, not even if Christ gets hold of it. It can only be reinterpreted as a "new law," domesticated by definition, but in fact going about its old business, accusing relentlessly.

The *Formula of Concord* salvaged what it could, in the process restoring the Lutheranism it recognized from the earlier confessions. But there is still a remaining question. Early in his theological studies, Luther recognized that the Greco-Roman assumptions characteristic of Aristotle could not provide the support necessary for the theological reflection on the gospel characteristic of effective witness. Going back, Melanchthon simply proved Luther's point. But as Robert W. Jenson has pointed out, Lutheranism has not gone forward from this point. An ontology worked out in the light of the justification of the godless that would serve preaching, as did Luther's apocalyptic thought, remains one of the challenges for contemporary theological reflection.[36]

Notes

1. The best single-volume introduction to the problem is *Luther and Melanchthon in the History and Theology of the Reformation*, ed. Vilmos Vajta (Philadelphia: Muhlenberg, 1961).

2. See, for example, Leif Grane's comments on Article 6 of the *Augustana* in *The Augsburg Confession: A Commentary* (Minneapolis: Augsburg, 1987) 83, and

Gerhard Ebeling's observations in "The Doctrine of Triplex Usus Legis," in *Word and Faith* (Philadelphia: Fortress, 1975) 66, 69.

3. Luther wasn't aware of the differences in the *Variata* until Johann Eck, his old enemy, used Melanchthon's restatement of Article 10 on the Lord's supper to show that the Lutherans no longer held to the real presence.

4. LW 31:346 (WA 7:51). (LW = the American edition of Luther's works; WA = the Weimar edition.)

5. Ibid.

6. Luther's Epistle Sermons, vol.1 (vol.7 of Luther's Complete Works), transl. John N. Lenker (Minneapolis: Luther Press, 1908) 280.

7. Ibid., 275.

8. LW 26:7 (WA 40/1:44).

9. LW 26:398 (WA 40/1:605).

10. LW 26:6 (WA 40/1:42).

11. "How Christians Should Regard Moses", LW 35:165-166.

12. LW 26:447 (WA 40/1:671).

13. Ibid.

14. Thesis 5.40, WA 39/1:356 (cf. Thesis 2.45 and 3.35, WA 39/1:349, 354.

15. Thesis 5.11, WA 39/1:354.

16. WA 39/1:433.

17. Thesis 5.41, WA 39/1:356.

18. Thesis 5.12, WA 39/1:355.

19. WA 39/1:413.

20. Robert Stupperich, "The Development of Melanchthon's Theological-Philosophical Worldview," *Lutheran World* 7/2 (1960) 169.

21. Wilhelm Pauck, "Luther and Melanchthon," in Vajta, *Luther and Melanchthon*, 15.

22. *Corpus Reformatorum* (Braunschweig: Schwetschke, 1858) 26:9-27. For a different version of this material, see the *Instructions for the Visitors of Parish Pastors*, LW 40:269-320.

23. P. Melanchthon, *Loci Communes Theologici, in Melanchthon and Bucer*, ed. W. Pauck, vol.19 of *The Library of Christian Classics* (Philadelphia: Westminster, 1969) 120-130.

24. Ibid., 122.

25. Ibid., 123.

26. In 1532, a couple of years after his engagement at Augsburg, Melanchthon went back to work on his Romans commentary. The most significant change in his treatment of the end of the law, as he discusses it on Rom 10:4, is the downplaying of the language of abrogation; *Melanchthons Werke in Auswahl* (Gütersloh: Gerd Mohn, 1965) 5:266.

27. *Corpus Reformatorum*, 21:459.

28. Clyde L. Manschreck, tr. and ed., *Melanchthon on Christian Doctrine* (New York: Oxford University, 1965) 198; see also the discussion beginning on 196.

29. Ibid., 199.

30. Ernst Käsemann, "The Beginnings of Christian Theology," in *New Testament Questions Today* (Philadelphia: Fortress, 1969) 108f. For other definitions, see Paul D. Hanson, *The Dawn of Apocalyptic: The Historical and Sociological Roots of Jewish Apocalyptic Eschatology*, rev. ed. (Philadelphia: Fortress, 1979), and J. Christiaan Beker, *Paul's Apocalyptic Gospel: The Coming Triumph of God* (Philadelphia: Fortress, 1982).

31. See Heiko Oberman, *Forerunners of the Reformation: The Shape of Late Medieval Thought* (New York: Holt, Rinehart and Winston, 1969); Klaus Aichele, *Das Antichristdrama des Mittelalters, der Reformation und Gegenreformation* (Den Haag: Martinus Nijhoff, 1974); Paul Althaus, *Die letzten Dinge: Lehrbuch der Eschatologie*, 5th ed.(Gütersloh: C. Bertelsmann, 1949); Ulrich Asendorf, *Eschatologie bei Luther* (Tübingen: Vandenhoeck & Ruprecht, 1967); and Jane E. Strohl, *Luther's Eschatology: The Last Times and the Last Things* (Ph.D. diss., University of Chicago, 1989).

32. See Oberman, *Forerunners*, 10f., 18.

33. Karl Holl, "Martin Luther on Luther," in *Interpreters of Luther*, ed. Jaroslav Pelikan (Philadelphia: Fortress, 1972) 9-31.

34. Strohl, *Luther's Eschatology*, 22-32.

35. Clemens Bauer, "Martin Luthers Naturrechtslehre," *Archiv Jar Reformationsgeschichte* 42 (1951) 100.

36. Eric W. Gritsch and Robert W. Jenson, *Lutheranism: The Theological Movement and Its Confessional Writings* (Philadelphia: Fortress, 1976) 108f.

LUTHER IN FRONT OF THE TEXT: THE GENESIS COMMENTARY

Luther's decade-long lectures on Genesis are the subject of this essay. Nestingen provides a helpful summary of the status of the texts from the Genesis lectures raised by Peter Meinhold (1907-1981), who held that the transcriptions had the fingerprints of their copyists, influenced by Melanchthon. Nestingen guides readers through the text-critical issues related to these lectures. Most importantly, though, Nestingen demonstrates how Luther reads Genesis with Christ present on every page. Not bound by the Enlightenment canons of historical criticism, Luther does not try to go behind or underneath the text but stands in front of the text, listening to the Triune God who is the Author and content of a narrative given for preaching, not dissection. Nestingen provides readers with an insightful window into Luther's Christological hermeneutic of the Holy Scriptures. This article was originally published in ***Word & World*** *(Spring 1994). JTP+*

When Luther finished his lectures on Genesis, which had lasted for about a decade, he deferred to commentators to follow: "This is now the dear Genesis," he said. "God grant that after me, others will do better."[1]

Some recent commentators may have provided the answer to Luther's prayer. Both Gerhard von Rad and Claus Westermann have produced more historically oriented commentaries that, at the same time, open up the text for preachers. Theirs are considered magisterial works.[2]

This said, there is still reason to examine Luther's work with Genesis. Beginning in 1535 and continuing until close to his death, Luther gave extended attention to the narrative. Though he sometimes appears historically naive, to listen to Luther's comments on Eve, Jacob, and the others is to move into an imaginative world in which the people of the story come to life both personally and theologically.

Living in an age that seems to resemble a tale told by an idiot and serving in a church recently described as having lost its story,[3] reading Luther's commentary is like walking into another world—one in which the narrative still functions with power to illuminate daily life. This commentary is extraordinarily helpful for preachers, showing how the narrative becomes effective both in the pulpit and in the larger life of the community of faith.

Before examining the commentary's gift, however, we need to address some preliminary questions: first, a historical problem with the original editing of Luther's lectures; second, given the fanciful character of some of Luther's reconstructions, his method of interpretation. After considering these matters, we will consider the narrative itself.

I. The Text of the Commentary

Over fifty years ago, Peter Meinhold, a German Luther scholar, provided a comprehensive analysis of the Genesis commentary, raising substantial evidence of theological alterations in its final editing.[4] A review of Meinhold's analysis, taken in conjunction with further consideration of the commentary's treatment of law, confirms that the altered readings touch on some of the most important aspects of the Lutheran dialectic. Because of this editing, Luther's commentary must be used in a measured way, particularly regarding theological issues that later became matters of dispute in the Lutheran community.

As in several of Luther's commentaries, his original treatment of Genesis came in lectures that were transcribed by his students. The man most responsible for the final form of the transcription was Veit Dietrich, who was also involved in a more minor way in the transcription of the lectures that became, after Luther's review, the great Galatians commentary of 1535. Luther did not take such a second look at the work on Genesis.

Tracing Dietrich's development as a theologian, Meinhold demonstrates that he, like most of the younger Wittenberg theologians of the 1530s and '40s, was critically influenced by Melanchthon's proposed revisions of the earlier Lutheran dialectic.[5] Meinhold tracks what he identifies as the footprints of a foreign theology in the commentary, showing the influence of Dietrich and the editors on matters like the word and faith, law and gospel, the work of Christ, and so forth. It is clear, Meinhold argues, that the lectures have been edited to enlist

Luther's authority in support of the theological revisions Melanchthon was espousing in the 1540s.[6]

Two additional factors support Meinhold's analysis. One involves some of Luther's discussion of law in the commentary; the other, more recent scholarship concerning Melanchthon's theological developments.

Luther was in the midst of the Genesis lectures when the antinomian strife reopened. Conflict between Melanchthon and Johann Agricola on the place of the law in the church surfaced in the summer of 1528. Agricola joined the theological faculty in Wittenberg in 1536. Soon after his arrival, anonymous documents circulated in the city arguing that the law belongs in the courthouse, not in the church. Luther challenged Agricola on the issue, and, beginning in 1537, they faced off in a series of six disputations that remain Luther's most important statements on the doctrine of law.

When Luther's arguments in the Antinomian Disputations are compared with some of his statements in the Genesis commentary, differences appear immediately. One is a simple matter of chronology—the Genesis lectures from the summer of 1535 refer to an issue that didn't arise between Luther and Agricola until 1536.[7]

More significantly, there is a critical alteration in the dialectic used repeatedly by Luther in his own later argument with Agricola. In the fifth Antinomian Disputation (theses 40 and 41)., Luther argues from two poles: first, "insofar as Christ is raised in us, so far are we without the law, sin, and death"; second, "insofar as he truly is not yet raised in us, so far are we under the law, sin, and death."[8] In the Genesis commentary, the first pole is rejected as a sign of antinomianism, the dialectic being smoothed out in a characteristically Melanchthonian way.[9]

Luther and Melanchthon were agreed, against Agricola, that the law had to be proclaimed to believers as well as unbelievers. But the end of the law as an actual cessation of its power in the conscience, so important to Luther in classical statements like the Galatians commentary and the Antinomian Disputations, has been severely qualified in the Genesis commentary, as it was in Melanchthon's contemporaneous work.[10]

A second external support for Meinhold's analysis comes from more recent scholarship. Clemens Bauer has demonstrated that in the early 1540s, Melanchthon began a programmatic reappraisal of his prior understanding of the law, one that led to critical theological readjustments.[11]

Summarizing the changes, Melanchthon attempted to base the eschatologically oriented biblical theology of Luther on the Aristotelian, substantialist ontology that Luther had rejected. He further attempted to revise the earlier Lutheran argument in a direction that he believed would make it more socially productive, emphasizing personal moral reform. Matters like the nature of the law, the bondage of the will, the nature of Christ's presence in the sacrament, repentance, and faith all became issues for Melanchthon and his students. The subsequent theological battles on these and other questions were finally settled in the Formula of Concord, which rejected Melanchthon's modifications while at the same time carrying forward his theological method.[12]

It has been important to examine these arguments, if only briefly, because of Jaroslav Pelikan's underestimation of Meinhold's significance in his preface to the American Edition of the Genesis commentary. There is no doubt that making Luther's work available to English—speaking readers was a major contribution. But Pelikan, apparently concerned that Meinhold's analysis cast doubt on the value of his work, caricatured Meinhold's analysis as "profound skepticism" and sought to limit the force of the argument to only the most peripheral matters—astrology and the like.[13] The tendentiousness of Pelikan's treatment is self-evident.

In summary, the Genesis commentary, in both the Weimar and American editions, is a compromised text. It was edited by Dietrich and his colleagues to use Luther's authority in support of Melanchthon's theological emendations. Consequently, it must be used very judiciously, particularly on those matters where the Philippists, as they were later called, found it necessary to make changes. The commentary can be safely used to illustrate or to amplify; in matters that remained uncontroverted in the Lutheran community, there would be no pressing reason for Dietrich and company to make revisions. But the text of the commentary cannot stand alone, as does Luther's work on Galatians or his earlier considerations of biblical texts. For example, the outstanding discussion of predestination in Luther's consideration of Gen 26:9 would have to be interpreted in light of the *Bondage of the Will* rather than vice versa.[14]

II. Luther's Interpretive Method

Luther's work with the Old Testament raises questions about his method. In his first lectures on the Psalms, begun in 1513, he literally found Christ everywhere present; in the Genesis commentary, though he goes about it differently, Luther still clearly assumes a historic continuity in the gospel. Abraham, Isaac, and Jacob, along with Seth and other lesser-known figures, emerge in the commentary looking like early Lutheran preachers.

The text may appear to have become pretext, leading readers to wonder whether there is any discipline at all.

The question of method can be addressed at two levels, one theological, the other historical.

Theologically, Luther would undoubtedly be surprised by the questioning of Christ's presence in the Old Testament. This is a modern problem, the result of a rigidly chronological, sequential, developmental understanding of time. In this view—a bequest of the enlightenment—Jesus of Nazareth simply could not be present in books written before his birth. He wasn't around yet.[15]

The notion of prophecy as foretelling, a somewhat more historical way of drawing a connection between ages, also becomes problematic under modern assumptions about time. Whatever people claim to know of the future comes under the suspicion of being an after-the-fact projection.

As a pre-enlightenment commentator, Luther was not so troubled. He was an apocalypticist who understood himself to stand at the brink of time in the face of Christ's impending return, the last stage in a progression of development. This conviction is sufficient by itself to make time seem inter-connected.

But the most important presupposition for Luther's assumption of the presence in the Old Testament of the gospel, as a specific word about Christ, is the doctrine of the Trinity with its assertion of Christ's preexistence. When the Old Testament is interpreted in a trinitarian perspective, Jesus of Nazareth—the crucified and risen Christ—doesn't have to be found there; rather, the second person of the Trinity is as continuously present as the Father and the Holy Spirit. For the three persons are inseparable—where the one is, the others are also.

When and if time became a problem under this trinitarian assumption, the notion of prophecy quickly resolved it. Once again, Luther's apocalypticism intensified a prior conviction of the church, going all the way back to the New Testament, that the birth, death, and resurrection of Christ were all prophetically foretold. Convinced he was on the edge of time, Luther was equally sure that he could see all the way back to the beginning. Everything that preceded Christ's original coming, as everything that now precedes his return, would be preparatory.

So with thc church's tradition, Luther took Genesis 3:15, what has been called the "proto-evangelion," as the original promise of the gospel. God comforted Adam and Eve in the face of their sin by promising to send his own son as the seed that would crush the serpent's heel.

Confident that God would bring such a gospel promise to Adam and Eve, Luther was equally sure they would treasure it, passing it on to their family, who would, in turn, speak it themselves.[16] What appears plainly imaginary to a historically conscious, contemporary reader has for Luther quite a matter-of-fact basis. It is just plain common sense, informed by the gospel.

There is a historical dimension to Luther's interpretation, however, one that frees the Old Testament from what might appear to be Christian imposition to speak on its own terms. It is this shift, evident in Luther's later work with the texts, which made him a principal in the recovery of the Old Testament in the church.[17]

From the time of Clement of Alexandria and Origen, some of the earliest commentators, formal interpretation of the Old Testament was set up on the distinction of letter and spirit. Using Paul's statement in 2 Corinthians 3:6, the church equated the letter with the literal meaning of the Old Testament, employing allegory to bring it to an appropriately spiritual and, therefore, life-giving level of significance.

In the medieval church, the letter/spirit distinction was taken over in the *quadriga*, or four-fold method of interpretation, whereby meaning was subdivided into literal, spiritual, anagogical, and tropological senses so that the doctrinal, eschatological, and moral implications of the texts could be isolated. The literal meaning had the approximate value of a golf tee.

Luther's apocalypticism was one of the critical factors in breaking the letter / spirit scheme and thereby freeing the Old Testament into a more historical dimension. Leaving behind the ontological equations of the prior interpretative tradition, whereby the letter equals the flesh and the spirit the soul, Luther moved to the distinction of law and gospel.

Law and gospel are not, as stereotypically misunderstood, a way of speaking of the Old Testament and New as literary forms. Nor is there merely a grammatical distinction dividing imperatives from indicatives. Rather, law and gospel are two different ways in which God rules. The law is anything that restrains or drives, be it legislative, literary, or the imaginings provoked by fright. Through the law, God holds the world in order for the promise and drives to it. The gospel is the specific word of grace in Christ which comforts, bringing peace and joy to a conscience smitten by the law. Through the gospel, God gives what the law demands, freeing a person for this life and the life to come.

Though his research was keyed to Luther's work on Psalms, James Samuel Preus's analysis works as well with the Genesis commentary.

Preus argues that following his interpretive shift, Luther saw the community of the Old Testament as parallel to the church. Both are eschatologically oriented communities: the people of the Old Testament awaited the Messiah just as the people of the New Testament now await the return of the Messiah.[18]

Thus, the community of the patriarchs in Genesis and the community of the faithful gathered in Wittenberg by the word share a number of common characteristics. Both live in a realm of law, battered by the powers of sin, death, and the devil. Both have heard a word of promise that has given them hope and the confidence of faith in the face of difficulties. Both communities experience tension as they struggle under the law, awaiting the realization of the gospel.

In a certain sense, Luther's work with Genesis could, therefore, be called historical. That term is most commonly used to refer to the factual representation of the past, but it may also be used to speak of the particularity—the down-to-earthness—of present existence. This latter sense applies to Luther's commentary. He is not nearly as interested in the world behind the text—the context that has so absorbed modern scholarship—as he is in the world in front of it, so to speak.

The world in front of the text is the one where the people in the narrative, as well as those in subsequent history, including our own time, must live—the historical world of everyday realities. It is the realm of law into which the gospel enters as an alien word, bespeaking righteousness and bringing forth the freedom that is the hallmark of the new age. The test of interpretation for Luther is not the theoretical reconstruction of what the text originally meant; rather, it is the opening of the text to the hearers as a word in which Christ is brought home, enabling life amid the hard particularities of present-day historical life. For such a purpose, Luther will use the historical data available to him and even allegory if he finds it necessary.

III. The Biblical Narrative

For preachers, Luther's approach to Genesis is at its greatest strength, just where current biblical criticism is at its weakest—in ferreting out the way the text addresses the hearer. Here, Luther's use of the text shows the way the biblical narrative has functioned in the past and should, once again, as the church seeks to recover its story.

The best way to see the strength of Luther's work with the text is to follow him through the traces, reading along as he develops his comments on particular people or situations in the narrative. The fact that the commentary covers eight volumes of the American Edition may make that task seem a little daunting—a sabbatical project—but it is well worth the required investment; the people in the narrative come to life, demonstrating the freshness and pertinence of the text. Two examples are Luther's treatment of Eve and Jacob.

Taking up the story of the fall, Luther argues that Adam and Eve were created for faith and lived in it until the devil led them from faith in God's word to faith in their own believing. "And this also reveals Satan's cunning," Luther writes. "He does not immediately try to allure Eve by means of the loveliness of the fruit. He first attacks man's greatest strength, faith in the word. Therefore, the root and source of sin is unbelief and turning away from God."[19]

Describing how this drawing away took place, Luther writes:

> The pattern of all the temptations of Satan is the same, namely, that he first puts faith to trial and draws away from the Word. Then follow the sins against the Second Table. From our own experience we perceive that this is his procedure. The events which now follow deal with the description of sin: what its nature is when it is active, and what it is later on when it lies in the past. For while it is active it is not felt; otherwise we would be warned and draw back. But because these lie hidden, we proceed smugly to the deed itself after we have forsaken our uprightness and faith. Eve trespassed similarly in the instance of the fruit after she had been persuaded, contrary to the Word of God, that she would not die.[20]

Moved from faith in the word to faith in their own faith, Adam and Eve have literally no one to whom they can turn. They are left hanging. The original sin is enthusiasm, a god-within-ism that assumes itself in possession of the promise and thereby attempts to propel itself beyond all earthly limit. Seeking to transcend itself, it gets stuck with itself. It only wakes up to what has happened after the fact when there is no alternative.

Luther's treatment of Jacob is equally revealing. As Luther moves through the narrative, the personality of Jacob emerges from the text with power and dimension. His call and his suffering are examined with a depth of compassion and understanding that is deeply moving.

> For when [Jacob's] household was in a most disturbed condition and full of great disasters and the worries by which we have heard that the saintly patriarch was afflicted, not so much on account of the enmity of his brother and injuries from his father-in-law, which he overcame

> with great courage, unconquerable faith, and wonderful patience, as on account of his domestic afflictions, Dinah's defilement, and the deaths of his nurse Deborah and his wife Rachel, and finally on account of the unspeakable incest of his son, who polluted the paternal couch—in these great difficulties, his one hope and comfort in old age and in troubles remained in the firstborn son of his deceased wife, Joseph, who with his piety and saintly life in one way or another healed and encouraged the sick heart of his father. Suddenly and unexpectedly he is also removed, so that the unhappy father after the loss of his dearest wife is also deprived of the son who was especially beloved.[21]

Jacob's experience, Luther's, that of Luther's hearers, and our own come together here in patterns of life recognizable to all. Yet in the midst of such troubled patterns, Jacob remains a person of deep faith: "but he nevertheless retains hope and confidence with wonderful constancy."[22] As such, he and the source of his hope offer consolation and solace to all.

No doubt, according to the strict historicism of our own day, Luther's reconstructions may appear tendentious. It sometimes seems as though Luther and Jacob had had a beer together the night before the lecture, talking over their family difficulties. Yet Luther's interpretation makes a direct connection between the text and the hearer, pulling together the common features of living amid conflict under the promise of the cross and the resurrection.

This is precisely the point where the historicism of much contemporary biblical work fails. Assuming a critical connection between the context and the text, it attempts scholarly reconstruction of the world in which the text was originally written, as often as not losing itself in obscurantist detail with only the remotest possible connection with the hearer. The preacher who follows this kind of scholarship into what can, at best, be the scholar's historically informed projection about what the ancient world must have been gets marooned there—all connections between the world of the text and the world of the contemporary hearer cut off by academic rules of evidence or claims of historicity.

It is no wonder that those who work the historical method most conscientiously complain of finding themselves with piles of notes and nothing to say. And it's no surprise either, in view of this situation, that lots of preachers appear to have simply given up on exegetical preaching, as though they were more capable of making contact with their congregations than the biblical word.

Luther interprets by a different standard, one about which he is very clear. "Christ is the Lord of the Scripture," he wrote to Erasmus, another scholar who insisted on the obscurity of the text and consequently the necessity of imposed interpretation, "take Christ out of them and what do you have left?"[23] Unabashedly, without apology or capitulation to literalism, Luther reads the text for how law or gospel or both law and gospel are set forth, prioritizing the promise and the gifts it bestows.

Luther then takes the narrative for what it already demonstrates: the junctions between the word and human experience. In the stories, the hearer has a dramatic account of how law and gospel intersect with the conscience, bringing about repentance and faith. Thus, it is a short step from the narrative to the pulpit. The storyline provides a ready-made sermon outline; points of pinch and release for the characters of the narrative provide immediate suggestions as to where the text is most likely to expose and/or bless the contemporary hearer. The narrative, in effect, introduces a meeting point between the world of the text and the world of the hearer where it is possible to rub shoulders in common experience.

In a recent essay, Robert W. Jenson offers a brilliant analysis of how narrative has functioned for the church historically.[24] The narrative assumes a comprehensible world, Jenson argues, one to which the biblical story gives access. Set side by side, the biblical story and the hearer's story interact, the text interpreting the hearer so that the common experience of law and gospel—of struggle and hope, daily crucifixion and resurrection with Christ—makes sense to faith.

By extension, it could be argued that whereas doctrine distills theology in thetical form, narrative embodies the truth of the witness more discursively, dramatically, in the form of a story. As the story unfolds, the hearer begins to see its implications, not so much in a distilled, propositional statement as in the hearer's being taken up, included, interpreted. The world in front of the text, in its past and present forms, comes together.

For this reason, while preserving its heritage doctrinally and confessionally, the church has insisted that there be regular contact with the biblical narrative—in the gospel readings, most of all, but also in the lessons. As the story of Jesus is told, his life intersects with that of the hearers. As Eve and Jacob, Abraham and Sarah, Mary, and Peter appear in the stories, they become—as they are, should be, and must be—our biblical neighbors, whose story is also and, at the same time, our own.

This is the lasting value of Luther's commentary. No doubt, masters of contemporary methodology like von Rad and Westermann, with their historical and theological work, anchor the text more firmly in the particular and thereby open it to further examination. But Luther's work with Genesis also has something to offer. For as Jenson so persuasively argues, the narrative has provided the framework of comprehensibility within which preaching has functioned and to which it has referred for its authorization. For all of its violations of the canons of contemporary historical-critical approaches to the biblical text, Luther's own exploration of the narrative offers a model for a living conversation with the text in which the storyline can be recovered.

Notes

1. Martin Luther, *Lectures on Genesis*, vol. 8 of *Luther's Works*, ed. Jaroslav Pelikan (St. Louis: Concordia, 1966) 333; Luther's Works hereafter cited as LW.

2. Gerhard von Rad, *Genesis: A Commentary* (Philadelphia: Westminster, 1961); Claus Westermann, *Genesis: A Commentary*, 3 vols. (Minneapolis: Augsburg, 1981-84).

3. Robert W. Jenson, "How the World Lost Its Story," *First Things* 36 (October 1993) 19ff.

4. Peter Meinhold, *Die Genesisvorlesung Luthers und ihre Herausgeber* (Stuttgart: W. Kohlhammer, 1936).

5. Ibid., 44-52.

6. Ibid., 370-428.

7. LW 1:107.

8. WA 39.1:356.

9. LW 1:109f.

10. Clyde L. Manschreck, tr. and ed., *Melanchthon on Christian Doctrine: Loci Communes 1555* (New York: Oxford University, 1965) 196ff.; compare *Library of Christian Classics* 19:120-130. Though published later, the 1555 *Loci* is consistent with the editions of the 1540s; it is inconsistent with the 1521 and earlier editions of the *Loci* where the end of the law is a significant emphasis.

11. Clemens Bauer, "Melanchthons Naturrechtslehre," *Archiv für Reformationsgeschichte* 42 (1951) 64-91; cf. also Lauri Haikola, "A Comparison of Melanchthon's and Luther's Doctrine of Justification," *dialog* 2/2 (Winter 1963) 31 ff., for an assessment of the critical importance of assumptions concerning the law in Lutheran dialectics.

12. The best introduction to the differences between Luther and Melanchthon, and their significance, is in Vilmos Vajta, ed., *Luther and Melanchthon* (Philadelphia: Fortress, 1962); see also Franz Hildebrandt, *Melanchthon: Alien or Ally?* (Cambridge: Cambridge University Press, 1946).

13. LW 1:xi
14. LW 5:42-50.
15. The definitive analysis of Luther's treatment of the Old Testament is still Heinrich Bornkamm's *Luther and the Old Testament* (Philadelphia: Fortress, 1969).
16. LW 1:191; 6:227.
17. Wai-Shing Chau, "The Letter and the Spirit: A History of the Interpretation from Origen to Luther" (Th.D. diss., *Luther Northwestern Seminary*, St. Paul, 1990) 262ff.
18. James Samuel Preus, *From Shadow to Promise: Old Testament Interpretation from Augustine to the Young Luther* (Cambridge: Belknap, 1969) 212-225.
19. LW 1:162.
20. LW 1:163.
21. LW 6:312.
22. LW 6:313.
23. J. I. Packer and O. R. Johnston, trs., *Martin Luther on the Bondage of the Will: A New Translation of De Servo Arbitrio (1525), Martin Luther's Reply to Erasmus of Rotterdam* (New York: Fleming H. Revell, 1957) 71.
24. See note 3.

LUTHER'S HEIDELBERG DISPUTATION: AN ANALYSIS OF THE ARGUMENT

Luther's Heidelberg Theses, presented in April of 1518, is theologically more significant than his Ninety-Five Theses, presented six months earlier. In these theses prepared for a disputation in Luther's Augustinian chapter, Nestingen points to significant shifts in Luther's thinking, particularly in his comprehension of the righteousness of God not as an activity of the believer but of God's salvific work. This essay first appeared in ***Word & World*** *(Spring 1992) JTP+*

With his *Explanations of the Ninety-five Theses*, Luther's *Heidelberg Disputation* of 1518, written at approximately the same time, remains one of the most important sources for understanding his theology of the cross. Using a recently recovered format of structured academic argument, Luther fielded, through one of his students, a set of assertions which, premise by premise, unfolded his developing insight into a way of thinking in which the cross and resurrection of Jesus of Nazareth function not merely cognitively but paradigmatically, shaping both theology and theologian.

The occasion of the presentation—a regular meeting of the German Augustinians assembled at Heidelberg—was set up in a strategy to defuse a potential explosion seen developing in Luther's protests. The strategy was a magnificent failure. The assembly could not contain the force of Luther's arguments. They echoed far beyond the cloistered world of the Augustinian order, escalating the indulgence controversy still further.

Compact, closely worded, as important to understanding Luther now as it was then, the Heidelberg Disputation challenges interpreters. The purpose of this essay, after reviewing the situation in which it was written, is to examine a significant analysis of the argument in the disputation and to propose an alternative reading—one more in keeping with Luther's apocalyptic.

An Escalating Controversy

Given the limits of sixteenth-century public communication, Luther's *Ninety-five Theses* spread with amazing speed across the Holy Roman Empire, roughly equivalent to modern Germany, into the surrounding areas. A combination of forces—nationalistic resentments, disgust with papal excesses, the reforming agenda of the current renaissance humanism, along with religious and other factors—coalesced behind Luther's protest to give these first theses a circulation far beyond anything he expected. Working in a recently established faculty at the eastern edges of German influence, Luther emerged from this double obscurity as something of a celebrity.[1]

Whatever his intentions may have been for public discussion, Luther clearly wanted to engage the Catholic authorities in some consideration of indulgence practices. He forwarded a copy of the Ninety-five Theses to the young Albrecht of Mainz, little realizing that the newly elevated archbishop planned to recoup a substantial investment in his recent appointment through Johann Tetzel's manipulations in the religious medicine shows of the time. Albrecht's partners in Tetzel's indulgence traffic were the Fuggers, the rich banking family from Augsburg, and the papacy itself.[2]

Receiving Luther's protest, Albrecht acted promptly, forwarding the copy of the Ninety-five Theses to Rome with the request that this upstart monk from far away Wittenberg be put to heel before his complaints caused some damage. If Albrecht's alarm seems a little out of proportion, the spread of Luther's protest and the quick escalation of the issues indicate that there was some basis for apprehension. The papacy responded quickly, initiating the first in a series of moves to contain Luther, all of which failed. Within just over three years, Luther would be excommunicated; a couple of months after that, outlawed.

Luther's appearance before his Augustinian brothers at Heidelberg was an early attempt to bring the controversy under control. Gabriel della Volta, the general of the Augustinian order headquartered in Rome, contacted Johannes von Staupitz, who was responsible for the order's work in Germany, telling him to cool Luther's ardor. It was something of a dilemma for Staupitz. He had mentored his younger colleague, promoting Luther through the ranks while serving as both his confessor and supervisor. Further, Staupitz played an important part in Luther's theological development, turning him to the crucified Christ for consolation in the face of Luther's agonies. But Staupitz was also a loyal churchman, intent on keeping his vows to obedience.[3]

Caught between loyalties, Staupitz worked out a simple, even-handed strategy that, in the normal vagaries of churchly academic life, would probably have been effective. If Luther had grown explosive with his studies of Paul and the Psalms, the most reasonable thing to do was to tap off the forces—failing that, to set off the dynamite in a situation where the damage could easily be contained. The annual meeting of the Augustinians would be just such a bomb basket. Luther would have his chance, but in a context of relative safety; the honor of the order would be preserved and possibly even extended. After some quiet excitement, things would settle down to the normal course once more.

Luther had his hands full through this period. He was lecturing morning and evening, with the preparation required; he had been supervising the Black Cloister, his monastery in Wittenberg, plus eight others; he was preaching regularly in the monastery chapel and taking his turns in the city church; in what time was left, he was at work on another document Staupitz had requested, the fuller exposition of the arguments appearing in summarized form in the Ninety-five Theses.

Upon Staupitz' further request, Luther added what was to become the Heidelberg Disputation to his already packed agenda. It was ready in late March or early April, when Luther and a brother from Wittenberg left for Erfurt to join some other brothers there in walking across Germany to the city of Heidelberg. The agreement was that the disputation would be presented at Heidelberg by Luther's companion, Leonhard Beier, with Luther presiding over the debate.

Arriving at Erfurt and his original monastic community, Luther soon learned that his attacks on scholastic theology were having more effect than he may have imagined. His old teacher, Jodocus Trutvetter, refused to see Luther because of his polemics. Sobered but undaunted, Luther departed with Beier and the Erfurters to travel the rest of the way. When they arrived, Luther quickly became the center of attention, drawing the interest not only of the Augustinians and their guests but also of people in the city he had reached through the comparatively new medium of print.

Beier's presentation of Luther's theses at Heidelberg set off a larger explosion than Staupitz had anticipated. Martin Bucer, a visitor in attendance from Strasbourg, spoke of being powerfully impressed, carrying away amongst his theological insights the memory of Luther's flashing black eyes. Through the reports of men like Bucer, word of the disputation traveled far beyond Heidelberg. Feted by his brothers, Luther rode back to Erfurt in a wagon owned by the monastery there. Upon his return to Wittenberg, the disputation was quickly published, adding to the growing number of tracts corning out of the city's printers.

Besides the political context of the Heidelberg Disputation, there is a more personal, intellectual one. The years 1516-1518 are especially important in Luther's development, for a number of important strands of his theological reflection either had come together or were in the process of doing so. A couple should be noted here.

One is what is traditionally described as Luther's reformation insight or discovery. The so-called "tower experience" may well have existed more in Luther's memory than in actual fact.[4] But even if that experience is notoriously difficult to pinpoint on the calendar, the language of Luther's later reminiscence is still significant:

> Then and there, I began to understand the justice of God as that by which the righteous man lives by the gift of God, namely, by faith. . . . From then on, the whole face of Scripture appeared different. I ran through the Scriptures then as memory served and found that other words had the same meaning, for example: the work of God with which he makes us strong, the wisdom of God with which he makes us wise, the fortitude of God, the salvation of God, the glory of God.[5]

There had been a shift in verbs, the "righteousness of God" now being understood as an act of God rather than of the believer. Luther's running through the Scriptures continued from this point as a hermeneutical re-appraisal. Rejecting the legal superstructure of both nominalism and classical Thomism, systems which require the combined efforts of both grace and the will in achieving a new obedience to the law, Luther insisted that salvation occurs *sola fide*, under the gracious sovereignty of God's all-sufficient, unconditional action for the believer in Christ.

This shift in verbs is closely related to another significant tum in Luther's thought at this point: his rediscovery of biblical apocalyptic. Luther could say that his spirit was not at home in the book of Revelation. But there is a New Testament apocalyptic beyond the speculation and vivid imagery of John's apocalypse. As Ernst Käsemann has argued, apocalyptic is the mother of Christian theology.[6]

Though it has taken a while for Luther scholarship to pull out of the static categories of German idealism, the critical force of Luther's own apocalypticism is now being recognized.[7] Later in his life, he constructed timetables based on biblical signs and wrote a commentary on Daniel. But his apocalyptic, early or late, was more like that of the earlier chapters of Isaiah, charged with an imminent expectation of the inbreaking day of the Lord. This expectation shaped Luther's perception of himself, the events of the Reformation leading him and many others around him to believe that he was a prophet on the order of John the Baptist or Elijah. It also shaped his perception of what has later been termed the Reformation, reducing it from something programmatic to a movement carried out for the improvement of preaching. Most importantly, here, it shaped the drive of Luther's thinking. His apocalyptic is characterized by a waiting, as Heiko Oberman has said, in which the anticipation is oriented toward God's action as both driving force and defining center.[8]

Thus, both Luther's reading of the Scriptures and his reading of the larger movements of church and society had undergone substantial change in the years around the time when the Heidelberg Disputation was written. While it is impossible to establish an exact date, the timing is close enough to assume that a correspondence between these shifts and the arguments in the disputation itself can hardly be coincidental.

Assessing Luther's Argument

Over the past couple of decades, some of the outstanding Luther scholarship has been the work of Roman Catholics. One such, a man named Joseph Vercruysse, has written extensively on the Heidelberg Disputation, offering a close analysis of Luther's argument. When the document is placed in the context of Luther's contemporaneous theological developments, however, critical assumptions in Vercruysse's analysis have to be modified to reflect Luther's assumption about the source of the action being considered in the disputation. When these modifications are registered, a different organization than that proposed by Vercruysse appears—one that is cruciform.

Considering the overall development of the arguments in the disputation, Vercruysse contends that "the whole disputation . . . forms a well-articulated and studied unity."[9] He then breaks the first twenty-four theses into three groups. In theses 1 through 12, by Vercruysse's analysis, Luther is arguing that the works of all people, whether justified or unjustified, are mortal sins when they are done without fear of

God; in theses 13-18, Luther rejects any notion that the person plays a part, through the exercise of a free will, in the reception of grace; in theses 19-24, the classical statements on the theology of the cross, Vercruysse interprets Luther as arguing that the true theologian must be aware that God deals with people through his alien work. The final theses, 24-29, deal with the relationship of faith and good works.

With this analysis set out, Vercruysse argues that the first twenty-four theses are held together by a common purpose. They "aim at nothing else than to stimulate this process of extinction and retrogression towards the awareness of being frightened and despairing sinners and towards foolishness and nothingness, 'finding in ourselves nothing but sin, foolishness, death and hell.'"[10]

As helpful as this analysis may be, there are a couple of critical problems with it. To begin with, there is a difficulty with the verbs. As Gerhard Ebeling pointed out some time ago in an essay on Luther's understanding of the uses of the law, the critical question concerns the user. If the law is known by its uses, who is using it?[11] Though commonly held, the assumption that the preacher or theologian is the user cannot stand without significant qualification.

In Luther's understanding of the law, there is a variety of possible users. The law may be its own user, a free-floating power which bears in on the conscience to accuse or expose it; the devil may use the law, driving it so deeply into a person's sense of self in relation to God and the other that the person loses all hope; the Spirit may use the law, taking hold of the weapon deployed by powers associated with the law, death, and the devil, to sink a person into Christ.[12] The preacher or theologian is only the user of the law in a limited way, in the proper distinction of law and gospel.[13]

Given Luther's hermeneutical breakthrough and the larger apocalyptic reorientation of his thought, taking into consideration his more fully developed understanding of the law, it surely cannot be assumed that it is the theologian's job—whether Luther or anybody else—to "stimulate this process of extinction and retrogression." Such a move would not only be inconsistent; it would raise all kinds of consequent theological and pastoral problems. If, as Jesus said, we are to fear more those who kill the soul than those who kill the body (Luke 12:4), this kind of "stimulation to extinction" would certainly appear to be out of bounds.

Another difficulty with Vercruysse's analysis involves the last theses, 25-28. If the first twenty-four form a "studied unity," why have the last several been left dangling? Are they a miscellany, an add-on? It seems odd that Luther would so carefully develop the bulk of his argument and then drop his concern for unity shortly before completing it.

But there is more than consistency at stake here. Luther's late catechetical reply to the question concerning the significance of baptism, "that the sinful self . . . is drowned through daily repentance . . . so that a new self might arise," reflects his understanding of the Pauline dialectic in Romans 6. With his extended work on Romans during the years 1515-16 not so far behind him, Luther clearly carried into the Heidelberg Disputation Paul's use of the cross and the resurrection as paradigm for the life of the believer—"If we live, we live to the Lord and if we die, we die to the Lord" (Rom 14:8). Or as Luther put it, "God does all this because it is his nature first to destroy and to bring to nothing whatever is in us before he gives us of his own, as it is written, 'The Lord makes poor and makes rich; he brings down to hell and brings back again' (I Sam. 2:7, 6)."[14]

On this basis, it is clear that the relationship of faith and good works is not simply an incidental theological problem for Luther. Rather, as he justifies the godless, Christ brings forth new life—a newness that is the present sign and power of the resurrection.

It is clear, then, that Vercruysse's analysis is critically faulted. He has not adequately considered shifts in Luther's thought at the time, assuming that Luther is acting to crucify the reader of the disputation; he has not recognized the interrelationship between faith and good works and the power of the resurrection in Luther's thought.

Given the problems with Vercruysse's analysis, an alternative is ready to hand: to register Luther's hermeneutical shift, the apocalyptic reorientation of his thinking and the force of the resurrection, and go back to the disputation. Following this procedure, a different organization appears—one in which Good Friday and Easter together shape the very form of Luther's thinking.

As Luther unfolds the argument concerning the theology of the cross in theses 19-24, he alternates expressions, sometimes speaking of the theology of the cross, sometimes the theologian of the cross. His use of the term "theology" in the phrase is sometimes perplexing; it almost seems in some of the theses as though a theology, i.e., a conceptual insight, is the working agency. So "a theology of glory calls evil good and good evil; a theology of the cross calls a thing what it is."[15]

But the alternating use of theology and theologian point to the shift for which Luther is at the same time arguing: there is a different conception of the relationship of subject and object. The "theologian of glory," the contrast Luther plays off against, assumes a subject-object relationship in which the theologian remains the detached subject, observing God as object. In the theology of the cross as a way of knowing, the theologian of the cross knows himself or herself as one comprehended by the one, true, and only subject: Jesus of Nazareth, crucified and risen from the dead. Thus, the source of the action, assumed throughout the argument, is neither the theology of the cross nor its theologian; the implied or stated subject of all of the verbs is Christ or the God who raised him from the dead. This is the unity which holds the disputation together.

On this basis, a different breakdown of the argument can be observed. The first seventeen theses are set up to establish the conclusion drawn in 18, that "it is certain that man must utterly despair of his own ability before he is prepared to receive the grace of Christ."[16] Even if the construction suggests the possibility of an active self, this despair can hardly be considered an achievement to be sought: it is worked by the conditions and circumstances of everyday life, the believer going down with Christ into the death administered in relationships and by demands which are out of control. So, theses 1 through 12 attack the notion that the law has a saving purpose or can contribute anything toward salvation; theses 13 through 17 reject the participation of the will in achieving its own death or rebirth. "Free will, after the fall, exists in name only, and as long as it does what it is able to do, it commits a mortal sin."[17]

Considering the force of both 1 through 12 and 13 through 17—which attack individually the elements to which the sinful self turns attempting to define itself—and their overall effect, the first eighteen theses of the disputation could be spoken of as the cross side of the argument. The sinful self, with all its evil deeds and desires to establish its hold by means of the law and its own will, is being crucified—not by the theologian but by the shape of daily life, ultimately by the one who originally put Christ to death upon the tree.

With this, then, theses 19 through 28 carry on the resurrection side of the argument. Theses 19 through 24 set out the dialectical relationship of the cross and the resurrection characteristic of the theology of the cross: 19-21 asserting the way of knowing under the sign of Good Friday and Easter, while 22-24 reject the false alternative, a theology of glory. Theses 25-28 show the force of the resurrection in the daily life of the believer, the risen Christ bringing forth new life. The knowing of theses 19-21 is already a sign of newness—only faith can know the crucified one. But this faith never rests at the level of knowledge—it overflows in the service of the neighbor.[18]

The dialectic of cross and resurrection in theses 18-24 remains the critical, transitional point in the argument. Shaped by the power of the resurrection, the way of knowing characteristic of faith is cruciform. Such knowledge occurs *sub contrario*, under the sign of the opposite. "The risen Christ always appears with his wounds," as Roy Alvin Harrisville repeatedly insisted in teaching the gospels. So, too, as Harrisville so often observed of Paul, the resurrection shows its power in enabling those raised with Christ to bear the cross.

It is thus with Luther. A theology of glory annuls the crucifixion, presuming that the observer can follow Christ out of the tomb into some ethereal world of the pious. A theologian of the cross knows the companionship of Christ's suffering in the stuff of everyday life, being "conformed to the image of the son" (Rom 8:29) while awaiting Christ's manifestation as destined Lord of all, "that we might be his own, live under him in his kingdom, and serve him in everlasting righteousness, innocence, and blessedness."

Notes

1. The most detailed account of events leading up to the Heidelberg Disputation available in English is that of E. G. Schweibert, *Luther and His Times: The Reformation from a New Perspective* (St. Louis: Concordia, 1950) 326-330; and H. Boehmer, *Road to Reformation* (Philadelphia: Muhlenberg, 1941) 206-210.

2. Scott L. Hendrix, *Luther and the Papacy: Stages in a Reformation Conflict* (Philadelphia: Fortress, 1981) 23-36.

3. David G. Steinmetz, *Luther and Staupitz: An Essay in the Intellectual Origins of the Protestant Reformation* (Durham: Duke University, 1980) 30-34.

4. Martin Brecht, *Martin Luther: His Road to Reformation 1483-1521* (Philadelphia: Fortress, 1985) 221-238.

5. Quoted from Luther by Wilhelm Pauck, "General Introduction," *Luther: Lectures on Romans*, ed. W. Pauck, *Library of Christian Classics* 15 (Philadelphia: Westminster, 1961) xxxvii.

6. Ernst Käsemann, *New Testament Questions Today* (Philadelphia: Fortress, 1969) 102. See also Roy A. Harrisville, "The New Testament Witness and the Cosmic Christ," *The Gospel and Human Destiny*, ed. Vilmos Vajta (Minneapolis: Augsburg, 1971) 39-63.

7. Robin Barnes, *Prophecy and Gnosis: Apocalypticism in the Wake of the Lutheran Reformation* (Stanford: Stanford University, 1988) 4.

8. Heiko Oberman, *Forerunners of the Reformation: The Shape of Late Medieval Thought Illustrated by Key Documents* (New York: Holt, Rinehardt, and Winston, 1966) 13.

9. Joseph Vercruysse, "Luther's Theology of the Cross at the Time of the Heidelberg Disputation," *Gregorianum* 57 (1976) 534. See '"DISPUTATO HEIDELBERGAE HABITA. . .": The Structure of Luther's Heidelberg Disputation (1518)' *Bijdragen* 35 (1974) 17-48.

10. J. Vercruysse, "Luther's Theology of the Cross," 538.

11. Gerhard Ebeling, "The Doctrine of the Triplex Usus Legis," in Word and Faith (Philadelphia: Fortress, 1963) 75.

12. WA 39/1.348.

13. G. Ebeling, "The Doctrine of Triplex Usus Legis," 78.

14. Quoted from *Luther's Lectures on Romans*, ed. W. Pauck, 240.

15. Martin Luther, "Heidelberg Disputation," *Luther's Works*, ed. Jaroslav Pelikan, Helmut Lehmann, et al., 55 vols. (St. Louis: Concordia; Philadelphia: Fortress, 1958-86) 31.53.

16. Ibid., 31.51.

17. Ibid., 31.48.

18. The philosophical theses, 29-40, provide support for the earlier arguments without being part of them. They are footnotes. So, 29 and 30 open the attack on a subject-object way of thinking by asserting the priority of faith as a way of knowing; Aristotle (31-35) and various other alternatives (37-39) are rejected, with one closing poke at Aristotle (40).

THE BOOK OF CONCORD: A HISTORICAL/CONFESSIONAL PERSPECTIVE

Originally published in ***dialog*** *(Spring 2001), this brief article comments on the then-newly released Kolb-Wengert translation of the Book of Concord. As he reviews the new translation, Nestingen offers some commentary on the state of American Lutheranism at the beginning of the 21st century. JTP+*

A deeply troubling irony dogs this new edition of the *Book of Concord*: its editors have produced the historically most sophisticated translation of the Lutheran confessions ever available to English speakers just at a time when American Lutheranism, caught up in the mechanics of interpretation, seems least inclined to join in the confessing that give the documents their value. It is to be hoped that the outstanding technical achievement will register in equally compelling interpretation, but as usual, such a hope can hardly find credit in sight.

Generally, American translations of the confessions have been brought forth by an intensified awareness of a troublesome third party. The first two parties are the traditional priorities: the text—the witness of the Lutheran confessional heritage as it has been shaped in conversation with Scripture, and the context—the particular situation in which the church is called to hand over the gospel.

In the US, ever since Lutheran immigration began, the disturbing third party has been the corrosive force of the American melting pot. This force is a deeply ingrained, ferociously militant cultural intolerance that makes individual rights its measure while steadily eroding alternative visions entrenched in key points of historic witnesses like the Lutheran confessions, such as the justification of the godless, the freedom of the gospel, the doctrine of vocation, the bondage of the will, the real presence and the like. So the Henkels, who published the first English translation at their press in Newmarket, VA, Friedrich Bente of Concordia Seminary in St. Louis, Henry Eyster Jacobs and later Theodore Tappert at the Lutheran Theological Seminary in Philadelphia, though in different circumstances and to their own degrees, all went to their work eagerly seeking to hand on the text to the context undiminished by the forces of acculturation.

The current editors, while certainly aware of the precarious position of the Lutheran witness in America, have had somewhat more modest intentions. Since 1959, when the Tappert edition was first published, there have been some significant scholarly and linguistic developments. As Tim Wengert spells them out in an article in *Lutheran Quarterly*, "Reflections on Confessing the Faith in the New English Translation of *The Book of Concord*," (14, 1 [2000], pp. 1-21) these include a more relational quality to theological language as well as a concern for inclusiveness. Wengert notes the relational dimension in justification both through and by faith, emphasizing the Spirit's work through faith and the gift granted in life by faith in Christ Jesus. He also notes an expansion of the term *Stand* or *Stande* from estate or estates, an obsolete English usage, to "walk" or "walks of life," again moving from a static, structural to a more relational translation. Using the New Revised Standard Version of Scripture, the new translation has similarly sought to broaden out particularly male terminology in more inclusive ways.

Honoring these relational concerns, the editors have also sought to preserve the historical anchoring of the confessional texts. They have done this by paying particular attention to the style of the various documents, recognizing the different historical circumstances from which they emerged, and also by taking over the now-established critical texts as a basis for the translations.

While general readers will not notice a pronounced difference between Tappert and the new edition, the net effect of the editors' labors is to provide the best-attested original texts, out of the Latin and German, in language that has an idiomatic English taste to it. Sometimes, as in the Small Catechism, the correctness of the words comes at some expense to the music, but the language is there, and so, with a little imagination, is the movement. Given the quality of the work overall, the new edition should stand—as Tappert did in the previous generation—for several decades.

But technical work, no matter how careful, will not defuse the power of the American third party. The Constitution, an elitist male document if there ever was one, so loads the balance in favor of individual rights that public documents—no matter what their historical precedence or truthfulness may be—are immediately reduced to matters of opinion. What Charles Saunders Pierce called "the argument from tenacity," rudimentary self-assertion that says "it's right because I say so," becomes the common coin.

Attempting to fight this, both the Lutheran Church-Missouri Synod and the Evangelical Lutheran Church in America have abandoned the open-endedness of confessing, imposing extra-biblical, extra-confessional standards as normative. In the process, they have become authoritarian. In Missouri, moving to the right, the synod guarantees not only interpretation of the confession but authenticity of the sacrament; the ELCA, moving to the left, celebrates its claims to inclusiveness while giving the churchwide secretary, with the support of the bishops, the last word in all interpretation. In the end, there is no difference—the Inquisitors, who can hardly be called grand, just wear different suits.

Kolb and Wengert, on the other hand, offer a concrete sign of hope. American Lutheranism sooner or later lost the generations of theologians that followed after Theodore Tappert, Martin Heinecken, Edgar Carlson, Robert Fischer, and their equivalents. The next age class, just going into retirement, for the most part, rejected a past they perceived as parochial; the generation behind them has generally found legitimacy not as much in the church as in the MR-SBL. Now, another class of theologians has come to the fore, maybe not as flashy, but much more inclined to recognize the dignity of the ordinary. They understand that the vocation of a theologian, historical or otherwise, is not to take captives but to free the understanding for witness and that the final test of that freedom is confessing, handing over the gospel of Christ Jesus in the midst of everyday life. Going by conventions, assemblies, and theological agendas, it may look for all the world as though American Lutherans have finally become simply Americans, a sentimental streak concealing the mean right hand. Yet there remain some still, small voices—maybe enough to stir God's memory.

LUTHER: DEATH AND RESURRECTION OF MOSES

In this essay published in ***dialog*** *(Fall 1983), Nestingen takes up the challenge from an Old Testament professor that the Jews understood the law as a gift and embodiment of goodness. Nestingen argues that it is precisely the goodness and giftedness of the law that is the problem for Gentiles, for it demonstrates what is lacking in sinners. As Christ shines, Moses fades. Luther speaks of Moses dying and rising in Christ. Raised with Christ, Moses now knows his place as a teacher but not the Savior. JTP+*

I. Debate with the Law

In the recorded account of one of the public discussions of Luther's Antinomian Disputations, there is an incident where Luther speaks to the law as if it were another person present for the debate.[1]

> Although, moreover, we say that despair is useful, it is not so by virtue of the law, but of the Holy Spirit who does not make a robber or devil of the law but a teacher. Thus whenever the law is dealt with, the nature and power and effect of the law is dealt with—that which it is able to do by itself. But when the law pretends that it follows or penetrates the gospel: Here, quiet down, O law, see lest you get out of bounds or jump your fences. You ought to be a teacher, not a robber, you can terrify, but beware, you may not crush entirely, as you once did Cain, Saul, Judas; remember that you are a teacher. Here is your office not of a devil or robber, but of a teacher. But these things are not by virtue of the law, but of the gospel and Holy Spirit as interpreter of the law.

Whatever it may also say about Luther, this statement can be taken as a summary of his view of law—of its dangers but more for consideration here, of its goodness.

The fact that the law is to be a teacher, thus providing both discipline and instruction, is already an indication of the goodness of the law. As things are currently constituted, however, the goodness is not to be had without the danger. The problem is that among the godless, the law seems to be inherently incapable of sticking to its jobs and, consequently, in the search for transcendence, becomes something entirely different: a devil, a robber, a killer.

In the psychologism of the contemporary American hermeneutic, the temptation is to assign such comments to the personal experience of the commentator. In fact, Luther's view of the law has been repeatedly subjected to this type of analysis. Ronald Hals argues to this effect in *Grace and Faith in the Old Testament*, holding that "the Lutheran tradition . . . has gone on to generalize on the basis of Luther's experience—and supposedly that of Paul as well—to create a pattern that describes how God works with each individual . . ."[2]

No doubt, there is something deeply experiential about Luther's understanding of law. A person does not imagine himself addressing the law, and preaching to it so passionately, without having had some fairly profound struggles with it. But the upper-middle-class picture of a detached individual working to make sense of his or her experience and then imposing an interpretive pattern on the world simply does not fit with the complexities of the law or Iife itself.

The experience that Luther describes is not simply a personal one, nor is it offered as a pattern. It is a descriptive analysis of the power of the law as it attacks the conscience. The law may lie dormant with a person, being silenced or "emptied." But when it "pretends to penetrate or follow the gospel," or when it attempts to "ascend into the conscience and to rule there," as Luther puts it in the Galatians commentary, it manifests itself insatiably.

Various attempts to forestall the law—arguments that the basis of its attack was an accident, happened by necessity, will never happen again, or will be atoned for in one way or another; arguments that a fear is baseless, that there is really nothing to worry about—may succeed for the time being. But thus denied, the law returns with greater force to convince the person that he or she is utterly alone, that no one else has had or could have such difficulty, that no one could ever help, that there is no way out. And then there is despair: the law becomes a dreadful, self-enclosing circle spiraling ever more deeply. And finally, death offers itself as a redeemer, an end to be preferred to the unceasing attack.

Unchecked, left to run its course to its end, the law produces another Cain, Saul, or Judas—a homeless wanderer or suicide.

When he speaks of the law in this manner, Luther is not referring to a stated requirement or a list of moral standards. The law is a force, linked with sin and death, which holds its power in league with them and, under the conditions of this age, announces its presence by doing what is in itself to do—that is, by threatening, accusing, and killing. "Whatever shows sin, wrath or death, it exercises the office of the law, whether it is in the Old or the New Testament," Luther argues in the Antinomian Disputations. "For to reveal sin is nothing else nor can be nothing else than law, or the most proper effect and power of the law." "A law which does not damn is imagined or painted, a mythological figure."[3]

II. Is the Law a Gift?

Hals and others have also argued that the goodness of the law can be had apart from these dangers. They contend that by beginning with his experience, Luther misses the law's fundamental Old Testament character as gift. The proper understanding of the Old Testament would free the law to be received as "God's gracious gift." Hals himself has acknowledged, in an interesting article following Heinrich Bornkamm's *Luther and the Old Testament*, that Luther could speak of the giftedness of the law—particularly in relation to the First Commandment.[4] But, there are several problems with Hals' type of argument.

To begin with, it is to be freely acknowledged and appreciated that Judaism—as one historical way of interpreting the Old Testament—understands torah to include both gift and regulation. But this giftedness has to be taken in its fullest sense: Judaism, as well as the Old Testament itself, is founded on the election of Israel, God's calling of Abraham, Isaac, and Jacob, and their descendants as a specific, historical people.

The relationship between the election of Israel and the election of the people of the "New Testament" has been a major problem for both Jews and Christians. In the first century, Judaism took steps—culminating at Jamnia—to formally detach itself from Christians who understood themselves eschatologically as in direct continuity with Israel. And though the church may have and may still speak of itself in terms of a spiritual continuity with Abraham, Isaac, and Jacob, in fact, the root event of the Christian witness is not the calling of Abraham but the death and resurrection of Jesus of Nazareth.

It is necessary to belabor the obvious in this way because it indicates the problem in Hals' assumption. The fact that the law is a gift and promise for the people of the Old Testament and Judaism is no indication whatsoever that it is also a gift and promise for Christians. For as both Jews and Christians have historically insisted, the root events of the two faiths are not the same. To recognize the Old Testament as the Old Testament and Judaism as Judaism is first of all to acknowledge the election of Israel as gift and promise—"the gift and the call of God are irrevocable," as Paul says in Romans 11. It is also to recognize that according to Judaism's own reading of its witnesses, Gentiles may not simply attach themselves to the people of Israel at will or take over their gifts in spiritualized versions, claiming all the rights and privileges attendant thereto.

The fact that *torah* is gift as well as regulation, then, does not strip the law of its danger for us *goyim*. Rather, it makes the law all the more dangerous. For the very characteristic that renders it gift for the people of the Old Testament and Judaism—the election of Israel—excludes us. To ignore the election of Israel as the gift at the heart of the torah, to treat it theoretically, or to regard it as a mere projection of Israel's national pride, is hardly any solution to the virulence of antisemitism!

Luther contended with a similar spiritualizing treatment of the law in his own time, meeting it among the Sabbatarians and others who wanted to take over the law of Israel to use it as a basis for advocating particular practices or observances. He argued as above in some colorful terms, insisting that Moses—as the personification of the Ten Commandments—is dead and that the attempt to resurrect him within the church is inappropriate. "We will not have Moses as ruler or lawgiver any longer. Indeed, God himself will not have it either . . . We must therefore silence the mouths of these factious spirits who say, 'Thus says Moses,' etc. Here you simply reply: Moses has nothing to do with us."[5]

Another problem with Hals' kind of argument is the implication that recognition of the law's giftedness somehow controls its aggressiveness. Among sinners, the fact that the law is a gift may register as interesting information. But the effect of this information, as it is taken "before God," may, in fact, be the exact opposite. The gift radicalizes the indictment, for it makes it clear that the accusing voice is not arbitrary or capricious but a voice that speaks justly and for our good.

Remarking on this, Alvin Rogness once commented that the most devastating proclamation of the law that takes place in the church happens in sermons on joy. The sense that it is only right, that Christians ought to be joyful, that if only things were a little different—just the very wistfulness of much of this kind of preaching—turns the gift intended into crushing weight.

It ought to be observed, too, that in the history of Israel, the law in no sense isolated the elect from scrutiny. Rather than sparing Israel, the presence of the *torah* in all of its giftedness and all of its requirement becomes the basis of the denunciations brought by Isaiah, Jeremiah, Amos, and even Haggai and the like. The fact that the law is a gift is no guarantee of obedience. Neither is it any protection against disobedience. It simply ups the ante, underscoring the law's right to damn.

No doubt, the law ought to be a teacher. But whether in the personal experience of those oppressed by it or the national experience of a people blessed with it, the law is never simply a gracious gift. The praise of the law in Psalm 119 and other passages of the Old Testament, and Paul's declaration that the law is "holy, good, just and true," is undoubtedly justified. But among sinners, the law's goodness is never unambiguous—it is so hidden that the law may well be taken as a robber or a murderer intent on nothing but death.

III. Luther's Dialectic

As usual in Luther's dialectic, one side is pushed to the seeming exclusion of the other. If the law now manifests itself as such a marauding power, how can it possibly be good? The answer is both predictable and explosively surprising, supplying the other side of the dialectic with at least equal force: the law can only be good among the godless, serving its proper purpose as a teacher, when it ends. It ends when it is taken under the agency of the gospel or the Holy Spirit, as interpreter of the law.

Theologically, Luther's nominalism made it possible for him to move from a structural notion of law to a more functional definition. Structurally defined, the law is understood statically, in terms of a world order built into the creation or a set of eternal moral requirements prescribing relationships with God and the neighbor. Functionally defined, the law is understood not so much in terms of the structures of things, or of what it says or requires, as it is in terms of what it does.

To put it in another way, Luther moves phenomenologically with the law when he speaks of it theologically. That is to say, he describes it in terms of what actually happens under the existing conditions of life when the law is spoken. The law constrains, and it exposes.

On the theological level, this way of defining the law makes it possible for Luther to speak of an actual abolition or abrogation of the law. Personifying the law under the name of Moses again, Luther can say that Moses is dead—he has been put to death by Christ.[6]

> Everyone ought to know that Moses and his law have been abrogated by Christ and are not binding on us Christians. Paul says this, "I have died to the law and live with Christ," Galatians 2:19; "Christ is the end of the law," Rom. 10[4]; "the brightness of Moses faded," and "the letter kills," 2 Corinthians 3:7,6 Christ himself says, "The law and the prophets were valid until the time of John," Matthew 11[:13), and again, "I have come to fulfill the law," Matthew 5[:17]. Therefore, anyone who wants to keep a single law of Moses as though he were obligated to do so must keep them all.

Luther is particularly fond of invoking this theme in the later Galatians commentary, scoring with it over and over again.[7]

While Luther's nominalism may have given him the conceptual vehicle for speaking of the abrogation of the law's function, it is his Christology—more appropriately, his faith in Christ rather than any theory about him—that is at work here. In this sense, "the end of the law" is virtually a Christological title in the later Galatians commentary. For it is the work of Christ that he brings the law to its terminus by attacking it at the point where it bears in upon the sinner to kill and to crush. He does this as the law's Lord, abrogating it, abolishing it through the forgiveness of sins.

The language of abrogation, both in Luther and the early Melanchthon,[8] is thus tied particularly to the function the law holds with sinners. When the gospel is declared in its eschatological fullness, as an unqualified bestowal of forgiveness and the future, the law can no longer threaten and accuse. It is silenced, emptied.

IV. The Law Fulfilled

It is here, in light of the gospel, that Luther can speak of the law as a teacher. But it is not the kind of teacher that hovers over the shoulder, scolding and nagging, anticipating the next false move. Rather, under the agency of the gospel, the law becomes the kind of teacher who knows a good thing when he or she sees it and can leave well enough alone—a teacher like the old missionaries who say, "If it works, don't fix it."

Melanchthon and his students, including those who were responsible for the Formula of Concord, take the more predictable course. For them, when the law becomes a teacher, it does so in a third use, that is, as a guide to Christian living. The old marauder has, in effect, been tamed by the gospel so that it can now give lessons for the pious. But like the pious, it is always nervous that the sins being forgiven might actually be real ones and that some honest-to-goodness, down-to-earth Mary Magdalene or Peter might come tripping into a pew.

But Luther does not know a law that can be so tractable. Neither does he know a freedom that can exist so hemmed in by overbearing qualifiers. Given the force and power of the law, as it works itself out upon sinners when the law ends, Luther can only describe its function as a teacher and thus its goodness eschatologically—in terms of the restoration of the creature and the whole creation. This can be seen in a remarkable series of arguments in the Antinomian Disputations. Here, Luther sets out this hope, cutting between the antinomianism of his old friend Johann Agricola and the emerging nomism of his even dearer friend, Philip Melanchthon.[9]

> 35. But in truth, faith in Christ justifies, alone fulfills the law, alone does good works, without the law. 36. It alone accepts the remission of sin and spontaneously does good works through love. 37. Truly, it is after justification [that] good works follows spontaneously without the law, that is, without help or coercion [of the law]. 38. In sum: The law is not useful or necessary, neither for justification nor for other good works, much less for salvation. 39. But on the contrary justification, good works, and wholeness are necessary to fulfillment of the law. 40. For Christ comes to save that which was lost and to restore all things, as Peter says. 41. Therefore the law is not destroyed by Christ, but restored, so that Adam might be just as he was, and even better.

Because the law's accusation has been abrogated, it is possible to speak of the law being fulfilled. This is no merely theoretical argument. In another part of the Antinomian Disputations, Luther speaks of a person being so terrified by the law that it is impossible for the person to make the "good resolve" that is a feature of repentance.[10] Fear and guilt paralyze, making it impossible for a person to move positively toward God or the neighbor. The release granted in the declaration grants freedom from fear and, thus, freedom for spontaneous service, which is an eschatological hallmark of the new creation.

Emptied of its accusing force, the law's rightness, its goodness, may then become apparent even to its victims. It is a kind of eschatological hindsight. As it moves forward toward the future, the gospel sets in relief what lies behind, in the past. When the Holy Spirit becomes the law's agent, the constraint, suffering, and death imposed by the law are exposed for what they are—means of driving toward Christ. Thus, and only thus, can it be said that "despair is useful." It is hindsight shaped by the conviction that Christ has expressed himself in the unconditional word of hope, thus bringing the despair to its end and fruition.

At the same time, the basic rightness and goodness of the law's requirement becomes apparent. Like a good teacher, the law backs off, letting the spontaneous joy of discovery become in itself the teacher. Only here, there is no backing off—the Holy Spirit, as the law's agent, silences the law even as the Spirit takes hold of the believer in faith. Then there is service—the law is fulfilled without the law.

But as Theses 40 and 41 make clear, this renewal of the individual is not to be detached from its eschatological context. It is part and parcel of the restoration of all things. As in Paul, it is earnest the downpayment on the reclamation of the whole creation. That is the goal, the hope that permeates Luther's whole witness, both theologically and in faith.

Finally, only in light of this hope is it possible to speak without qualification and with certainty of the law's goodness. As long as there is sin and death, the law will always be dangerous—forever bursting at its restraints to get away and attack. But when the whole works has been restored in Christ, the law will be fulfilled—not simply theologically or merely at a personal level but in reality. Then, the law will be good without danger; it will "be removed happily," as Luther puts it, and Moses, too, will be able to boast of a resurrection—but only because one was raised before him.

Notes

1. WA 39.1, 445.
2. Ronald M. Hals, *Grace and Faith in the Old Testament* (Minneapolis: Augsburg Publishing House, 1980) p. 62.
3. WA 39.1, 348, 358.
4. Ronald M. Hals, "Luther and the First Commandment: You Belong to Me," in Fred W. Meuser and Stanley D. Schneider, eds., *Interpreting Luther's Legacy: Essays in Honor of Edward C. Eendt* (Minneapolis: Augsburg Publishing House, 1969), pp. 2-13.

5. LW 35, 165.

6. LW 46, p. 145.

7. *A Commentary on St. Paul's Epistle to the Galatians*, Philip Watson, ed. (Cambridge and London: James Clarke & Co., Ltd , 1953), pp. 24, 147, 266, 312, 326, 332, 337, 351, 357 and 419.

8. See, for example, the *Loci Communes* of 1521 in LCC 19, pp. 120ff. With a growing appreciation for Aristotle and a more structural view, Melanchthon moves away from the language of abrogation later in the 1520s.

9. WA 39.1, p. 354.

10. WA 39.1, 346.

APPENDIX

Funeral Sermon by Dr. Steven Paulson on Luke 7:36-50

This sermon, based on Luke 7:36-50 was preached by the Rev. Dr. Steven D. Paulson at the funeral service for Dr. James Arne Nestingen at Saint James Evangelical Lutheran Church in West Saint Paul, Minnesota, on the Epiphany of our Lord, January 6, 2023. Dr. Paulson was a student of Dr. Nestingen and later his colleague on the faculty of Luther Seminary in St. Paul. The sermon is a testimony to the decision that God in Christ Jesus had made for Jim and the power of that promise, which enlivened Jim's faith and ministry. JTP+

Grace and Peace to you from God our Father and our Lord and Savior Jesus Christ. Amen.

God has made a decision about you! That is not only true, it is one of the most famous opening lines in all literature, like "Call Me Ishmael," and it came from Jim Nestingen's *Free to Be*. That opening salvo is right up there with Luther's Heidelberg Disputation: "The Law of God, the most salutary doctrine of life, cannot advance a man on his way to righteousness, but rather hinders him." Then Jim (and Gerhard Forde) added: not only has God made a decision about you, "He hasn't waited to find out how sincere you are!" That is the first commandment, "You shall have no other gods," and Luther's explanation: "We are to fear, love, and trust God above anything else." More precisely, God's decision for you (without checking your own sincerity) is the preface to that commandment: "I am the Lord *your God*." That means you have a God—and are not one yourself! He is speaking to you, a creature, as Isaiah once declared (using Jim's own flare for the particular): *as you are* with "tears and dung, trampled as Moab like straw in a dunghill" (Isa 25:9).

That preface to the first commandment is not a command. It is a promise. When he says, "I am the Lord your God" he is speaking to you in the most down-to-earth way possible—not vaguely or in general. One thing you can say about Jim is that he was not vague. "I am the Lord your God" means *you as you are*—living, with life in you, with your strengths, gifts, talents, abilities—and also with a lot of "tears" (as Isaiah says—a lot of dung that God will trample down). But still, despite the dung, God has decided to call you to his feast on the mountain with red wine and meat dripping down to the marrow. God knows Jim loves that: "It will be said on that Day, behold, this is our God—we have waited for him that he might save us" (Isa 25:9).

But therein lies the problem with God's decision for you, since there are two "yous"—and one of you doesn't like God's decision. Old Adam wants to be the decider. He wants to invite himself to the feast, without Christ and without his cross—as life without death. He thinks he can get the aged wine and meat to the marrow by himself. Your Old Adam is like Peter, running for his life from the crucified, screaming, "God just cursed him! Messiah can't die! Peter wanted no part of that cross. He thought: Jesus is impure! He has sin on him! We are on the wrong side of history, boys! So it was that Peter, seeing a fresh grave with no Christ in it—ran for his life. Mary Magdalene was not much better—she did not know what to do with a dead Jesus, but to weep and wonder where he went. She, too, fled.

But Jesus won't let this unfaith stand with Peter running from the grave and Mary weeping. So, Jesus "takes you by the ears" and gives you faith when you have none. Jim, it's over! The running and weeping is finally done. This is a good time and place to rest, for He gives you a dwelling place; a mighty fortress (Psalm 46) where no enemy, no sin, no death, and no devil can conquer you. Our God, who has decided for you and has already set for you a dwelling place—and it is Himself! He is a *faith to have* and your place to go. As you said once: I would like on my tombstone these words from Christ on the cross: τετέλεσται: It is over! It is done! No more fighting for the preaching of the Gospel. No more carrying the weight of the church and world that you have carried so long. That is, after all, our calling in life—especially, Jim, your specific calling to preach. Callings are not pursuing your passion or trying to make a difference in the world. They are like a sow with dozens of piglets suckling away—and Jim had much milk and many piglets! It wears a person out to give people the good news day after day! You would think, "I forgive you!" would be cheesecake! But try it sometime; say, "I forgive you," and see what happens. More often than not, this is what you hear back: "You can't say that to me! Who are you to forgive sins? Are you without sin? Besides, how do you know I need it? A lucky guess?" Then the devil chimes in: "Thank you, pastor. But Absolution is not needed here; this is the company of the saints! We have the third use! When things got particularly difficult in the church and Seminary, I wore my tee shirt with one of Jim's slogans: "We have to stick together, or the pious will pick us off one by one." It is also why Jim slipped his hockey stick under his alb during communion when the Wild were playing to talk smack to the Devil.

Jim was a strong, skilled, and truly amazing teacher. He is talking to me right now, telling me—no eulogy! At a funeral, tell them that God does the calling, starting in your baptism—then God wants a family where absolving can take root. Just so, Jim had a set of callings in this old world. He was Husband to Carolyn, Father to his boys, and Teacher of the church. He loved each, especially his family, but the hardest was the last—Teachers of the Church. Melanchthon was right when he (begrudgingly) admitted at Luther's death that sometimes, in the church, it takes a harsh doctor to treat us. Then again, sometimes it takes the words of sweetest honey to address the bruised reed—and Jim could skillfully dole out either as needed—a harsh doctor to false teaching and the kindest heart who would out-weep you in your own sorrow.

So, Jim, you rest now. This is your final sending-off—your last Absolution. The next voice you hear will be your Christ's voice; the trumpet will sound, and he will call you by name: James Arne Nestingen! You will then do what the prophet Joel and our Paul said to do: Call on His name: Christ, have mercy! You know better than any of us that that moment of arising is not the time to hold up your accomplishments and fame—nor to weep over your sin. Instead, just say: I plead Christ! Christ only! He is my justification by faith—alone! Then, Jim, what you have wanted all this time will be well underway: "The smorgasbord will be spread—aged wine and meat and marrow—will all flow at table with the Lord. After all, God likes humans to be human. He made them with flesh and bones—and for loving a good meal with each other and the telling of many, many stories and jokes. If you think Jim told stories here on Earth, wait until you hear him in heaven. Then we will trade his favorite limericks: "There was a young lady of Norway who hung upside down in the doorway!'

For God is right now swallowing your death whole. Who cares if it is a big mouthful! Like Luther once said, "I'm tired of doctors telling me not to eat red meat, let's give the worms a fat doctor to feast on!" So Christ is opening wide now. Your death has already been defeated. The enemy is done for, as Christ declared to his disciples: "I have already conquered the world!" (John 16:33). Then, when the feast begins, the final enemy—death itself is put to death. Death, you have no sting! You can't bind us now!

Now, I can't resist giving you another story here, as Jim would, to tell you what decision God has made concerning you—and what you have coming yet. Even this funeral is God's orchestration, and he intends to use it to speak to you. One of Jim's teachings was that when the old Adam finally dies, we can sum up his life especially from one of the stories of Scripture. Each of us is made for Scripture this way—meaning we are interpreted by it. He knew that everything in history, and in life, is really a story—and ultimately a story about one thing: how Jesus positioned everything in life to get to the thing he wants for you most of all: a good, solid—deadly—forgiveness of sin. I am convinced Jim's, or perhaps my own (it is hard to tell the difference), is this story in Luke 7 of the woman anointing Christ for burial starting at verse 36:

One of the Pharisees asked him to eat with him, and he went into the Pharisee's house and took his place at the table. The Pharisee in this house thought he was deciding things! Come eat with me—and Jesus did!

And behold, a woman of the city, who was a sinner. . . (when Jim preached on this text, of course, he noticed with a chuckle: "How was it that this woman of the streets knew her way so well around the Pharisee's house?" As Luther put it, "Whoever thinks he is not a sinner—is one." But the point in Luke's telling of this woman is clear: she was a sinner, there is no getting around that. Now, anyone who has come into contact with Jim for very long is not only going to converse with a sinner but become one himself—since, as he liked to quote Luther saying—"If you think you are not a sinner, then you are one." And *when she learned that he was reclining at table* (like the Lord of Hosts preparing aged wine and fatty ribs) *in the Pharisee's house, brought an alabaster flask of ointment.* There is Jesus, reclining at the table in the Pharisee's house—like Yahweh (Isaiah 25) at his dinner with rich food, surrounded by his own chosen people. But Jesus knows we are people who forget this word daily and cling to the law as old Adams always do, and so he would not have the woman shrink back. She didn't run away from her Christ; she went in to him. To those watching, none of this seems appropriate. The flask of ointment is too expensive! Bible historians spend their whole lives like accountants for the Lord, figuring out how much it must have cost. Indeed, the expense of the things is what stuck in Judas' craw and led him to betray Christ. But the point here is not the capitalist expense; it is what she intended to use the oil for. The Pharisees thought that there must be more important things for Christ to be doing (like unseating a Herodian king, or conquering Roman imperialism, or at least redistributing money to the suffering poor). But remember, everything in life is a story, not a systematic doctrine. When our stories intersect with Christ, things start to get interesting. Therein, God decides! The Holy Spirit orchestrates everything for this one moment—the good, solid, deadly Absolution. Jim knows perfectly well that his death is now Christ's way of bringing you folks in to receive the great gift—and so we shall make use of this last part of the woman's and Jim's story especially: *and standing behind him at his feet, weeping, she began to wet his feet with her tears and wiped them with the hair of her head and kissed his feet and anointed them with the ointment.*

Weeping, wiping, oiling, kissing! It seems all so wrong, so fleshly: hair and lips—and so many tears! Remember, in the end, our Lord will swallow death and wipe away every tear! But, for now, this woman is anointing Jesus with oil, kissing and weeping all over him—not to make Jesus into a Messiah but to hide the smell of his impending death—for her sake. *Now when the Pharisee who had invited him saw this, he said to himself, "If this man were a prophet, he would have known who and what sort of woman this is who is touching him, for she is a sinner."*

Sinners are always talking to themselves! It is their special trait. Yet, they did manage to ask a good question! Why is Jesus letting this pathetic display play out at their table? The Pharisees thought it was perhaps sexual—or strangely liturgical—and yet somehow all very wrong. What happened to the legend of Jesus in Samaria knowing all about the woman at the well and her many husbands? If Jesus really were a prophet, he would know what sort of woman is touching him—as the Pharisees clearly know by experience! She is a sinner! Or does Jesus really know the way this appears to them and nevertheless encourages such debauchery against God's holy law?

And Jesus answering said to him, "Simon, I have something to say to you." And he answered, "Say it, Teacher." Jesus doesn't even bother teaching or answering the Pharisee. He turned instead to Simon (the betraying escape artist), saying, "I have something to say to you!"

Now, let me assure you, my congregation today, that Jim never asked me in this way for the right to talk! He said what he wanted when he wanted to. But Simon said to Jesus—go ahead, "Say it, Teacher! We all know what it is that you will say anyway. You always end up saying one thing—and that always at an inconvenient, inappropriate time and to the wrong sorts of people. Go ahead, Jesus—let the bird fly! Deliver the goods! No one can shut you up when you want to say your big thing anyway! No one is going to stop you."

But then, instead of giving his promise and really delivering the goods, Jesus did something awful. He gave a "parable test" (another story) to Simon, saying, *A certain moneylender had two debtors. One owed five hundred denarii, and the other fifty. When they could not pay, he cancelled the debt of both. Now which of them will love him more?"* There were two debts, both large, but one much larger—and summarily canceled! Now, which will love the banker more?

Now, do you know what is worse than Jesus absolving sinners right and left? It is when Jesus only talks about the Gospel but doesn't give it. It is when Jesus tells a story rather than what he actually came to earth to do among us sinners. Come on, Jesus! No more parables! No more stories! Nevertheless, *Simon answered, "The one, I suppose, for whom he canceled the larger debt." And he said to him, "You have judged rightly."* Simon is thinking: "I've been through this a hundred times already Jesus, and the answer is always the same for the only exam Christ ever gives! The one who gets more—the one whose debt is bigger when canceled!" Jesus loves to use Simon as his Boso. This is as close as we ever get to Jesus giving a "Socratic Dialog" to his disciples, which is to say that Jesus doesn't really care about "dialog" at all. Jesus wants to get to his preaching *per se*. Jesus wants to give his magisterial, categorical declaration that forgives sin, since God's decision is already made. For this, Jesus is using Simon as a preacher—that is to say, Jesus' pawn, tool, or puppet to deliver God's plan at the right time and place. So, Jesus says to Simon: "You have justified justly! You get an A+ for understanding the chief doctrine of justification! Now we just have to teach you to give it! Deliver the goods!

Jesus continues: listen to the way you, Simon, are to give the Gospel to a sinner: *Then turning toward the woman he said to Simon, "Do you see this woman? I entered your house; you gave me no water for my feet, but she has wet my feet with her tears and wiped them with her hair. You gave me no kiss, but from the time I came in she has not ceased to kiss my feet. You did not anoint my head with oil, but she has anointed my feet with ointment.* Poor Simon! He is surely an eager student trying to follow

Jesus—but he has no idea yet how to forgive someone. And Jesus did not hold back regarding his preaching stiff: he gave the full force of the law and condemn Simon right there: "*You gave* me no water for my feet—*she gave* tears! You gave me no kiss! She is kissing my feet constantly! You did not anoint my head with oil—since I am Messiah—and she even anointed my feet! After that, Simon shuts up, dead as a doornail.

But now comes the Catechism—Jim's favorite part. He loved the Catechism because it teaches us the difference between the law and the Gospel: what we are to do (and never do) and what God does (and always gets it done!). Listen now to the difference between the commands and the creed: *Therefore I tell you, her sins, which are many, are forgiven—HENCE!!! [not because] she loved much. But he who is forgiven little, loves little.* What is she doing? Acts of kindness? Is this a woman making sacrifices to Christ like Israel was supposed to make to Yahweh? No. She was crying her sins onto Jesus. She kissed them into Christ. And when that was not enough, she oiled them into Jesus' skin. Did Jesus object?! Did he stop her for indecency? No, Jesus lay there like a corpse and took it! Her sins became his! That is why Jesus is here on earth! Jesus didn't come in order to wait for someone to notice him and give him credit for being Messiah. Jesus wasn't displaying to the world his divine qualities in hope that someone would "believe." This sinner, this woman, knew what faith was and didn't simply hang around Jesus or try to "follow" him like a disciple. She figured out how to practice the art of laying her sins on Jesus. And hope he would take them as she poured them on him, rubbed them into his skin, in just the way John the Baptist told her to do: "He is the Lamb of God, who takes away the sin of the world" (John 1, Isaiah 53 and 25).

Meanwhile, Peter was trying to get credits for deciphering a parable from Jesus. But Jesus is saying, Peter! You are going to have to come up with much more sin than you currently have if you want to love me like she! After the death of Martin Luther, when everything Lutheran looked like it was going to hell from the outside (from the pope and emperor) as well as from the inside (from the Philippists and Gnesios alike), the church was reduced to exactly four faithful pastors (much as it had been in Athanasius' say. This little group following Luther was led by one Andreas Poach—who recognized that when Jesus forgives, the law actually ends! Could "end" mean "finished and fulfilled?" Of course, but not without the conclusion: over, done, caput! That means Paul meant exactly what he said in Romans 10:3. The law ends! Its accusation is silenced. The woman at Jesus' feet found that he not only took her sins but defeated them all—one by one. She oiled them into him and he not only took them, he defeated them forever. He swallowed them up, and with them, he inhaled her death, the law, and all of her accusers. There went the Pharisees! Her accusers were inhaled by Christ. Poach, this woman, and Jim have all learned the same lesson: that faith does not make the promise; the promise makes faith.

Now, the thing about faith is that it, unlike my own things in this life—actually holds. The woman knows: I am righteous by it! Her sins were swallowed up by sin. No more death penalty for me! The law does nothing to save you! Nothing? I say nothing at all. What if people stop trying to be good? Who cares? Jesus doesn't! This is what it means for Paul to say that Death has lost its sting. The sting being sin—but your sin is gone! Where did it go? Jesus swallowed it! Jim was right, then, when he went off to Toronto to do his doctoral dissertation with the Roman Catholics. There, he chose the crucial passage: Romans 10:3: Christ, the end of the law! And Jim learned it means what it says: Christ fulfilled the law by suffering it, and even more—it means once Christ speaks to you—there is no more law. Not only is all accusation over, the law itself is over and done.

Now that you have gotten your Catechism, here comes the real thing: the great Absolution: *And he said to her, "Your sins are forgiven."* That is it! The Gospel! So short and sweet! That is what Jim taught us is the simple, clear "grammar of the Gospel": 1) The subject of your word is Christ. 2) The direct object is "you"—the sinner. 3) The verb is present tense, "*are forgiven,*" and then learn 4) to give it unconditionally—no "ifs" or "ands" or "buts" added at the end. As Paul said, "Even though we were dead, he made us alive!" (Ephesians 2). Jesus gave the full, present, simple, total Absolution to the woman: "Your sins are forgiven!"

Now what? *Then those who were at table with him began to say among themselves, "Who is this, who even forgives sins?"* Onlookers to the Absolution never like it! They saw their law and its accusation *vamoose*—and they were not happy. Observers may say the same thing about me in a moment, but you hearing this will be free. This is the way Jesus, raised from the dead, finally corrals all his fearful, running-away disciples who have betrayed him and tells them what he now tells this sinful woman: "*And he said to the woman, "Your faith has saved you; go in peace."* Faith is God's decision. He gave it to you the first time he baptized you: giving you your name and His name—and making a promise to you—that whoever (that is you) believes and is baptized *shall be saved*" (Mark 16:16).

This forgiveness is not only his gift to you (grace), but it is the specific promise that he has not only taken this woman's sin upon himself but has taken yours, too. Faith knows that Jesus did with our sins what we could not. He was crucified with them, and there nailed them to the cross (as Peter learned later). The sins belong to him—and he will never let you have them back. Your story has now been taken up in his story, and he has made you—with the old Adam dead and gone—into a new "you" with faith that he has done this!

Jim is sleeping now in Christ; his work is done. He is made righteous by a decision of God, and the gift of the Absolution. It couldn't have happened to a better sinner, and now we remember that the power of this forgiveness is given by Christ to his preacher, including Simon and Paul—and Jim, and now even me. And I recall to you this truth: it is not the forgiver that does these things, but the mighty word of Christ that not only says, "I forgive" but accomplishes it. I only hand over the goods; Christ is the goods.

The Holy Spirit has connived and manipulated, organized and plotted so that you would hear this word that belongs already to Jim as a sure and certain promise: by Christ's own mouth and authority, by the power of the word itself: *I declare to you the entire forgiveness of all your sin.*

Your sin now belongs to Christ. Leave it there. None of us can come to a death, especially of one we love, without sin, fear, and remorse—without wondering, "If only I could have spoken one last time to him. Did I say enough? Did I do enough? And what of the sin that laid on Jim and I never forgave?" There is plenty of sin in this room, and it flowed from Jim and back to him for many of you. But it is gone now. We now commend Jim to our Lord. He is sleeping in Christ; his work is done. Jesus swallowed his death and now has done the same with yours. The law is over. Your faith—alone—all by itself—*sola*, has saved you. Christ ate it—whole. What, then, is left? Not the law, not your sin, not your accusation. Only These words: *Your faith has saved you; go in peace*—God doesn't lie.

Pr. Steven D. Paulson
Saint James Lutheran Church

A BASIC CHRONOLOGICAL NESTINGEN BIBLIOGRAPHY

1975
Free to Be co-authored with Gerhard O. Forde. Augsburg Publishing House (revised edition 1983).

1977
Faith and Freedom: The Christian Faith According to the Lutheran Confessions—A Leader's Guide. Augsburg Publishing House.

1979
Roots of our Faith: A Six-Session Course on Lutheran Teaching. Augsburg Publishing House.

1982
Martin Luther, His Life and Teaching. Fortress Press.

1983
The Faith We Hold. Augsburg Publishing House.

1985
Christ is the End of the Law: Romans 10:4 –An Historical Exegetical Problem. (PhD Dissertation).

1990
"Ministry in the Early Church" (25-34) in *Called & Ordained: Lutheran Perspectives on the Office of the Ministry* ed. Todd Nichol and Marc Kolden. Fortress Press.

1992

"Luther's Heidelberg Disputation: An Analysis of An Argument" (147-154) in *Word & World Supplement 1* :Essays in Honor of Roy A. Harrisville Jr (147-154)

1999

Manger in the Mountains. Augsburg Publishing House.

2001

Sources and Contexts of the Book of Concord co-edited with Robert Kolb. Fortress Press.

2003

- "Approaching Luther" (240-256) in *The Cambridge Companion to Martin Luther* ed. Donald K. McKim. Cambridge University Press.
- *Martin Luther: A Life.* Augsburg Publishing House.
- "The Lutheran Reformation and Homosexual Practice" (41-58) in *Faithful Conversations: Christian Perspectives on Homosexuality* ed. James M. Childs, Jr. Fortress Press.

2004

"Examining the Sources: Influences on Gerhard Forde's Theology" (10-21) in *By Faith Alone: Essays in Honor of Gerhard O. Forde* ed. Joseph A. Burgess and Marc Kolden. Eerdmans.

2008

"Seeking a Biblical Confessional Future" (69-84) in *The Banff Commission.* American Lutheran Publicity Bureau.

2009

"Ministry to the Sexually Conflicted" (15-26) in *The Jasper Commission.* American Lutheran Publicity Bureau.

2012

- "Preaching Repentance" (230-246) in *Justification is for Preaching.* Pickwick Publications.
- *The Lutheran Confessions: History and Theology of the Book of Concord* co-authored with Charles Arand and Robert Kolb. Fortress Press.

2017

"Speaking of the End of the Law" (169-184) in *The Necessary Distinction: A continuing Conversation on Law & Gospel* ed. Albert B. Collver III, James Arne Nestingen, and John T. Pless. Concordia Publishing House.

2019

- "Foreword" (xiii-xv) in *The Essential Forde: Distinguishing Law and Gospel* ed. Nicholas Hopman, Mark C. Mattes, and Steven D. Paulson. Fortress Press.
- "Luther on the Sharing of Attributes" (125-141) in *Luther@500 and Beyond: Martin Luther's Theology Past, Present, & Future* ed. Stephen Hultgren, Stephen Pietsch, and Jeffrey Silcock. ATF Press.
- "The Eschatology of Forgiveness" (155-160) in *Promising Faith for a Ruptured Age: An English-Speaking Appreciation of Oswald Bayer* ed. John T. Pless, Roland Ziegler, and Joshua C. Miller. Pickwick Publications.

2021

- "The Grammar of Absolution" (19-28) in *Take Courage: Essays in Honor of Harold L. Senkbeil* ed. Timothy J. Pauls and Mark Pierson. New Reformation Publications 1517.
- "The Two Kingdoms Distinction: An Analysis with a Suggestion" (188-196) in *One Lord, Two Hands? Essays on the Theology of the Two Kingdoms* ed. Matthew C. Harrison and John T. Pless. Concordia Publishing House

2022

"Bound and Free: Christ as the End of the Law in the Life of the Christian" (25-30) in *Free and Locked Up!* edited by John W. Hoyum. 1517 Publishing.

2023

- "Distinguishing Law and Gospel: A Functional View" (182-189) in *Lutheran Preaching? Law and Gospel in Proclamation Today* ed. Matthew C. Harrison and John T. Pless. Concordia Publishing House.
- "The Theology of the Cross in the Lord's Prayer" (516-521) in *Luther's Large Catechism with Annotations and Contemporary Applications.* Concordia Publishing House.

GENERAL INDEX

SCRIPTURAL INDEX

LUTHERAN SOURCES INDEX

MARTIN LUTHER'S WRITINGS

THE CONFESSIONAL WRITINGS